GENERAL JOHN BUFORD

Brigadier General John Buford, ca. 1862 (National Archives)

GENERAL JOHN BUFORD

Edward G. Longacre

COMBINED BOOKS
Pennsylvania

PUBLISHER'S NOTE

Combined Books, Inc., is dedicated to publishing books of distinction in history and military history. We are proud of the quality of writing and the quantity of information found in our books. Our books are manufactured with style and durability and are printed on acid-free paper. We like to think of our books as soldiers: not infantry grunts, but well dressed and well equipped avant garde. Our logo reflects our commitment to the modern and yet historic art of bookmaking.

We call ourselves Combined Books because we view the publishing enterprise as a "combined" effort of authors, publishers and readers. And we promise to bridge the gap between us—a gap which is all too seldom closed in contemporary publishing.

We would like to hear from our readers and invite you to write to us at our offices in Pennsylvania with your reactions, queries, comments, even complaints. All of our correspondence will be answered directly by a member of the Editorial Board or by the author.

We encourage all of our readers to purchase our books from their local booksellers, and we hope that you let us know of booksellers in your area that might be interested in carrying our books. If you are unable to find a book in your area, please write to us.

For information, address:
COMBINED BOOKS, INC.
151 East 10th Avenue
Conshohocken, PA 19428

Library of Congress Cataloging-in-Publication Data
Longacre, Edward G., 1946-
General John Buford / Edward G. Longacre.
p. cm.
Includes bibliographical references (p.) and index.
ISBN 0-938289-46-2
1. Buford, John, 1826-1863. 2. Generals—United States—Biography.
3. United States. Army—Biography. I. Title.
E467.1.B785L66 1995
355'.092—dc20 95-30002
[B] CIP
Printed in the United States of America.
Maps by Paul Dangel

for
Jarold and Penny
Gene and Ann
Charley and Maryann
Jacquita and Walter

CONTENTS

MAPS

Acknowledgments

Especially given the lack of a body of Buford correspondence, this book could not have been written without the assistance of several individuals who located other valuable sources pertaining to the general. I am deeply indebted to my research assistant, Patrick A. Bowmaster, a graduate student at Virginia Tech, who uncovered little-known material on Buford's life and career and shared with me the results of his labor toward a biography of Buford's pre-Civil War colleague, Beverly H. Robertson. I also benefited from the invaluable assistance of Bryce Suderow of Washington, D. C., whose work among various document groups at the National Archives supplemented my own research at that institution. Others who assisted me at the National Archives included De Ann Blanton, Mike Pilgrim, and Michael Musick of the Military Reference Branch.

My knowledge of John Buford's early life was considerably increased by Ruth Coyle of the Woodford County Historical Society, Versailles, Kentucky; Lucille Sampson of the Rock Island County Historical Society, Rock Island, Illinois; and Judy Beelan of Augustana (Illinois) College. Valuable information on Buford's Military Academy career was provided by Lisa Malden and Judith Sibley of the United States Military Academy Library and Archives, West Point, New York; I am also grateful for the assistance of Major Steven Hoffpauer, USA, formerly of the West Point faculty. Sources of information on the general's prewar career were directed to my attention by Thomas Metsala and Bill McKale of the U. S. Cavalry Museum, Fort Riley, Kansas; Arnold Schofield, historian and dragoon reenactor at Fort Scott, Kansas; and

Jim Potter and Eli Paul of the Nebraska State Historical Society.

In researching Buford's service in the Regular Army and the volunteers, I was assisted by E. Lee Shepherd and L. Eileen Parris of the Virginia Historical Society; Lynda Lasswell Crist of Rice University, editor of the Jefferson Davis Papers; and Scott McIntosh of the Margaret I. King Library, University of Kentucky. Brief conversations with a couple of fellow Virginians, Clark B. Hall of Upperville and Bob O'Neill of Stafford, provided some research leads. Dr. David G. Martin of Hightstown, New Jersey, shared his extensive research on the first day at Gettysburg and contributed an extremely helpful reading of my original manuscript. Dr. Perry Jamieson of Crofton, Maryland, helped me understand the influences that shaped Buford's battlefield tactics. John J. Hennessy of the National Park Service verified some of my findings about the general's role in the Second Bull Run Campaign and brought some obscure sources to my attention. My understanding of Buford's medical history was enhanced by Colonel Adrian Wheat, Chief of Surgery, McDonald Army Community Hospital, Fort Eustis, Virginia, an authority on Civil War medical and surgical practices.

For encouragement and support throughout this project I thank Bob Pigeon and Ken Gallagher of Combined Books. My wife, Melody Ann Longacre, once again joined me in tramping over battlefields, visiting libraries and museums, and helping me turn a rough draft into a finished manuscript.

Finally, I thank two of my colleagues, Dr. James George, who provided pictorial support, and Major John Dabrowski, USAR, who, in the immortal words of Grant, is "worthy of favorable mention in dispatches."

Introduction

When, several years ago, a publisher approached me with a proposal for a biography of John Buford, I rejected the idea out of hand. At the time I was busy with other projects but I also feared that a notorious scarcity of first-person sources—especially the lack of a substantial body of Buford papers—would prevent the development of a fully rounded life study. In the intervening years I have often regretted my decision, for Buford, who never received a biographer's tribute, manifestly deserves one—not only because of his role in helping shape the pivotal battle of Gettysburg but because of the major influence he exercised on mounted tactics through much of the Civil War and well into the twentieth century. Even so, short of the discovery of a substantial collection of Buford correspondence I seriously doubted that I would ever attempt to write the book to which Buford's achievements entitled him.

Over the past three years, a couple of factors combined to change my mind. One was the realization that archival material relating to Buford and the published and unpublished observations of his comrades and opponents might help fill the research void. A second factor was the 1992-93 effort to film Michael Shaara's Pulitzer Prize-winning novel about Gettysburg, *The Killer Angels*. Despite its numerous inaccuracies, Shaara's novel had long been one of my favorite works of historical fiction; I had featured the book not only in the freshman composition classes I taught as a Ph.D. candidate in English but also in the courses I taught after switching fields of study and receiving my doctorate in American history.

My affection for the book and my long-time interest in film prompted me to volunteer my services to Turner Pictures, producers of *Gettysburg*. My stint as a technical advisor to Sam Elliott, who portrays Buford in the movie, rekindled my interest in the general's life and career—an interest shared by the publishers of this, the first full-life biography of Buford during the 132 years since his death.

John Buford left an enduring imprint on mid-nineteenth-century mounted operations, precursor of the mobile, mechanized warfare of today. Once he ascended to high rank he almost singlehandedly overturned the practice, prevalent in virtually every theater of operations, to cast the mounted forces of the Union in the mold of European heavy cavalry. In place of the mounted, saber-reliant shock tactics the army's hierarchy had borrowed from the Age of Napoleon, Buford substituted the light cavalry tactics he had mastered during prewar campaigns against the Plains Indians. His emphasis on dragoon-style operations featuring dismounted fighting with carbine and pistol helped transform the Yankee horsemen from a poor imitation of *cuirassiers* into a potent, mobile, versatile arm of the service capable of taking its rightful place in battle beside infantry and artillery comrades.

Buford also had much to do with turning the Union cavalry, initially lax at reconnaissance, into an expert intelligence-gathering arm of the service. His determined efforts to provide his superiors with accurate, timely reports of enemy movements—coupled with his tenacious defense of strategic ground—helped decide the outcome of Gettysburg.

Had his earlier efforts at intelligence gathering been appreciated by his superiors, the battle of Second Bull Run might also have ended as a decisive Union victory rather than an ignominious defeat.

His army's tardiness in recognizing Buford's contributions—he was denied a command until the second year of the war and rose to division rank only six months before his untimely death from disease and overwork—can be attributed to many factors. A native Kentuckian, his allegiance was a matter of speculation among some members of the Union hierarchy, and he lacked the sort of political support that brought high rank and position to many officers of lesser ability. He entered the war as a staff officer in the Inspector General's Office, where his talent as a field commander lay hidden from view. He began his combat service under Major General John Pope, whose deserved unpopularity following Second Bull Run hampered Buford's ability to gain a prominent position under Pope's successors and was largely responsible for his inactivity during the campaigns of Antietam and Fredericksburg. Finally, Buford's self-effacing personality, his tendency to shun publicity, and his cordial dislike of reporters ensured his inability to gain the newspaper coverage that colleagues parlayed into high rank and prominence.

Despite Buford's tardy arrival on the scene of active operations in the eastern theater and his early departure from it, his influence was potent and enduring. Through high-ranking disciples such as Wesley Merritt, Thomas C. Devin, and George H. Chapman his tactical precepts shaped mounted operations up to, and beyond, Appomattox. One measure of the belated recognition his contributions elicited from comrades throughout the service was the tribute paid him by artillery Colonel Charles S. Wainwright, who eulogized Buford as the finest cavalry general in the Army of the Potomac, "straight-forward, honest, conscientious, full of good common sense, and always to be relied on in any emergency." This was lofty praise indeed for any cavalryman, and it still resonates with the ring of truth.

CHAPTER I

The Origins of a Soldier

John Buford was born into a fighting family. A fellow cavalry commander, Major General James Harrison Wilson, observed that Buford "came by the virtues of the strong hand by inheritance." He could trace his lineage to Norman warriors who for centuries had battled to protect hearth and home along the disputed borders of western Europe. Several of the more peripatetic Beauforts—as the family originally spelled its name—accompanied William the Conqueror to England in 1066. One chronicler notes that once settled in England, family members "became knights, dignitaries of the church, merchants, husbandmen, yeomen, and men of position in every walk of life." Family occupations might be several, but, significantly, the warrior class topped the list.[1]

By the early seventeenth century, the main branch of the family in England, which called itself "Beauford," was again ready to relocate. On 1 August 1635 eighteen-year-old Richard Beauford boarded the ship *Elizabeth* at Gravesend, bound for the North American colony that earlier settlers had named in honor of the Virgin Queen. Ambitious and acquisitive, young Richard flourished in Virginia; by 1656 he was making a prosperous living from 300 acres of Rappahannock River country in Middlesex County. Subsequently, Richard moved with his family to Lancaster County, where he lived the balance of his life while his descendants fanned out to virtually every corner of the Old Dominion.

The family remained Virginia-bound until its homes and lands suffered at the hands of British occupation forces during the Revolution. In 1789 several sixth-generation brothers—the first generation to call itself "Buford"—pushed westward to settle what would become known as the Bluegrass State. The most enterprising member of the clan, Simeon Buford, became a successful farmer, a wealthy landowner, a social light in Barren and Warren Counties, and, after Kentucky attained statehood in 1796, a legislator. His children and those of his brothers intermarried with the Dukes, the McDowells, the Adairs, and almost every other Kentucky family of prominence.[2]

Simeon's eldest son followed his lead as a pioneer, planter, and politician. In 1801, twenty-three-year-old John Buford moved with his wife, Nancy, to Versailles, the seat of Woodford County, Kentucky. There the couple reared a son and a daughter; the boy's hero-worshipping father gave him the grandiose name Napoleon Bonaparte Buford. In the family circle he was known simply as "N.B."

In 1825, a year after Nancy Buford's sudden death, John married Anne Bannister Howe Watson, widow of a Frankfort physician and daughter of an army captain who had served under "Light Horse Harry" Lee. By his second wife John Buford fathered three sons. The eldest, born on 4 March

1826, was known until his father's death in 1847 as John Buford, Junior.[3]

John, Jr. spent his boyhood in a large and comfortable home, "Rose Hill," outside Versailles. Forty-five slaves helped the family tend an extensive tract of farmland at neighboring Spring Station. The Bufords earned a second income from a stage line that John, Sr., established in the early 1820s to carry passengers and freight between Frankfort and Lexington.

A man of politics as well as of commerce, John Buford, Sr., for seven years represented Woodford County in the state legislature. His political contacts included a close acquaintance with President Andrew Jackson. By all accounts "Colonel" Buford cut an imposing figure in local society. One acquaintance described him as "a large, powerful man, rough in manner, but genial," with scholarly proclivities, an unswerving dedication to the Democratic Party, and a pious devotion to Presbyterianism. These several traits he bequeathed to John, Jr., as well as to his brothers, Thomas Jefferson Buford and James Monroe Buford.[4]

No youngster who loses his mother before he reaches ten—Anne Buford died in June 1834—can be said to have enjoyed an idyllic youth. Even so, John, Jr.'s boyhood does not appear to have been a gloomy, tragic period. His formative years were spent amid the woodlands and rolling hills of the Kentucky Bluegrass. The outdoor life brought him good health, a robust physique that left him "well grown for his age," and a perennial tan that made him appear older than his years. The boy spent countless hours hunting and fishing, but his great passion was riding. Like so many Kentuckians, the Bufords surrounded themselves with blooded stock able to "get up and go." In such a household, it was only natural that young John should become an accomplished equestrian and a keen judge of horseflesh.

In early youth John also developed an abiding appreciation for things military. To some extent this interest derived from his father's love of martial history and the family's long tradition of citizen-soldiering. Within that tradition, special emphasis was placed on Simeon Buford and his kinsman, Colonel Abraham Buford, both of whom had rendered distinguished service in the Virginia Line during the Revolution.[5]

A more influential factor in young John's interest in soldiering was his half brother's choice of a military career. Three years before John's birth, Napoleon Buford had secured an appointment to the United States Military Academy, graduating in the Class of 1827. Among John's earliest memories were visits that N.B., proudly clad in the uniform of a lieutenant of engineers, made to the homestead in Woodford County.

The young officer not only stoked John's martial ardor but fostered his desire for a good education. N. B. had distinguished himself scholastically, graduating in the top seventh of his West Point class. Later, by War Department permission, he would study law at Harvard College. Later still, his engineering and mathematical skills would land him a position on the faculty of his alma mater, there to teach the demanding physical science course known as natural philosophy. By his middle teens young John had begun to consider the possibility of following his half brother to West Point.[6]

Napoleon Bonaparte Buford appears to have exerted yet another influence on John and his family. Some years after he graduated from the Academy, the Corps of Engineers sent him to explore the rapids of the upper Mississippi. The assignment—the first military survey of that region—took him to a country recently wrested from the Blackhawk Indians and soon to spawn the villages of Davenport, Iowa, and Moline, Illinois.[7]

Impressed by the natural beauty and the abundant resources of the area—fertile farmlands, broad and deep rivers, bluffs rich in mineral deposits that would support a prosperous mining industry—Lieutenant Buford brought word of this "New Jerusalem" to his relatives in Woodford County. In recounting his travels he appears to have infected his father with wanderlust, for in 1838 John Buford, Sr., sold his home and farm, divested himself of his business ventures (and, presumably, his slaves), and transported his family and his remaining possessions to the scene of his eldest son's explorations.

The Bufords put down roots in Stephenson, Illinois, a nondescript grouping of cabins, huts, and houses that wandered along the Mississippi levee. There John, Sr., went into the mercantile business, building the first general store in Stephenson, "a small frame structure with a very high front, gorgeously painted to imitate granite." In time he also became the first United States postmaster to serve his village. Largely through his influence, that village changed its name, in 1841 becoming the nascent city of Rock Island, seat of the newly formed county of the same name.

Colonel Buford's civic-mindedness impelled him to take the lead in building streets, improving the levee, and draining the sloughs that encircled the town. As his local stature grew he was persuaded to reenter political life. Soon he was travelling to the new state capital to represent his district in the Illinois senate. In Springfield, where he regained prominence in Democratic circles, he became a friendly opponent of a tall, raw-boned Whig legislator named Abraham Lincoln.[8]

While his father enjoyed business and political success anew, John, Jr., whirled through adolescence. In his early teens he worked long hours in the family store and post office; in his spare time he tended to the horses that his father trained as a profitable side-enterprise. When his chores were done, he would ride for pleasure everywhere that his fancy took him. Neighbors recalled seeing the boy "scampering through the streets and over the bluffs of the town on a bareback horse that no other boy in the town could ride," while Napoleon Buford would tell of John's "hairbreadth escapes as a dare devil rider...."

As he approached young manhood, John devoted increasing attention to his educational and professional future. Never having relinquished his dream of following in the footsteps of his half brother, by 1843 he was positioning himself for a West Point appointment. In all likelihood he supplemented his regular studies with private tutoring in an effort to meet the scholastic requirements of the Academy. The West Point curriculum leaned heavily on higher mathematics and science-related subjects not taught in the school that John attended on the Davenport side of the river.

While the teenager had no assurance of gaining entrance to the Academy, he felt reasonably certain that his hard work would bear fruit. Despite his family's local prominence, however, his quest to gain admittance was an extended one. Not even letters of recommendation from influential friends to the local Congressman, J.C. Spencer, touting the applicant as "a fine promising young man ...of excellent mind and morals," secured his appointment. The fact that other family members including his first cousin Abraham Buford had already received a West Point education appears to have hurt his chances in those early months of 1843.[9]

Undeterred, John resolved to make himself—educationally, at least—more acceptable to Academy officials. Leaving home for Galesburg, Illinois, he enrolled at highly regarded Knox College. After completing his freshman year, however, he left the school to live in Cincinnati with his half brother, who, having resigned his commission, was seeking a teaching position at Woodward College.

Unwilling to see John denied the educational advantages he had enjoyed, N.B. launched another letter-writing campaign in his behalf. This second effort achieved results; on 20 April 1844, eighteen-year-old John Buford, Jr., proudly returned to Secretary of War William Wilkins his acceptance of an Academy appointment as well as his pledge to serve the army for the next eight years.[10]

As John prepared to leave the wilds of western Illinois for the civilized East, events on other coasts hinted that his military career would be busy and perhaps violent. In mid-1844 America and Great Britain appeared on the verge of hostilities over a border dispute involving the Oregon Territory and Canada. Cries of "Fifty-four Forty or Fight!" trumpeted America's boundary claim and her intention to wage a third war with England if that claim were rejected. While this confrontation would finally be defused through diplomatic negotiation, another international conflict appeared to be brewing hundreds of miles to the south and east. Officials of the Republic of Texas were debating whether to seek admission to the Union despite Mexican threats that such an act would bring bloody retaliation. In fact war with Mexico was less than two years off when John Buford, Jr., left Illinois in the late spring of 1844 and traveled by stage line, steamboat, and train to the institution that would transform his martial ardor into the skill and knowledge required of a professional soldier.

* * *

The week-long journey was lengthy and arduous enough to daunt an experienced traveller twice his age. Even so, when he reached his destination in the first week of June, the more unpleasant features of the trip passed quickly from his mind.

Alighting from a Hudson River steamer, he was immediately captivated by the pomp, tradition, and scenery that met his eye at every turn—what a fellow-newcomer called "the whole grandeur of West Point." He was not the first visitor to be dazzled by the beauty of the Hudson highlands. Only two years earlier, for example, an English novelist named Dickens, making his maiden journey to America, had rhapsodized over a succession of valleys "shut in by deep green heights and ruined forts, and looking down upon the distant town of Newburgh, along a glittering path of sunlit water ...hemmed in, besides, all round, with memories of Washington and events of the revolutionary war." The Briton decided that the nation's foremost military school "could not stand on more appropriate ground, and any ground more beautiful can hardly be...."[11]

Of course, John Buford could not afford to spend his time gazing open-mouthed at the local vistas. As soon as he set foot on the grounds of the Academy he reported to the adjutant and treasurer's clerk. His business with those officials completed, he followed an upperclassman to a cell-like room in one of the Academy's two barracks, each cubicle thirteen feet square and adorned by a chimney, a single oil lamp (which, according to another new cadet, John Tidball of Ohio, gave the room a smell "which Jonah must have experienced during his sojourn in the whale's belly"), a row of shelves to hold books and personal articles, a washstand and mirror, two narrow iron bedsteads, a pair of cast-iron tables, and two wooden chairs. Amid these spartan surroundings John would spend most of his waking hours—when not in the classroom or on the newly graded drill plain—over the next four years.

After making the acquaintance of several other "plebes" and numerous upperclassmen whose only function appeared to be to devise novel ways to harass, intimidate, and embarrass the newcomers, young Buford furnished his room with articles procured from the Academy store: a pair of blankets, an arithmetic text, a slate, a broom, a washbasin, a bar of soap, a candlestick, and a few candles. The blankets gave off a foul odor, "as though made of wool that had not been cleared from the essential oil of the sheep." The peculiar stench would combine with the smell of lamp oil to provide one of John's most pungent reminders of West Point.[12]

After donning cadet gray, he plunged into his first summer encampment. He spent hours drilling alongside awkward, gangly comrades fresh from farm, village, and city. He walked tour after tour of guard duty. He became conversant with the care and handling of muskets, sabers, and other tools of war. And he immersed himself in the textbooks that fourth class students must devour. Given his strenuous, out-of-doors upbringing, he easily met the physical demands imposed on him, and he called on reserves of patience and self-discipline in withstanding the hazing of upperclassmen. He developed a reputation as being of "a serious turn of mind," speaking infrequently, briefly, and always to the point. He was not a loner but neither did he share his father's gifts as a politician.[13]

About three weeks after his arrival on the Hudson John took the battery of physical and scholastic tests required of all plebes. To his great relief, the entrance exam proved less demanding than he had anticipated. The physical portion was a perfunctory affair that certified only the basic characteristics of good health. "We were made to bend and twist," recalled John Tidball, "and our chests were thumped for soundness of wind. Our teeth were examined for decay and our feet for bunions." The eye examination consisted of the surgeon's holding up a coin at the far end of the dispensary and the student deciding whether it was heads or tails.[14]

The scholastic portion of the examination, held in the

Academic Building before the full faculty, was only slightly more rigorous. A cadet of the 1850s, Morris Schaff of Ohio, recalled the examination as being "thorough, as it should have been, but it was extremely simple. I wondered ...that any boy who has had a fair training at a common school should have failed to pass it." At length, Schaff concluded that a more difficult exam would militate against the Academy's intent to educate a cross-section of the population, the wealthy and the impoverished, the sophisticated and the homespun: "Any exaction that puts admission beyond the reach of a farmer's or mechanic's boy ...ought not to be adopted without overwhelming reasons."[15]

Given his above-average education, John Buford easily weathered this initial scholastic challenge, becoming officially a member of the Class of 1848. He passed the remainder of the summer encampment with growing confidence and poise, poring over his textbooks, reciting his lessons in class, drilling in various formations three times daily, and trying to digest the "miserable" fare served up by the mess-hall, which he described as "bull beef and bread, and bread and bull beef continuously. It would be quite a luxury to miss a meal." He also inured himself to walking guard, policing the campus, and handling the myriad chores—chopping wood, hauling well-water, blacking shoes—that every senior cadet levied on every plebe. As John Tidball pointed out, such menial labor was "not hard physically, but it was petty and disagreeable, taking all conceit out of us," as in fact it was designed to do.[16]

In his first year at the Point, John made numerous acquaintances and a few lasting friends. Shared values and influences drew him to the other Kentuckians in his class, Benjamin D. Forsythe, Joseph C. Clark, and William N.R. Beall. Other Southern-born classmates with whom he developed ties included future Confederate generals Nathan G.

Evans of South Carolina, George H. Steuart of Maryland, and William E. Jones of Virginia. As an Illinoisan of six years' standing, it seems likely that he also kept company with fellow Northwesterners John Tidball, Nathaniel H. McLean and Hugh Boyle Ewing of Ohio (the latter a foster brother of William T. Sherman, Class of 1840).

Curiously enough, John's closest friends in the cadet corps were upperclassmen such as stocky, jovial Ambrose Burnside of Indiana (Class of 1847) and fellow horse enthusiast George Stoneman of New York (Class of 1846). He failed notably, however, to become friends with Stoneman's roommate, a dour ascetic from western Virginia, Thomas Jonathan Jackson, who some seventeen years hence would win the enduring appellation "Stonewall."

Not every fellow-cadet merited his high regard; the Class of 1848 contained its share of Yankee sharpers, haughty Southerners, and quick-tempered Westerners. At the end of his first summer encampment he observed pointedly that "there are a good many fine fellows in the corps of cadets, and a great many d——d rascals—some that would 'steal acorns from a blind hog.'"[17]

In a move unusual among fourth classmen, he became close with some faculty members including one he would not study under for a couple of years. While a number of professors seemed distant and standoffish—notably Albert E. Church, chairman of the department of mathematics, and Hyacinth R. Agnel, the newly appointed French instructor—others proved to be approachable and sociable.[18] The closest relationship John developed was with Professor William H.C. Bartlett, an internationally acclaimed expert in natural and experimental philosophy. An 1826 honors graduate of West Point, the brilliant scientist was the closest rival in notability to Dennis Hart Mahan, who taught the civil and military engineering course at the heart of the Academy curriculum. Cadet Buford may have had an ulterior motive in courting the good professor, for through him John met Bartlett's "mighty pretty daughter." If the object of his interest was Bartlett's eldest child, however, the cadet was destined for disappointment. Several years after John left the Academy, Harriet Bartlett would wed Lieutenant (and future Commanding General of the Army) John M. Schofield, Class of 1853.[19]

John's scholastic career began in meteoric fashion. At one point in the early going he placed sixth in general merit among his class of fifty-seven cadets. He hoped to do even better but as the semester wore on the sheer weight of his studies—chiefly mathematics and French—and his plethora of duties outside the classroom combined to bring him down. By year's end, he ranked thirty-eighth in math, nineteenth in French, and twenty-eighth in general merit.[20]

Another factor in his steep slide was the forty-nine demerits he accumulated during his fourth class year. The number was not excessive by contemporary standards—200 demerits assessed in one year constituted grounds for dismissal—but it was more than he received in any year except his last, when, assured of graduating, he lowered somewhat his own standards of deportment.[21]

Under the rigid system by which the Academy logged infractions against its code of conduct, each delinquency carried a numerical value depending upon the severity of the offense. Certain infractions not only earned demerits but punishments such as the loss of privileges, confinement to barracks, extra duty, even expulsion. The delinquency system gained the almost universal disapproval of the cadet corps. John Tidball decided that while the process was "supposed to be ...the great agent by which the discipline and good order of the institution are maintained at such a high standard," it was rife with inequities, levied penalties that were out of proportion to most offenses, and through its complicated system of appeals promoted "excuse-making, thus cultivating a skill ...more suitable for some other than the military profession."[22]

Cadet Buford's early delinquency record reveals no heinous crimes. Most of his initial year's demerits arose from a simple lack of punctuality: he was late for roll call, for reveille, for dress and undress parade. Other repeat offenses included inattention to marching formation, failure to turn out to receive the officer in charge, and failure to come to "arms front" when addressed by the officer of the day. That the quiet and reserved Buford could be something of a social animal was evident in the numerous demerits—nearly half the year's total—he gained for visiting in other cadets' quarters after hours. Although his adherence to Presbyterianism failed to prevent him from cultivating a taste for fine liquor, he was never gigged for sampling the off-bounds hospitality of that storied cadet hangout, Benny Havens's Tavern.[23]

By the outset of his second year of study, John had settled into the flow of Academy life and had gained the self-confidence that came from surviving his plebe year. It had become clear that, if he was not the intellectual equal of his half brother, he knew how to get the most from his mental and physical abilities. Already it was evident, as a later admirer commented, that he was "at all times conscientious and thorough in his work."[24]

His grades reflected his determination to improve. At the close of his second year at the Academy, his standing in math rose to thirty-fourth and he had moved up five places in French. Although declared deficient in English grammar midway through the year, he worked hard enough to raise his standing in that subject by almost twenty files. He accumulated only fourteen demerits for the year. This almost unblemished record of deportment gave him an Academy-wide ranking of forty-sixth out of 213 cadets in conduct. His improved performance in the classroom and the proficiency he consistently displayed in the tactics courses—thus far limited to infantry and artillery instruction—also accounted for his rise, within his own class, to twenty-fifth in general merit.[25]

* * *

During John's third class year, events on the Rio Grande stirred the martial dreams of the cadet corps. Early in 1845 the annexation of Texas became a reality; true to her promise, Mexico reacted violently. Retaliatory acts resulting in numerous American casualties led President James Knox Polk in May 1846 to secure a declaration of war. The news had an immediate and electric effect at West Point. "War at last sure enough!" exclaimed George B. McClellan of Pennsylvania, second-ranking member of the Class of '46. "Ain't it glorious!"

As the army prepared for combat and volunteers flocked to the colors to augment the regulars, several of John's acquaintances in the graduating class—among them McClellan, Stoneman, Jackson, and two other young Virginians, George E. Pickett and Ambrose Powell Hill—headed south to join the fighting. John left no record of his reaction to the war news, but doubtless he was disappointed that he must remain behind while comrades took position on the firing lines.[26]

The war continued through his second class year, punctuated by battlefield successes that brought fame and glory to many officers including more than a few West Pointers. Indeed, at conflict's end Commanding General Winfield Scott declared that, deprived of the abilities of Academy graduates, American forces would have required twice as long to win the war, "with, in its first half, more defeats than victories, falling to our share." While the incessant flow of war news was a distraction, John Buford tried to rivet his attention on his studies. The effort was largely successful; in 1846-47 he greatly improved his ability at drawing while grading high in chemistry. Only Professor Bartlett's notoriously difficult science course kept him from rising higher than seventeenth out of forty-three cadets in general merit.[27]

He continued to perform ably in the non-graded courses in infantry and artillery tactics, though neither captured his imagination or challenged his abilities. During his second class year, however, he was introduced to the recently expanded course in equitation, which ran the gamut of bareback riding to group drill in full panoply. Students learned to bridle and saddle, to manage their mounts at various gaits, to jump low obstacles, and to direct saber blows at dummies. In that same year the Academy opened an indoor riding hall, permitting enthusiasts such as John to polish their horsemanship on a year-round basis.[28]

Not surprisingly, Cadet Buford excelled in every aspect of the course. Under the tutelage of Lieutenant James M. Hawes of the Second United States Dragoons, he adapted readily to the European cavalry tactics that constituted the standard of instruction. He derived special enjoyment from those occasions on which Lieutenant Hawes staged mock charges—evolutions that Cadet Thomas K. Jackson of South Carolina characterized as "a riot of yells, of flashing sabres and fierce riding." Not even the inferior quality of the horses and saddles furnished the cadets diluted John's enthusiasm for a course that seemed designed especially for him.[29]

In some respects John's first class year, July 1847 to June 1848, marked a departure from the course he had maintained during his first three years. Now a cadet lieutenant, he carried a much heavier burden of responsibility than heretofore. At the same time, his self-discipline slipped to the point that he netted demerits for such serious infractions as neglect of duty while serving as officer of the day and on a later occasion when acting as division inspector. He continued to violate the prohibition against visiting after lights' out, and only a few weeks before graduation he was gigged for smoking in his quarters (by his senior year he had developed a fondness for both pipe and cigar tobacco, which he would indulge throughout his life). It is doubtful that he regarded his delinquency log with alarm, for he realized that although they continued to award demerits Academy officials were more tolerant of misbehavior during a cadet's graduation year.

Still, the relatively high number of delinquencies caused him to drop to 124th place in conduct.[30] Scholastically, John maintained upward mobility, attaining a class ranking of fifteenth, nineteenth, and sixteenth, respectively, in engineering, ethics, and geology. While insufficient to win him a berth in the top quarter of his class, his steady academic progress indicated a degree of perseverance and a commitment to self-betterment that augured well for his career.[31]

Clouds darkened his horizon as graduation approached. The conflict in Mexico dragged on through the spring of 1848, although large-scale fighting had ceased with the capture of the enemy's capital the previous September. Although war fever remained high at West Point, a sectional debate had already begun as to the social, political, and economic repercussions of the struggle. Some Northern and Western cadets expressed concern that the territory being wrested from Mexico would serve to perpetuate the institution of slavery. Within the Academy, the slavery question triggered discussion and occasionally provoked argument. The growing disharmony raised the unsettling though as-yet-distant prospect that when they fought their next war West Pointers would not have to leave the country.

If sectional discord troubled John Buford—as it was bound to trouble a Northwesterner with Southern, slave-holding roots— it was not the only force that jarred him during his final year at the Academy. Early in that period he received the unexpected news of his father's death. Unable to make the long journey home for the funeral, John mourned inwardly, privately, even as he walked guard duty and recited in class. The blow thus dealt may have dazed him enough to prevent a final rise in the class standings. On graduation day he ranked sixteenth in his thirty-eight-man class—neither a brilliant record nor one to provoke bitter regret.[32]

In fact, such a ranking redounded to his benefit when service assignments were announced. The top students were most often posted to the topographical or construction engineers—an elite branch that held no charms for the new graduate. Those on the next tier were usually commissioned in artillery or mounted units—a less prestigious assignment than the engineer corps but clearly preferable to the lowly infantry. Virtually assured of gaining his preference, even before graduating John had requested a berth in a mounted unit. Thus he was highly pleased when, on 1 July 1848, he was commissioned a brevet second lieutenant in the First United States Dragoons. Since its organization in 1833, the regiment had amassed the most creditable service record of any unit of horse in the service. John Buford could think of no better way to embark on a career to which he looked for personal satisfaction as well as professional fulfillment.[33]

CHAPTER II

The Young Dragoon

The regiment to which Brevet Second Lieutenant Buford had been assigned boasted an impressive history. Organized in 1833 at Jefferson Barracks, Missouri, to subdue the Plains Indians, the First Dragoons had done an effective job of guarding the routes of expansion as far west as the Rocky Mountains and as far south as the Red River. In the Mexican War, under Colonel (later Brigadier General) Stephen Watts Kearny, the First had embellished its record, serving with distinction in numerous engagements in what was to become California and New Mexico.

Its achievements in safeguarding settlers and helping acquire territory for its nation had made the First Dragoons, by 1849, the most distinguished of the three mounted regiments then in service (the Second United States Dragoons had come into being in 1836, the Regiment of Mounted Rifles a decade later). Such distinction, however, carried a price: the First had suffered heavily in casualties, especially below the Rio Grande. To refit and to make good these losses, by early 1848 the regiment had reestablished its headquarters at Jefferson Barracks, outside St. Louis. From that point it funneled recruits and replacements to its ten companies, some of which were engaged in occupation duty in Mexico, others scattered along the frontier from the Indian Territory to California.[1]

From the time of his posting Buford looked forward to reporting to his regiment, not only because of its distinguished past but because in its ranks he would serve alongside his cousin Abraham, then first lieutenant of Company H. For all his eager anticipation, however, the new subaltern did not reach Jefferson Barracks until 24 October, at the close of the sixty-day furlough granted him as a recent graduate of West Point. By the time he reported at regimental headquarters he was more anxious than ever to take up his ordained duties: two months amid the pleasant but slow-paced world of Rock Island, Illinois—much of that time doubtless devoted to legal matters involving his father's estate—had dispelled any residual longing Buford might have felt for the joys of civilian life.[2]

At Jefferson Barracks he was greeted by the newly appointed executive officer of his regiment, Lieutenant Colonel Edwin Vose Sumner (Colonel Richard B. Mason was on temporary duty at Monterey, Mexico). Sumner assigned the newcomer to Company F, led by Captain Philip Roots Thompson and First Lieutenant Patrick Noble. Buford quickly developed a close relationship with these and other officers at Jefferson Barracks, but he was disappointed to find few familiar faces at regimental headquarters. Cousin Abraham's company was currently stationed at Fort Gibson, Indian Territory, while West Point acquaintances were serving at other far-off stations: Second Lieutenant George Stoneman had been posted to California, Brevet Second Lieutenant Samuel D. Sturgis was also at Fort Gibson, and

Second Lieutenant John Adams was serving with Colonel Mason below the Rio Grande.[3]

After only a few weeks outside St. Louis, Buford found himself at Fort Scott, Missouri, a post established along the Marmaton River seven years before to protect the military road between Forts Gibson and Leavenworth. There he experienced good times and bad; soon after arriving he was laid low by illness, but upon recovering he made the acquaintance of a new superior, First Lieutenant Delos B. Sacket. The New York native, a graduate of the West Point Class of '46, would become one of Buford's closest friends in the service. Under the tutelage of Sacket, an accomplished horseman who had won battle honors in Mexico, Buford embarked on his apprenticeship as a dragoon; he would credit much of his success in the mounted arm to the New Yorker's patient guidance.[4]

Despite Buford's native expertise as an equestrian, his formative training period was long and arduous, for dragoon service demanded a high degree of dexterity and versatility. Later generations would come to regard the dragoon as a species of mounted infantryman, riding a horse only to the field of action and there dismounting to fight on foot with carbine, rifle, or pistol. Mid-nineteenth century dragoon tactics, however, stressed one's ability to fight in the saddle and afoot with equal effectiveness, as conditions warranted. The typical dragoon was armed with weapons appropriate to both mounted and dismounted operations. In addition to a Model-1843 North-Hall breechloading carbine—a compact, lightweight shoulder arm with a shorter range than a musket but able to be loaded more quickly and easily—each First Dragoon was equipped with a heavy, European-style saber as well as with single-shot percussion pistols or a 44-calibre Colt "Hartford Dragoon" revolver.[5]

The multi-faceted nature of dragoon operations demanded a body of tactics that kept pace with fast-moving developments in weapons technology. As the U.S. Army approached mid-century, advances in the manufacture of long-range rifles—to be expedited in the early 1850s with the perfection of the hollow-based, expandable minie ball, which bit into the grooves inside a rifle barrel—was altering the role of horsemen in battle. Mounted charges were becoming increasingly perilous under the intense and accurate fusillades that foot soldiers were capable of delivering. Even so, when Lieutenant Buford joined the First Dragoons tactical theory stressed Napoleonic concepts including the mounted attack and the double-rank formation, while calling for the infrequent use of firearms. Little thought was given to the use of cavalry in close cooperation with units of other arms or in the taking and holding of disputed ground. These and other inflexible rubrics, based on outmoded theories of warfare, threatened mounted troops with extinction.[6]

Change would come slowly, painfully, and at heavy cost. Buford, however, would embrace innovative thinking and modern tactics. As one admirer later noted, at an early period in his career the Kentuckian decided that mounted troops should not be restricted to a single mode of fighting. He could appreciate the moral and physical value of the mounted attack, especially when striking a disorganized force or harassing an enemy in flight. At the same time, he entertained "no prejudices in favor of fighting with the saber, or against fighting dismounted when the circumstances of the case called for or seemed to justify it." In sum, Buford was a rare commodity among the mounted officers of his era, "a true dragoon, as well as a true cavalier...."[7]

* * *

Buford's association with the First Dragoons was remarkably brief, even by the standards of the mid-nineteenth century army, which featured short stints of service and frequent transfers from one duty station to another. In the spring of 1849, less than six months after joining the First, he found himself elevated to the full rank of second lieutenant. The only vacancy then existing was in the Second United States Dragoons, which had suffered the recent loss of Lieutenant Bezaleel Wells Armstrong to a fatal illness. In accepting the promotion, Buford not only broke ties with his original outfit but made a transfer from line to staff duty, a position he would occupy, at frequent intervals, for years to come.[8]

Although he was destined to forge a long and satisfying relationship with the Second Dragoons, Buford would have been pardoned had he expressed hesitancy and even trepidation at the thought of joining the regiment. Established in 1836 to help overawe recalcitrant Seminoles, the outfit had achieved indifferent success in the Florida everglades but had won its share of battle honors against Native American tribes in the Southwest as well as against the defenders of Vera Cruz, Buena Vista, and Mexico City. Following the Mexican campaigns, the Second Dragoons had been "kept continually in the saddle in their active duties, under [a] burning sun, upon the plains of Texas."[9]

Along with numerous campaign streamers and a penchant for dash and swagger unmatched by the other mounted outfits of the army, the Second Dragoons had acquired a reputation for rowdiness and insubordination. Soon after the regiment reached Mexico in 1846 a staff officer complained that "there have been several disgraceful brawls and quarrels, to say nothing of drunken frolics. The dragoons have made themselves a public scandal...." One of the ranking commanders in the Mexican campaigning, Brevet Major General William Jenkins Worth, noted in a letter from the battlefield that "on my left are the Second Dragoons, an Augean stable, but I fear [with] no Hercules to cleanse it."[10]

The regiment's blemished past was owing in part to erratic leadership. Its original commander, Colonel David E. Twiggs, an impetuous, profane Georgian, had ruled the regiment with an iron hand that he applied unevenly and sometimes illegally. An early acquaintance described him as "an arbitrary, overbearing officer" whose favorite punishment—meted out to officers and men alike for offenses great and small—was flogging. Some observers considered Twiggs's excesses a symptom of mental instability; at least one critic described him as a wild animal.[11]

For all his shortcomings, Twiggs was a hard fighter whose combativeness marked him as worthy of promotion. When he attained a brigadier generalship at the outset of the Mexican War, regimental command devolved upon Lieutenant Colonel William S. Harney, who exhibited only slightly more restraint in his approach to command. A burly, rough-hewn Tennessean, Harney too could be autocratic and overbearing in his relations with others, not excepting his superiors. While he comported himself ably enough in Mexico, he gained a greater reputation as an Indian fighter, although his record of success was far from unblemished. An unadmiring subordinate described Harney's ambivalent attitude toward Native Americans: "The Indian was always Harney's favorite foe, and paradoxical as it may appear, about his only congenial friend. Why 'this was thus,' no mortal could ever tell, unless it was that both Harney and the Indians had somewhat similar ideas of warfare, and did not differ materially in their degrees of intelligence."[12]

Any qualms Buford might have entertained about entering the ranks of the Second were eased by an unusually lengthy transition period. Before he could join the regiment in Texas, he was placed on detached duty and transferred to the garrison at Santa Fe, New Mexico Territory. There he was reattached to the First Dragoons, with whom he would serve for the next three years as "acting" regimental quartermaster.

Despite his anomalous duty status, Buford enjoyed his stint in New Mexico and the varied service it entailed. While not a combat command, his position was a highly important and responsible one, involving as it did the handling of many thousands of dollars in government funds and encompassing a vast spectrum of duties. Not only did he supply the garrison with all manner of clothing and equipment, he oversaw the care and distribution of its horses and mules, blacksmith facilities, supply wagons, forage, tools, and building materials. When in the field he was even responsible for selecting and laying out campsites.[13]

From the outset, Buford proved to be an energetic, efficient, and honest administrator—qualities that would also stand him in good stead when he returned to field command. One indication of his success in his demanding position was his ability to fill it to the apparent satisfaction of a succession of commanders not only at Santa Fe but later at Las Vegas, New Mexico, and later still in Texas. During the decade of the 1850s the versatile officer would move frequently and comfortably between line and staff positions, giving consistently creditable performances in both roles.[14]

* * *

In the late summer of 1851, Buford laid aside his many duties and left Las Vegas on the first extended furlough of his active-duty career. He probably returned to his family's home in Illinois; he also may have visited his Kentucky kinsmen, for he maintained a deep allegiance to Woodford County, one that years of estrangement would fail to diminish. At about this time the young officer appears to have begun courting one of the most eligible young women in that section of the Bluegrass, and one quite familiar to him: twenty-one-year-old Martha McDowell Duke. Cousin of future Confederate Brigadier General Basil Duke, "Pattie" Duke was also a third cousin to John Buford, their great-grandfathers having been brothers. Although John was a quiet, diffident sort incapable of a whirlwind courtship, gradually the romance blossomed; it would take almost three years to culminate in marriage.[15]

When he returned to duty early in 1852, Lieutenant Buford found himself transferred to Fort Mason, Texas, an outpost established along the Llano River the previous July by Brevet Brigadier General Harney. At that garrison, which defended nearby villages populated by German immigrants, Buford at last joined the regiment with which he would be intimately associated for the next decade. Like the First Dragoons, the various companies of the Second Regiment were scattered from the Southwestern frontier to the Central Plains. In his new station, however, he forged a cordial relationship not only with General Harney and ranking subordinates including the scholarly, avuncular Major Philip St. George Cooke of Virginia, but with many younger officers, many of whom would make their marks in years to come.[16]

As the junior member of Company A of the Second, Buford came under the command of Captain Charles May, whose storied exploits and conspicuous gallantry in Mexico had won him three brevets including that of colonel. Like Delos Sacket before him, the dashing, athletic May, at six-foot-four a man of imposing presence and "marked character," exerted a major influence on Buford's early training as a dragoon officer. Another influential superior was May's first lieutenant, Samuel H. Starr, an Irish-American from New York with twenty years' army experience and with whom Buford would be intimately associated over the next dozen years. Among the subalterns of the regiment, Buford became closely acquainted with First Lieutenant Alfred Pleasonton, a suave, self-confident Easterner whom he had known briefly at West Point; Second Lieutenant Jonas P. Holliday, an introspective New Yorker; and a personable Virginian, Second Lieutenant Beverly H. Robertson.[17]

While Buford had been on detached duty and on leave, his new outfit had been heavily engaged in field service, some of its companies fighting Apaches in Texas and New Mexico, other units battling the Sioux and the Cheyennes on the central plains. Buford probably expected to join in such campaigning at an early period; instead, no sooner did he reach Fort Mason than he was again detailed to quartermaster duty. Over the next several months the closest he came to mixing with the enemy was to escort Indian prisoners to departmental headquarters at San Antonio. Such service helped break the monotony of garrison routine on the Llano as did an occasional detaching to Fort Leavenworth and Jefferson Barracks.[18]

Buford seemed destined to embark on a long stint in the field when, in July 1853, he received notice of his promotion to first lieutenant in Company H of the Second Dragoons. The following month he relinquished his administrative chores at Fort Mason and headed west to join his new unit at Post of Albuquerque. Again, fate intervened to deny him a chance for active duty. Within five months of his arrival, Buford's company was chasing bands of Jicarilla Apaches along the banks of the Cangillon and Moro Rivers as well as across the rim of the Grand Canyon. It did so, however, without the lieutenant, who once again was serving on detached duty at Jefferson Barracks.[19]

Aware that only through combat service would he gain professional experience and opportunities for advancement, Buford must have felt frustrated by such frequent and inopportune assignments to inactive theaters. And yet, a stint of detached duty enabled him to bring Pattie to Jefferson Barracks, where they were wed on 9 May 1854. The union—by all accounts an enduring, affectionate one—would produce a son, James Duke Buford, born in July of the following year, and a daughter, Pattie McDowell Buford, born in October of 1857. Tragically, neither child would reach adulthood, Pattie dying short of her sixth birthday, James while still in his teens.[20]

Blue Water (Ash Hollow)

When a long-deferred opportunity to take the field finally beckoned, for a time it appeared that yet again Lieutenant Buford would be relegated to staff rather than field service. This time, however, he would not be among the missing when the trumpet signalled the Second Dragoons into action.

In the early spring of 1855, as the regiment grouped at Fort Riley, Kansas Territory, General Harney joined Buford at St. Louis. There the Tennessean assumed command of a punitive expedition put together by Secretary of War Jefferson Davis and Commanding General Winfield Scott. Briefly shifted to Fort Leavenworth and then returned to Jefferson Barracks, the expedition was designed to chastise Sioux warriors implicated in numerous depredations including the waylaying of a mail party in November. The most serious crime, however, was the August 1854 massacre of a thirty-man detachment under Brevet Second Lieutenant John L. Grattan of the Sixth Infantry, near Fort Laramie, Nebraska Territory. Through conspicuous retaliation Harney's force hoped to curb the warlike tendencies of the Sioux, thus protecting settlers in exposed sections of the Kansas-Nebraska frontier.[21]

Harney was just the man for the assignment; his youthful affinity for Native Americans notwithstanding, the general was determined to levy a punishment of almost apocalyptic proportions upon Little Thunder, chief of an especially bellicose band of Brule Sioux recently camped along the Platte River east of Fort Laramie. To Harney's mind, a simple thrashing would not impress the enemy. As he informed the Adjutant General's Office in Washington, "a victory, in our acceptance of the term, is no victory at all, in the eyes of the Indians," unless suffering was widespread: "Savages must be *crushed* before they can be completely conquered." This theory demanded not only a large number of kills but also an impressive number of captives including women and children.[22]

Harney would have enough manpower and firepower to accomplish his purpose. For the mission he had been assigned a four-company battalion of the Second Dragoons that included Buford's unit (although only Companies E and K would actually accompany the expedition, under the command of Major Cooke), as well as five companies of the Sixth Infantry, a company of the Tenth, and a "prairie battery" of the Fourth U.S. Artillery. The combined force of 600 soldiers—most of them armed with newly issued rifles capable of killing at distances of up to 1,000 yards—could stagger a force of Native Americans many times the attackers' size.

Apparently, Harney feared otherwise. By early June he was asking the War Department to permit him to add the rest of the Second Dragoons to his expeditionary command. In the end, however, he had to withdraw his request; the six companies of his old regiment, then stationed at Fort Riley, were deemed critical to protecting not only local settlers but also the emigrant trails to California and the Oregon Territory.[23]

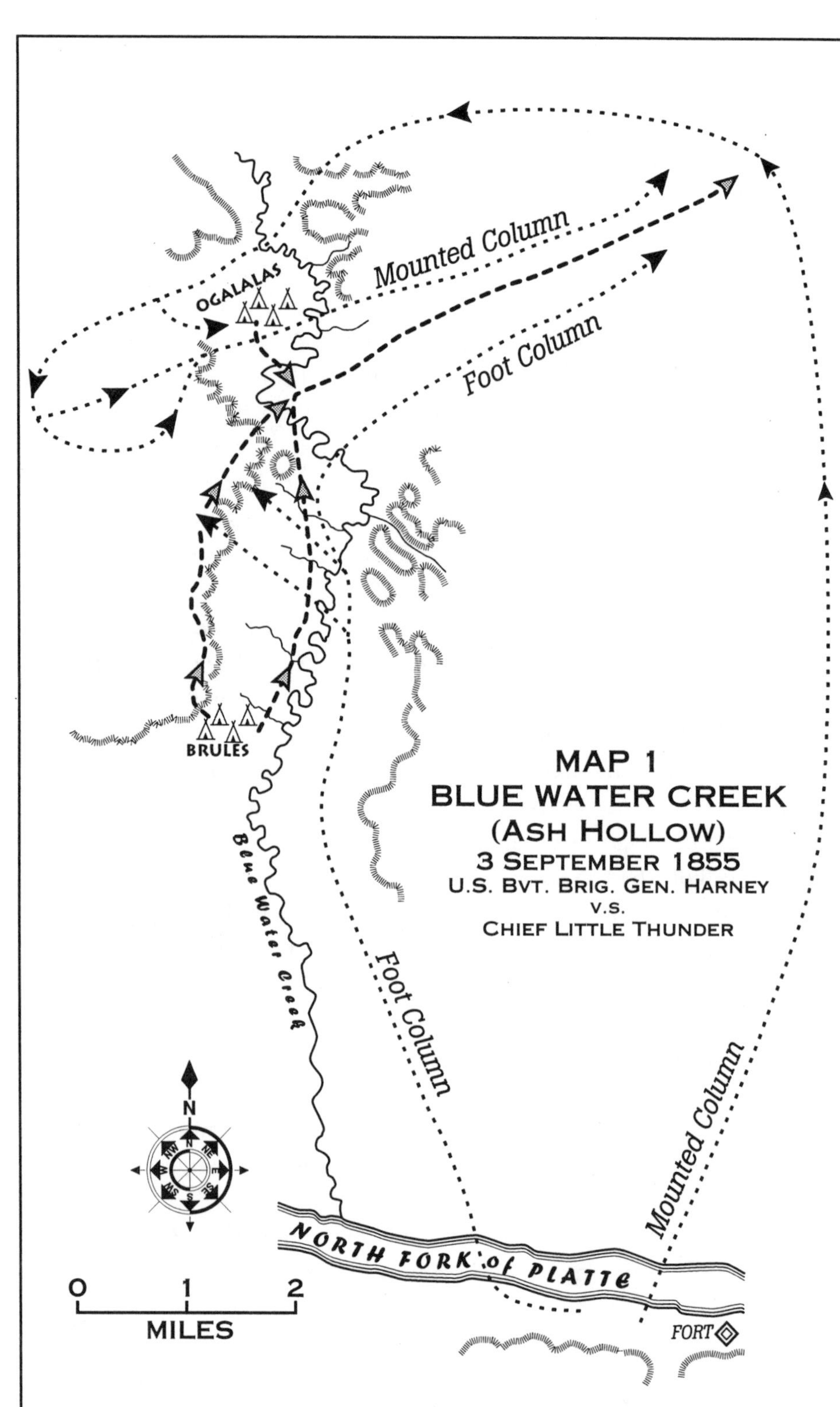
Mounted Column
OGALALAS
Foot Column
BRULES
MAP 1
BLUE WATER CREEK
(ASH HOLLOW)
3 SEPTEMBER 1855
U.S. BVT. BRIG. GEN. HARNEY
V.S.
CHIEF LITTLE THUNDER
Blue Water Creek
Foot Column
Mounted Column
N
NORTH FORK of PLATTE
FORT
0
1
2
MILES

For a time Buford wondered if he too would be left behind when the expedition rolled forward. Three weeks after arriving at St. Louis, Harney reassigned the lieutenant from line to staff duty. Pleased with his performance as acting quartermaster of the regiment, Harney now recommended him for the permanent post of quartermaster of the Second Dragoons. There is no evidence that Buford, who took pride in his managerial abilities, sought to evade the assignment. But he must have pondered whether he would ever rejoin Company H on anything approaching a permanent basis.[24]

Although it would be October before Secretary of War Davis got around to approving the appointment, Buford immediately donned the administrative responsibilities he had shed when leaving Fort Mason. These included the Herculean task of outfitting Harney's command with a full spectrum of equipment and provisions. To oversee the process, early in May 1855 Buford bade farewell to his young bride and journeyed to Fort Leavenworth, jumping-off point for the expedition. There he worked with military and civilian assistants to provide Harney with sufficient quantities of small-arms, ammunition, accoutrements of all types, horse equipments, medical stores, and weather-protective clothing, while putting together an extensive column of supply wagons and pack-mules capable of hauling everything. The work was intensive, fatiguing, and nerve-wracking; the initial contingent of infantry was scheduled to depart the garrison for the Platte River country before the month was out.

Through dint of great exertion, Buford validated the trust Harney had placed in him. When the detachment of the Sixth Infantry left Leavenworth for Fort Kearny on 28 May, it marched in full panoply, trailed by dozens of vehicles carrying every imaginable article of clothing, weaponry, and support equipment.[25]

After the infantry's departure, Buford spent the next two weeks storing up supplies for his comrades in the Second Dragoons. These were ready and waiting when Major Cooke and his four companies reached Leavenworth in mid-June. Cooke brought good news to Quartermaster Buford: General Harney deemed his services so integral to the success of the expedition that Buford would accompany Cooke's battalion against the Sioux. As soon as the quartermaster train was put in motion, Cooke led the force westward, Buford riding in company with Captain Pleasonton and Lieutenant Robertson, puffing contentedly on his pipe.

After a journey notable only for the large herds of buffalo encountered en route, Cooke's battalion reached Fort Kearny on 23 June. The dragoons joined the detachment of the Sixth Infantry that had preceded them to what one of the latter's officers called "a dreary looking place ... the most undesirable place I have ever seen in the army." As the combined units settled in to await the arrival of General Harney, Lieutenant Buford made last-minute efforts to ensure the serviceability of the equipment he had stockpiled. In his off-duty hours he tried to make himself comfortable in the fort's cramped barracks, where he wrote melancholy letters to Pattie. When outdoors, he rode along the base of the sandhills that alone relieved the monotony of the flatlands surrounding Kearny. On 18 July he even accompanied Pleasonton and Captain John Todd of the Sixth Infantry on an impromptu buffalo hunt, each of the party dropping a bull or cow "with the long range rifle." As an officer of horse, Buford was not intimately acquainted with the capabilities of the new weapon; on this occasion, he must have been impressed by its extended killing power.[26]

Not until 20 August did General Harney reach Fort Kearny in company with Captain Albion P. Howe's light battery of the Fourth Artillery and Captain Henry Heth's mounted Company E, Tenth Infantry. Four days later, Buford's preparations complete, the expeditionary force set out on its journey to the South Fork of the Platte, which it struck some few miles beyond Kearny.

Over the next week the command marched up the riverbank, camping beside it every night and dispatching scouting parties to fix the location of Little Thunder's band. On the morning of 2 September Harney led the column across the South Fork. After marching northward for eighteen miles, the advance guard reached the North Platte opposite a long ravine known as Ash Hollow. That night the column made a difficult crossing of the North Fork in the midst of a violent thunderstorm. Once across, it camped on the upper bank within easy reach of a large Sioux encampment—perhaps forty lodges—thought to be Little Thunder's. Well before dawn on the third Harney and his six companies of infantry, under the immediate command of Major Albermarle Cady, moved cautiously up a wide valley along a Platte tributary that the Indians called "Mee-na-to-wah-pah" and which the whites knew as Blue Water Creek. Their heading would carry them into the midst of the hostiles.[27]

Despite Harney's stealth and the pre-dawn gloom that cloaked his movements, Little Thunder's scouts detected his approach and sounded the alarm. Before the infantry could reach them, the Sioux—hundreds of men, women, and children—struck their lodges and began moving up the valley in an effort to clear harm's way. Harney, however, had taken steps to block their escape. Ninety minutes before Cady's men struck camp, the expeditionary leader had dispatched Cooke's dragoons, Heth's mounted infantry, and Howe's battery, with directions to pass eastward around the Sioux camp and gain a place of concealment above it. When Cady's detachment attacked the enemy's front, its firing would signal the horsemen and cannoneers into action from the other side.

Lieutenant Buford and his comrades in Cooke's column carried out their part in Harney's strategy with admirable efficiency. Breaking camp at three A. M., they made a rapid circuit of the sand hills east of Blue Water Creek, fording the stream north of Little Thunder's retiring band. Shortly before dawn, after discovering and bypassing another Sioux camp—eleven lodges occupied by members of the Oglala tribe—the flanking force took up a position behind a tall ridge. There Buford and his comrades waited for the command to strike south.

For two hours they remained concealed, until some roving scouts from the Oglala camp detected their presence. By this time Little Thunder's people, having halted their retreat, were crowding a rugged bluff three-quarters of a mile to the south. Though the element of surprise was fast fading and while tempted to move against the Sioux before they could resume their flight, Cooke withheld his blow until an inconclusive parlay between Harney and Little Thunder broke up and Major Cady's foot soldiers were ordered forward.[28]

As expected, the reports of Cady's rifles spooked the Sioux into headlong flight northward and westward, while propelling Cooke's troops into a charge. Buford and the others swung into their saddles, put spurs to their mounts, and raced south. As soon as within range they unleashed a volley against the leading ranks of the Sioux—Brules and Oglalas mingled together, some mounted, most afoot. As he closed the distance to his target, Buford had a clear view of the destruction being inflicted on Little Thunder's band from the south. Cady's riflemen were dropping warriors by the dozen, including many on horseback who apparently believed themselves beyond effective range of the sharpshooters. The slaughter smacked of the buffalo hunt in which Buford had recently participated.

Many of those who fled the infantry's fusillade sought refuge along a range of hills just below Cooke's position. Swiftly converging on that point, dragoons and mounted infantrymen swarmed over the fugitives. At such close quarters firearms gave way to sabers as the mounted troops sliced through their enemy, cutting down all in their path regardless of age or gender. It is not known how many, if any, Buford personally dispatched, but in his campaign report Major Cooke lauded the quartermaster for his "good service" in this phase of the fighting.

The blow delivered unexpectedly from the rear completed the rout of Little Thunder's people, who were soon "flying in every direction." Although a cadre of warriors stood their ground and fought to the death, the majority raced eastward across the creek in utter panic. For a great distance—Cooke estimated it at up to eight miles—the dragoons and mounted infantry pursued them, screaming a facsimile of a war-whoop as they shot, sabered, and ran down the ever-dwindling band of survivors. By midafternoon, when Cooke finally recalled his far-flung detachment, seventy-four warriors including Little Thunder had fallen before the savage pursuit. Perhaps a hundred others—mostly women and children—had been wounded, and forty-three uninjured Sioux had been rounded up as prisoners. Cooke's detachment had suffered only a dozen men killed, wounded, and missing.[29]

In common with the majority of his comrades, once the passion of battle subsided Buford must have regretted the heavy loss among noncombatants, which sullied the victory. No one doubted, however, the effectiveness of this fight as a means of subduing the Brule Sioux. The chief's successors never again engaged in acts liable to provoke military retaliation. In this respect Harney's campaign, its excess casualties notwithstanding, stood as both a strategic and a tactical success.[30]

The battle of Blue Water (or Ash Hollow) provided lasting memories to Lieutenant Buford, and not merely because it marked the only Indian engagement in which he participated. The tactical implications of the fight would shape his view of mounted warfare for years to come. He had been greatly impressed by the effect of the infantry rifle on mounted warriors. Few of Little Thunder's people had been able to move beyond its range and even fewer of those who came under its fire survived the fight. The lesson Buford took to heart was that, even when the numerical odds favored them, mounted men were no match for well-trained foot troops wielding rifles. At the same time, the battle had validated the effectiveness of the saber in stampeding an enemy already disposed to flee. The moral and physical effects of the *arme blanche*, at least when wielded against an incoherent force at a psychologically critical movement, appeared undeniable. Buford would remember these and other principles illustrated along Blue Water Creek. It was just possible they would come in handy some day.

CHAPTER III

From Bleeding Kansas to the Valley of the Saints

Harney's troops camped near the battlefield for some days after the fight, tending to their own and their opponents' casualties and working on Fort Grattan, a sod work erected by the mouth of Ash Hollow. On the ninth the column started westward toward Fort Laramie, wounded and able-bodied prisoners in tow. Reaching that garrison a week later, most of the expedition lay over for a month before turning north to Fort Pierre, Dakota Territory. Before September ended, however, Major Cooke led Buford and his comrades back to Fort Kearney and from there to Fort Riley, where they rejoined the balance of their regiment. Harney had detached Cooke in the belief that only the entire outfit could ensure "superintendence" of the Kansas garrison.[1]

The move eastward effectively divorced the Second Dragoons from General Harney's expedition, which would remain operational until the following July. But if Cooke's horsemen believed they were leaving the scene of strife for the quiet comforts of garrison service, they would soon be disabused of the notion. Their transfer to Fort Riley—a move completed before the close of October—would embroil the regiment in a prairie war between white antagonists every bit as bitter and bloody as any encounter between the army and the Sioux. This war—which pitted Kansas pro-slavery-ites against "Free Staters" in a struggle to influence the political, economic, and social orientation of a territory poised for statehood—would constitute a prelude to a much larger and more sanguinary conflict five years hence.[2]

At first John Buford was much too busy to devote close attention to this volatile climate of affairs. Soon after reaching Fort Riley he was joined by Pattie, whom he had not seen in six months, as well as by the son—now three months old—he had never laid eyes on before. While made happy by the resumption of his family life, Buford must have felt oppressed by his return to administrative duties. The job of quartermaster was demanding enough, but just before year's end he took on the duties of regimental adjutant while the incumbent served on detached duty at Fort Leavenworth. For several months in 1856, Buford also became assistant commissary of subsistence to the Second Dragoons. To cap off his additional duties, at intervals he was sent to posts along the Missouri-Kansas-Nebraska frontier to inspect horses recently purchased for the army.[3]

In June 1856, Buford's regiment became intimately involved in what its commander, now-Lieutenant Colonel Cooke, called a "rehearsal for a tragedy." On the twelfth of that month Kansas Governor Wilson Shannon, a pro-slavery Democrat, ordered every available member of the Second Dragoons to report to him at the territorial capital of Lecompton, fifty miles southwest of Fort Leavenworth. Only three weeks before, 700 pro-slavery zealots had sacked and burned the Free State enclave of Lawrence; anti-slavery bands were vowing vengeance. Shannon was especially concerned by reports that a mob of "Border Ruffians" from Missouri was massing near Lawrence to fight the Free Staters, thus "threatening the peace of the whole Territory."[4]

Next day a disgruntled Cooke left Fort Riley at the head of 134 officers and men including Quartermaster/Adjutant/Chief Commissary Buford. The detachment—reinforced in later weeks—reached Lecompton on the sixteenth to find that a portion of Colonel Sumner's First Dragoons, also summoned by the governor, had already chased the invaders back to their home state. Cooke hoped that his presence in the territory was no longer needed; he wished to return to Fort Riley without delay—a sentiment doubtless shared by Buford and most of his comrades.

Cooke was concerned that his Regulars were out of their element in a local war zone where they might be caught in a crossfire. In his view, the earlier blood-feud nature of the Kansas wars had diminished: "The disorders in the Territory," he wrote, "...consist now of robberies and assassinations," the purview of Governor Shannon's militia. The colonel wished to avoid "the petty embroilments of armed constabulatory duty," though he admitted that under certain circumstances his well-armed, well-disciplined detachment could "exercise a very beneficial moral influence."[5]

Agreeing with the latter proposition, and fearful that the crisis had not abated, Shannon refused to let the regiment go. Short on options, Cooke directed Quartermaster Buford to select the site for a temporary camp ten miles east of Lecompton, on the trail to Lawrence. Once his men were under canvas, the colonel wired Washington for instructions, only to receive a reply that pained him: the dragoons would remain in their present location indefinitely. In fact, the detachment's tour of duty among pro- and anti-slavery fanatics would last throughout the summer and well into the fall.

Although the Second Dragoons were not committed to a pitched battle during that period, numerous false alarms kept them tense and uneasy. Late in August, with the recently deposed Shannon en route to Washington and his successor, John White Geary, not yet on the scene, Acting Governor Daniel Woodson issued a proclamation declaring the territory to be in "a state of open insurrection and rebellion." In addition to calling on law-abiding citizens to support him in suppressing violence, Woodson tried to place Cooke's dragoons directly under his authority. He went so far as to direct the colonel to march west to Topeka, where Free Staters had set up a rival government, to disarm a force led by the fiery abolitionist James H. Lane. Believing that the governor's order conflicted with the instructions of the War Department, Cooke refused to comply—wisely, in the view of his departmental commander at Fort Leavenworth, Brevet Major General Persifor F. Smith. Had Cooke obeyed, Smith feared the order "might have resulted in the death of two or three hundred citizens on the mere vague denunciation of the acting governor."[6]

General Smith also endorsed Cooke's even-handed attitude toward the warring factions, whose leaders the colonel warned with equal severity against violating the peace. Cooke's neutral, impartial stance undoubtedly mirrored the sentiments of John Buford, a political moderate and a dedicated servant of the government. As a native Kentuckian whose family had owned chattels, Buford could sympathize with settlers who wished to make the "peculiar institution" legal in Kansas. On the other hand, he despised lawlessness in any form—especially that directed against federal institutions, which he saw as the bulwark of democracy. He resented the claims of many pro-slaveryites that the army's presence in Kansas would provoke trouble rather than preempt it. He especially abhorred the outspoken belief of some pro-slavery men that the federal government was their sworn enemy. Other settlers whom Buford became acquainted with—recent emigrants from Georgia and the Carolinas—ranged beyond the local controversy to assert that the only way the South could safeguard her political and economic rights was to leave the union. Secessionists were as despicable to Buford as they were to Lieutenant Colonel Cooke, a native Virginian whose Southern roots ran several generations deep.[7]

Under Cooke's prudent but firm control, the Second Dragoons did a masterful job of maintaining the peace and tranquility. By concentrating his troops midway between Lawrence and Lecompton, he kept the warring parties apart and prevented settlers between the lines from being plundered, beaten, or shot. On at least one occasion, he forestalled an attempt by Free Staters to raid Lecompton. At another time, Cooke came within a few hours of capturing John Brown, "the notorious Ossawatomie outlaw," who had supervised the murders of five pro-slaveryites in revenge for the sack of Lawrence.

The unobtrusive but ubiquitous presence of the Second Dragoons staved off large-scale violence until early in September, when Governor Geary arrived to take office. An anti-slavery Democrat open to compromise but willing to resort to stern measures to suppress lawlessness, Geary strove to end "the embarrassments arising from the combinations of different parties" that had reduced Shannon and Woodson to ineffectiveness. He worked in tandem with Cooke's dragoons and other Regular forces but disbanded unruly militia units and disarmed vigilantes. Though his bold policies made powerful enemies in both camps, ultimately he succeeded in imposing an uneasy armistice upon the territory. For a time, at least, "Bleeding Kansas" quit hemorrhaging.[8]

John Buford did not remain in the territory to see Geary's labors reach fruition. By late September he had returned to Fort Riley to reunite with his family and to serve as commissary officer of the post. Still, he would have been pleased to hear that the crisis in Kansas continued to ease following the national elections that fall, the results of which seemed to reflect a compromise between extremist positions. The embodiment of this compromise was President-elect James Buchanan, a Northern Democrat who appeared to be sympathetic toward, but not controlled by, the pro-slavery wing of his party.

The contest settled, a friend of Buford's living in Kansas noted that "pro-slavery and Free State [men] agreed to keep the peace and frown down every disturbing element." Within a week of the election, in fact, General Smith was informing the Adjutant General of the Army that "order and tranquility have gradually resumed their legitimate sway, the laws have again been put in operation, and the administration of justice revived."[9]

The new climate permitted the departmental commander, with the governor's consent, to withdraw federal troops from the territory. By early December the Second Dragoons, along with Sumner's regiment and a battalion of infantry also sent to the troubled frontier, were back at their permanent duty stations.

The troops must have been greatly relieved to escape from a land of fanaticism and fratricide, where every man faced the daily prospect of becoming a bushwhacker's target. The Second Dragoons could not have known, however, that after only a few months' respite they would be back in another disputed corner of the frontier, this time opposing religious zealots as well as political firebrands.[10]

* * *

In the early months of 1857 Governor Brigham Young of the Utah Territory, president of the Church of Jesus Christ of the Latter-Day Saints, threw down the gauntlet at the feet of the federal government. As Secretary of War John B. Floyd complained in his annual report of that year, Young and his followers had "substituted for the laws of the land a theocracy, having for its head an individual whom they profess to believe a prophet of God.... Running counter, as their tenets and practices do, to the cherished truths of Christian morality, it is not to be wondered at that, wherever these people have resided, discord and conflict with the legal authorities have steadily characterized their history."[11]

To be sure, Young and his flock had ample reason to distrust the central government, which had failed to protect them against bigots in Illinois, Missouri, and elsewhere who had driven the Saints from their borders into the wilderness of the Far West. Still, even gentiles sympathetic to the Mormons' plight believed that by mid-'57 Young had gone too far. The Prophet ruled his Mormon Zion with a righteous fist that struck down those who questioned his authority or faulted his policies. His tentacles of power reached into every corner of local government. Territorial courts tried civil and criminal cases alike; few important disputes were referred to federal judges and when they were Mormon jurors were instructed how they should find.

Already jealous of Young's power base and outraged by polygamy and other Church tenets that ran counter to Christian orthodoxy, federal authorities needed little urging to strike at the Mormons. When Young's followers tried to intimidate federal magistrates, marshals, and surveyors—slaying some of them—Washington acted, declaring Young, as a religious leader, constitutionally ineligible to act as a civil official. The governor vehemently refused to stand down and defied the government's authority to depose him, whereupon President Buchanan ordered an expeditionary force sent to Utah, to install a gentile governor in whom Washington had confidence. Once word of this action reached the Prophet, he forbade the army from entering the Valley of the Saints unless first disarmed by Mormon militia. A bloody confrontation appeared inevitable.[12]

The military expedition, which would comprise 2,500 troops of all arms including the Second Dragoons, was originally assigned to William Harney. In mid-July the forward contingent of his force, the Tenth Infantry, left that familiar starting-point, Fort Leavenworth, bound for Young's territorial capital at Great Salt Lake City; other Regular troops set out in succeeding weeks. By mid-May Buford had again taken leave of his family and Fort Riley. Sent to Fort Leavenworth along with six companies of his regiment under the immediate command of Lieutenant Colonel Cooke, for the third time in two years the quartermaster labored to outfit a sizeable column that would be many days on the march.[13]

It took several weeks to put together an adequate supply train and to stock it with enough provisions to sustain Harney's force in a barren, desolate country. The work was prolonged by an interruption late in July, when Buford's detachment of the Second Dragoons was abruptly returned to Kansas. Hard-pressed to counter a renewed outbreak of violence in the southeastern part of the territory, the new governor, Robert J. Walker, directed Colonel Cooke to establish a temporary camp outside Lawrence, a task Cooke delegated, as usual, to Buford. At this site the dragoons spent the next month holding together the truce they had helped fashion the previous autumn.[14]

Some of the men suspected they would proceed from Lawrence directly to Salt Lake City. In early September, however, all returned to Leavenworth, where they were joined by another territorial governor, Alfred Cumming of Georgia, recently appointed to succeed the still-defiant Brigham Young. With Cumming were three federal judges appointed to courts in Utah.[15]

At Leavenworth the dragoons also met the new leader of the expedition, Colonel Albert Sidney Johnston, commander of the recently organized Second United States Cavalry. Because the expedition was getting off to a belated start, it would not reach its destination before winter weather descended upon the prairie. Snow would block the passes of the Rocky Mountain before the vanguard of the column could penetrate Brigham Young's stronghold. Bothered no end by this prospect, General Harney had asked to be relieved of the assignment and the War Department had reluctantly selected Johnston to take his place.

By the time Johnston reached Leavenworth in early September, all but Cooke's rear guard and the civilians entrusted to its care had taken to the road. The main body of the expedition—the Fifth United States Infantry, eight companies of the Tenth Infantry, and two light batteries—was then nearing Fort Laramie, forcing Johnston to ride hard to overtake the troops short of Utah. Johnston, who had a reputation for incisive thinking and careful but inspired planning, would need all his native resources to make a success of an operation that from the outset appeared destined for trouble, if not disaster.[16]

On 17 September, following some hectic last-minute preparations that better planning at the departmental level would have avoided, Cooke's six companies started out on their 1,100-mile journey, Lieutenant Buford riding with the mule- and horse-train he had so ably crafted. The first leg of the journey, like the recent mission to Lawrence, returned the detachment to familiar territory. During the balance of the month it crossed the same well-rutted ground it had covered on the expedition to punish Little Thunder. By 4 October the column was stopping for the night at Fort Kearny and eleven days later it was passing the now-deserted battlefield where the year before Buford had tasted combat for the first time.[17]

Thus far the march had proceeded smoothly; the dragoons had made good time—on most days covering twenty miles and more—and the mule train carrying Buford's carefully stored supplies had held up well. So had the pipe-smoking Buford, although his continuing responsibilities made him, as one chronicler puts it, "the hardest-worked man in the command." As he left Ash Hollow behind, Colonel Cooke noted that already the supply column had surmounted obstacles of terrain and weather that would have disarranged a less carefully organized train. "This must be attributed," the colonel wrote in his campaign report, "to the excellent management of that most efficient officer, First Lieutenant John Buford, Regimental Quartermaster."[18]

Cooke had particular admiration for Buford's ability to keep the train at peak efficiency. Along the Big Blue River during the Fort Kearny leg of the march, the quartermaster had exchanged tired mules for fresher ones hauling a contractor's train bound for Utah via a less forbidding route. The civilian employee in charge of this column, Percival G. Lowe, formerly a noncommissioned officer of dragoons, was well known to the lieutenant. While sorry to see Buford "taking our best and leaving his worst," Lowe observed philosophically that "we were going where forage was plentiful; they were approaching winter, where forage of all kinds would be scarce. Buford trusted to me, and I gave him the best."[19]

By the third week in October the dragoons reached another familiar port-of-call, Fort Laramie. There Buford won Cooke's praise for locating an expanse of good grass where his animals could graze for the first time in weeks. At the colonel's direction, Buford made a critical examination of the mule and horse herds. He culled out fifty-three animals deemed unable to withstand the rigors of the march and certified 278 as fit to proceed.

The expedition tarried at Laramie for several days, awaiting the arrival of trains of corn, a provision Cooke considered "absolutely necessary" to a successful campaign. During the layover, the colonel considered invoking the discretionary authority Johnston had given him to winter in Nebraska instead of trying his luck in topping the snow-swept Rockies. At length he decided to leave behind the laundresses who had accompanied the command as well as any trooper who was thought to be even mildly ill, and to push on with the rest.[20]

The colonel also used the respite at Laramie to try to combat an instance of political intervention in army affairs. He composed an eloquent memorial to Secretary of War Floyd criticizing the recently imposed ban against dragoon officers accepting field rank in the First and Second Cavalry. Doubtless none of the dragoon officers believed Cooke's protest would accomplish anything of value. Still, such discrimination should be attacked, and ten officers in Cooke's detachment, including John Buford, endorsed the petition.[21]

Having gotten certain grievances off their chest, the dragoons pushed on from Fort Laramie on the afternoon of 26 October. Soon after they hit the road, an ominous portent appeared. A few miles beyond Laramie, Cooke received a message written eight days before near South Pass by Colonel Johnston, now riding with the main body. The expeditionary leader reported that bands of Brigham Young's militia had begun to enforce their leader's proclamation banning the army from the Valley of the Saints. The Mormons had interposed between two widely separated segments of Johnston's column and had burned many of its supply wagons. The attackers had also torched much of the scarce grassland east of their mountain stronghold. Despite the losses, Johnston was pushing on through wintry weather, hoping to establish a temporary camp somewhere between South Pass and Salt Lake City. He trusted that Cooke's detachment would waste no time closing up on the main column so as to help forestall further depredations.

After perusing the dispatch, Cooke halted his column, called up Buford and the other officers, and read Johnston's message aloud. The colonel added "a few words expressing my confidence in their every exertion to meet the kindly-announced expectations of the commander of the army." He believed that his pep-talk would prompt his subordinates to strain every nerve to reinforce Johnston before their enemy struck again.[22]

For the next several days good weather facilitated progress. Through the rest of the month the column followed the northwestward course of the upper Platte before turning toward the mountains early in November. With November, however, came meteorological obstacles including sleet and frigid headwinds. Fatigued horses had to be led by hand and the difficulty "of walking up and over the high hills, in the face of the wind, was very great."

As provisions were consumed, Buford sent empty wagons back toward Fort Laramie. He could only hope that the remaining supplies would prove sufficient to support the column on the most difficult stretch of the journey, which lay ahead. He was troubled to find, however, that instead of picking up speed the lightened column seemed to proceed more slowly than before. Finally, as the expedition trundled through Devil's Gate, the mountainous rim of the Sweetwater Valley, it came to a virtual standstill, bogged down in snow. At first the precipitation came down in moderate amounts, but it quickly grew heavy. Presently, as Colonel Cooke reported, "the air seemed turned to frozen fog; nothing could be seen" in any direction.

Crossing a frozen stream on 5 November, the snow-buffeted travelers sought shelter from the storm behind a granite outcropping that could shield only a portion of the command. Throughout the night they huddled in ankle-deep snow, with the wind howling about them and the herds of famished mules "crying piteously." The blizzard continued next day as the column struggled to cover a few miles through treacherous drifts.

When the snow finally ceased, frozen fog returned, chilling everyone to the bone. On the eighth, soon after the column straggled across Sweetwater Creek, the temperature dropped to forty-four degrees below zero. The conditions took a heavy toll of mules and horses, but despite the suffering of soldiers and civilians alike, morale remained high. In his report Cooke recalled that "It was not a time to dwell on the fact that from that mountain desert there was no retreat nor any shelter.... No murmurs, not a complaint, was heard...."[23]

The storm abated and the sun came out on 9 November; thereafter the detachment recaptured something of its early momentum, making close to twenty miles through the high-piled snow. Raw, biting winds returned on the tenth, however, and when temperatures plummeted so did progress. To facilitate speed, Buford directed that some of the wagons, including one stocked with horse equipments and sabers, be left behind. This expedient helped increase the pace, but so many horses were dropping in their tracks that the dismounted men threatened to exceed the mounted. On the eleventh a number of those reduced to walking suffered severely frostbitten feet and toes.

The final week of the journey—which carried the column

through South Pass and across the northeastern boundary of the Utah Territory—was a reprise of what had gone before: sub-zero cold, snow, frigid fog, and no grazing ground for the grass-starved animals. Because the mules were becoming unmanageable, Buford had them lashed to the sides of the wagons. He watched helplessly as the desperate brutes gnawed their way through ropes, wagon-tongues, and wagon covers. Those who got free had to be hunted down in the snowdrifts; the exertions demanded of the hunters decreased what remained of their physical endurance. The list of disabled men quickly reached thirty-six troopers and teamsters.

Under Colonel Cooke's tenacious prodding, which seemed as unlikely to let up as the cold, the expedition persevered. On 15 November it crossed Green River, only forty miles from its destination; two days later, for the first time in weeks, the guides located an extensive tract of grassland. As the ravenous animals ate, Cooke made camp on Black's Fork. The next day, with their final destination nearly in sight, the column made thirteen miles, and fourteen miles the day after that. Such progress brought them home free. On the nineteenth the column passed the camp of one of the infantry units in Colonel Johnston's vanguard. Three miles below the trading post of Fort Bridger—recently reduced to blackened stone and charred timbers by Young's troops—an exhausted but relieved Buford laid out the perimeter of a permanent camp.

All rejoiced that the long, dreadful ordeal was over. For all its perils, it might have been worse: Cooke's column had lost 144 horses, an indeterminate number of pack-mules, but only one traveler—a soldier who died not of hypothermia or frostbite, but of lockjaw. Summing up a journey neither he nor any of his troops would ever forget, Colonel Cooke waxed eloquent: "The earth has a no more lifeless, treeless, grassless desert; it contains scarcely a wolf to glut itself on the hundreds of dead and frozen animals which for thirty miles nearly block the road with abandoned and shattered property; they mark, perhaps beyond example in history, the steps of an advancing army with the horrors of a disastrous retreat."[24]

* * *

What followed the dragoons' arrival at Fort Bridger smacked of anticlimax. With little option but to wait out the balance of the winter, Johnston camped his various detachments pretty much where journey's end had deposited them. The main force resided in a city of tents, dubbed Camp Scott in honor of the army's commanding general, that sprawled along Black's Fork south of Fort Bridger. Cooke's dragoons, however, wintered at Camp Johnston, the cantonment Buford had established on Henry's Fork, several miles to the southeast.[25]

Throughout the cold-weather season, the dragoons were kept considerably busier than their comrades at Camp Scott. Whenever the climate permitted, Buford and the others drilled regularly in saber, pistol, and carbine practice in anticipation of combat with Young's militia. When not on the makeshift drill plain, they spent hour after hour scouring distant valleys for herds of oxen, mules, and horses and guarding the animals against Mormon raids.

Because the captured horses did not supply the detachment fully, Buford purchased ponies from gentile settlers. To fill the gap that remained, he furnished dismounted troopers with converted pack-mules. A bugler noted sarcastically that "we will have all kinds of fun breaking them [the mules] into the use of the army, as most of them never had a man upon his back."[26]

Despite all their preparations, the expected clash with the

Army of the Saints never materialized. Shortly before spring returned to Mormon country, Governor Young—perhaps surprised by the resolution and stamina Johnston's force had displayed—left the bellicose path he had followed for the past year. He directed his people to adopt a conciliatory attitude toward the government and its military representatives. To Johnston, Young announced that his followers would evacuate the Valley of the Great Salt Lake, allowing the army to enter and occupy the territorial capital without molestation.

Washington, too, was seeking an accommodation. Unaware of Young's change of heart, President Buchanan dispatched a commission to Utah carrying conditional pardons for the governor and his subordinates contingent upon their pledge to obey all applicable federal laws. After two months of negotiation, the governor agreed and the Mormon War came to a quiet end.[27]

On 13 June 1858 now-Brevet Brigadier General Johnston started his forces, including the Second Dragoons, on the road to Zion. From Camp Scott the long column wended its way southwestward across Bear River, down Echo Canyon, and through the Wasatch Mountains to the Valley of the Saints. The army entered all-but-deserted Salt Lake City on the twenty-sixth, observing strict prohibitions against harming Mormon property. Passing out of the city, the troops continued down the banks of the Jordan River, many of them disappointed that their antagonists had offered no resistance. Some thirty-five miles below the city they established a permanent post of occupation known as Camp Floyd.[28]

In later weeks, Young's followers curtailed their flight and returned to their capital, where they observed a fragile truce with the army. John Buford, however, did not remain to witness the aftermath of hostilities. In mid-August he left Utah on an extended leave that marked an end to three years of service as quartermaster of his regiment. In company with Lieutenant Colonel Cooke—en route to Europe, where he would observe foreign armies and begin work on a body of cavalry tactics for the army—Buford retraced the route he had taken to Fort Bridger nine months before, this time in balmy weather.[29]

He returned home by way of Jefferson Barracks, where he was reunited with Pattie, their son, and their infant daughter, born not long after her father set out on the march to Utah. By stage and train the family accompanied him to Washington, D.C., where in January the lieutenant reported at the Adjutant General's Office. A few weeks later the Bufords were in Georgetown, Kentucky, visiting Pattie's relations.[30]

While at his in-laws John Buford received the welcome news that he had been promoted to captain of Company B, Second Dragoons—a major milestone in a decade-old career. Although anxious to join the first unit he could truly call his own, he did not leave Kentucky until the end of summer, when his extended furlough ran out. When he returned to Washington, he appears to have left Pattie and the children behind; they would remain in Georgetown for the next three years.[31]

He spent some weeks in Washington, awaiting orders to rejoin his regiment in Utah. Finally, on 15 October, he reported to the cavalry rendezvous at Carlisle Barracks, Pennsylvania, where he took charge of a detachment of recruits. The raw levies were bound for service in the Oregon Territory, where a campaign was underway against the Snake Indians, attackers of miners and emigrants. Shortly before the year ended, Buford and the recruits set off on their long and roundabout journey—probably via ship down the Atlantic Coast, then by train through the jungles of Panama, and by steamboat to California. They may have been delayed en route, for the records suggest that as of March 1860

Buford had yet to reach San Francisco. When he finally arrived he debarked, leaving his erstwhile charges to continue up the coast without him. Assuming that weather permitted, he would have travelled directly to Utah, reaching Camp Floyd some time in April.[32]

Upon arriving he made a disappointing discovery: under the command of junior officers, Company B had left Utah for the Oregon frontier. Rather than follow the unit, Buford remained at Camp Floyd. There he mingled with old comrades—including another recent returnee, now-Colonel Philip St. George Cooke, new Commander of the Department of Utah—and he introduced himself to newcomers. Then he took up staff duties, some of which he continued to perform even after Company B's return on 10 September. He appraised horses, beef cattle, and (on one occasion) 327 tons of hay offered for sale to the Department. He inspected camp equipage and quartermaster's and ordnance stores. He served on numerous courts-martial. The work was unchallenging and perhaps unfulfilling as well. He longed to get on with the duty he had been waiting so long to perform: company command.[33]

When his unit finally returned from fighting the Snake Indians and escorting wagon trains to the Columbia Valley, Buford eagerly ministered to its battle-wounds, while training it to his standards of efficiency and readiness and alerting it to the possibility that their Mormon neighbors might rise up in opposition to the presence of the army and the administration of Governor Cumming. In tending to these chores he was ably assisted by subordinates old and new, the latter including a young New Yorker fresh from West Point: Second Lieutenant Wesley Merritt, whose faultless deportment and aptitude for mounted operations quickly impressed his commander and mentor.[34]

Buford's rigorous training regimen was not tested in combat, for neither Mormons nor Indians disturbed the placid course of life in the Valley of the Great Salt Lake. When the new year came in, however, Buford noticed a palpable change in the atmosphere surrounding Camp Floyd—a change that was affecting the country as a whole. Angry clouds had been gathering on the national horizon for many years, spawned by the same provocations and animosities Buford had witnessed first-hand in Kansas. Volatile, divisive, but seemingly isolated acts such as John Brown's raid on the United States arsenal and armory at Harpers Ferry the previous October, "black Abolitionist" Abraham Lincoln's presidential victory the following month, and the secession of South Carolina just before Christmas 1860 had lent the storm warnings a heightened sense of danger. By the early months of '61 the general population—and the army—had begun to batten down in anticipation of the coming conflict.

Even in its isolated corner of the wilderness, Camp Floyd could not escape the effects of discord and division. In March, after Buchanan's Secretary of War resigned his cabinet post and proclaimed his fealty to Virginia, Colonel Cooke changed the name of his installation to honor the loyalist Senator from Kentucky, John J. Crittenden. Meanwhile, several of Buford's Southern-born comrades at Fort Crittenden, including Beverly Robertson and Major Henry Hopkins Sibley, declared that they would resign their commissions and join the military forces of their state should Virginia follow South Carolina into secession.[35]

Southern-born officers who placed loyalty to state above love of the Union expected their brethren to share their sentiments. In some instances, they were disappointed. After much soul-searching, Colonel Cooke informed his Virginia relatives that his allegiance would remain with his nation and its army. John Buford suffered no such anguish in deciding where his loyalties rested. Although Buford's native state would never leave the Union, thousands of her sons opted to defend the newly formed Confederate States of America. According to one account, early in 1861 Kentucky's secessionist governor, Beriah Magoffin, tendered Buford a command in the pro-Confederate state militia, an offer its recipient quickly rejected. At about the same time, authorities of the provisional Confederate government offered Buford a general officer's commission, which reached him by mail at Fort Crittenden. A well-known anecdote has him wadding up the letter while angrily announcing that whatever the future had in store he would "live and die under the flag of the Union."[36]

Such an outburst seems rather out of character for the unostentatious Buford, but he never wavered in his devotion to the federal government and its institutions. Even so, he would always maintain a conservative political outlook; doubtless he harbored misgivings about some of the more sweeping military and social policies of the Lincoln administration. Certainly it appears untrue—though some accounts have it otherwise—that Buford's name made a covert list, compiled early in 1861, of Army officers suspected of disloyalty.[37]

After South Carolina troops opened fire on the U.S. Army garrison at Fort Sumter, Charleston harbor, in April, war seemed a *fait accompli.* In later weeks Virginia and her neighbors in the upper South followed the Cotton States into secession, and their native sons streamed out of the army. July brought a fateful communication from the War Department: the remnant of the Second Dragoons in Utah—one four-company battalion—would help strike Fort Crittenden and would then accompany other units on an overland march to Fort Leavenworth. From Leavenworth, the dragoons would proceed by train to Washington—presumably to prepare for field campaigning farther south.

As he made ready for the journey that would carry him to the seat of war, John Buford must have recoiled from the prospect of fighting against his homeland and many of his kin. An artillery officer at Fort Crittenden, John Gibbon, who had grown up in North Carolina, no doubt spoke for his Kentucky-born comrade when he anguished over the realization that "all our hopes of peace were blasted.... our once happy and prosperous country was plunged into the horrors of civil war, the end of which no man could foretell."[38]

CHAPTER IV

On the Sidelines

Marching-distance records were broken when the column commanded by Colonel Cooke made its trek from Fort Crittenden, which it departed on 27 July 1861, to Fort Leavenworth, where it arrived on 8 October. The course was rugged and rations and forage were not to be found in quantity short of Fort Laramie. Even so, horses and men held up well and the column—which in addition to companies B, E, H, and K of Buford's regiment included two companies of the Tenth Infantry and three artillery batteries—managed to keep ahead of bad weather. The small force assimilated detachments, including two more companies of dragoons, at outposts along the route, but the additions did not impede progress: on the leg to Leavenworth the column averaged twenty-five miles per day including rest-stops.[1]

For a time it appeared that the troops might face obstacles other than terrain and weather. While passing south of Salt Lake City, Buford and his comrades were alert to rumors that Brigham Young's followers aimed to steal their horses and provisions. When the column turned westward without incident, the troops focused on potential troubles farther along the route. In the first days of August a Pony Express rider brought the column word of the 21 July battle near Manassas Junction, Virginia, twenty-some miles southwest of Washington, the first large-scale engagement of the war in the eastern theater of operations. The majority of the travelers, loyal Unionists, shook their heads at the news that the Northern troops had suffered heavy losses in the day's fighting, followed by a panicky retreat to the capital. "Great God," exclaimed one listener, "there will be no Government when we get there."

As the eastward journey continued, it became increasingly difficult to avoid the reality of the crisis that loomed ahead. Reaching Fort Laramie, the troops found the garrison depleted by the defection of numerous Southern-born officers to the Confederate forces. Nearing Fort Kearny, the men heard reports (which proved unfounded) that Rebel forces out of Missouri were planning to waylay the column. And when they reached Fort Leavenworth, seventy-four days out of Utah, they found what Captain Gibbon called "evidence of the disturbed condition of the country," including newly erected breastworks and nearby camps filled with volunteer troops.[2]

From Fort Leavenworth, the caravan proceeded northeastward to the railroad hub at St. Joseph. There Buford and his comrades turned over to the local quartermaster the mounts they had cared for so attentively that they appeared to Lieutenant Merritt "in better condition for service than when we commenced the march." The suddenly dismounted troopers joined the other detachments in boarding a train bound for the East Coast. A week later Buford's contingent—minus Colonel Cooke, who had proceeded by stage from the Platte River to a new assignment in St. Louis—found itself in the nation's capital.[3]

When his unit went into camp outside the city on 19 October, Buford would have been pardoned had he felt lost. For one thing, he and his comrades seemed out of place in their new surroundings. Despite the reverses its troops had suffered at Manassas, Washington appeared to be thriving on the business of war—a war entrusted to volunteer troops, not Regulars. Buford's outfit—depleted by years of lax recruiting, more recently by defections to the Confederacy—looked puny and insignificant in comparison to the huge, well-equipped regiments of citizen-soldiers encamped on all sides of it.

Also troubling to Buford was his perception that old truths had lost their validity. Not only was his unit no longer the first line of national defense, it was no longer a dragoon regiment. Recent changes in army organization had resulted in the outfit being redesignated the Second United States Cavalry. It was as though thirty years of history had been swept away with the scratch of an administrator's pen. With the old name went a sense of identity, the loss of which Buford would have felt keenly. As the cold winds of change blew about him, he must have wondered if he had a place in this new order, a place in which he could do credit to himself, his service, and his profession.[4]

He realized that he must come to terms with the new military. Wherever he walked in the capital he found himself crowded off the streets by mobs of civilians with eagles and leaves on their shoulders. It must have rankled him to salute men so obviously ignorant of their profession and with so little claim to the positions they held. Still, this was the way it was to be; thus, Buford resolved to make his peace with the situation, that he might play a meaningful role in what was surely the most important event of his life.

Naturally reluctant to promote himself, he forced himself to make the rounds of the War Department, seeking out what few contacts he enjoyed there. It did no good. Although other Regulars and former Regulars had gained field command in volunteer regiments, no such opportunity came his way. A major reason was that army headquarters hoped to use the regular service as a nucleus of experience to train and enlighten the volunteers; therefore, it discouraged professional soldiers from transferring to the volunteer establishment.

Another obstacle in Buford's path was his lack of political support. The Southern sympathies of some Kentucky legislators had cost them their seats in Congress. Those who remained, including Senators Lazarus Powell and Garrett Davis, were conservative Democrats whose lukewarm enthusiasm for the war barred them from the circles of power. In any case, none appeared able or willing to help Buford, nor did any member of the Illinois congressional delegation.[5]

Three weeks after reaching the capital, with his outfit's duty status still in limbo, Buford finally landed a position of some significance, and a promotion to boot. Perhaps through the assistance of his old mentor and friend, Delos Sacket, now a colonel in the Inspector General's Office, Buford made inquiries of another former comrade, Colonel Randolph Barnes Marcy. A companion of Buford's at Camp Douglas, Marcy had led a daring rescue mission to the New Mexico Territory in the fall of 1857 to keep the main body of the Utah Expedition from starving. He was also the father-in-law of Major General George B. McClellan, the recently appointed commander of the Army of the Potomac, the vast force now flooding the training camps of the capital. Largely through McClellan's influence, in August Marcy had become senior inspector general of the Regular Army as well as a member of his son-in-law's staff. Whatever the extent of Marcy's solicitude toward an old colleague with long experience in army administration, Buford was offered the position of assistant inspector general at the regular grade of major. He accepted the appointment, which was dated 12 November.[6]

In the scheme of things, the new post did not compare with the rank and power being lavished on political appointees in the volunteers. Still, it was a start; John Buford had gained a foothold in the war effort, and opportunities for further advancement—preferably in the mounted arm—were not beyond the realm of possibility.

* * *

While it must have been difficult for Captain Buford to sever his twelve-year association with the erstwhile Second Dragoons, he had the satisfaction of knowing that the vacancy he created enabled a deserving subaltern, First Lieutenant John K. Mizner, to win promotion. It also eased his mind to learn that he would not have to linger close to his former comrades. Only ten days after transferring out of the field, Buford said his good-byes to Wesley Merritt and the other officers and men of his old outfit. Then, armed with orders from the office of Adjutant General Lorenzo Thomas, he strode to the railroad depot, where he boarded a westbound train that would take him to the site of his initial inspection duty.[7]

Despite his mixed emotions at leaving Washington, the trip had a pleasant denouement, for it returned him to that section of the country he continued to think of as home. On 27 November he left the train at Louisville, Kentucky, only eighty miles west of Pattie and the children in Georgetown. At once he reported to the headquarters of the Department of the Ohio, whose commander, Brigadier General Don Carlos Buell, ordered him down the Ohio River to the post at Calhoun. At Calhoun, commanded by Brigadier General

Thomas L. Crittenden, son of the former senator, Buford for the first time scrutinized the volunteer troops of the Union.[8]

From the first, his reports were cogent and pithy yet sufficiently detailed and descriptive to constitute a well-rounded evaluation of a unit's overall condition. Buford's commentaries touched on many aspects of military life: unit dress, deportment, and discipline; the quality and quantity of weapons, ammunition, equipment, quarters, animals, and transportation; the general health of the unit and the medical facilities available to it; and the training progress of officers and men.

Perhaps Buford's most valuable quality as an inspector was his ability to evaluate fairly and objectively, doling out praise and criticism as warranted, commending as often as he condemned. The troopers of a Kentucky cavalry regiment training at Calhoun he judged to be "hardy, fine horsemen, and gallant men," while a neighboring unit of infantry he described as "under no restraint, much like a herd of wild animals." The soldiers of one outfit exhibited an appearance indicative of "a crack regiment." Another unit, composed predominately of Irish-Americans, he considered "the most incongruous mass I have yet seen.... made up of hard featured, ill shaped and dissipated men from the City and Steamboats. Many of them had their eyes blackened, faces bruised, and presented a most rowdy appearance."[9]

Despite their sometimes unprepossessing look, the inspector was cautiously optimistic about the military potential of the citizens-in-arms. Many of the rank-and-file appeared to know next to nothing about their assigned duties, but Buford expected that time and experience would provide a cure. The officers were a different matter. Some struck him as "zealous and able," "active, intelligent and competent," holding the welfare of their troops uppermost in mind. More than a few, however, he considered "deficient in every respect" and "scandalously ignorant of all of their duties." A large number he found to be lazy, apathetic, uninterested in learning the basics of leadership; others exercised no discipline over their men, or punished them severely for minor infractions. Some did not even know how to drill their units. On the practice field captains and colonels shouted out "commands of their own, more suitable for 4th of July occasions than for service." Buford pulled few punches, even when critiquing the big brass. He declared, for example, that neither General Crittenden nor any member of his staff possessed even a rudimentary knowledge of military affairs.

Buford did not consider it proper to tutor a general officer in the responsibilities of his position, other than to provide a few hints toward more effective training. Whenever possible, however, he dispensed general information, explaining to regimental personnel "the proper method of keeping their books, the manner of raising and spending Company funds, and the proper way of giving commands"—in short, "anything in the regulations that was not understood." His patient, helpful attitude was much appreciated by those who wished to learn. Buford was happy to note that such soldiers constituted the majority of the personnel he encountered.[10]

As might be expected, he devoted his sharpest attention to supply officers. Quartermaster Durham of the Forty-third Indiana Volunteers at Calhoun he judged to be "incompetent for his position ...lazy and careless.... His accounts are all irregular, his vouchers incomplete, his stores neglected and exposed to the weather and his forage wasted." Quartermaster Wood of the Thirty-first Indiana, while basically competent, kept incomplete and "backward" accounts. Moving upriver in early December, Buford found the quartermaster of the Ninth Pennsylvania Cavalry, stationed at Jeffersonville, Indiana, guilty of purchasing "very inferior horses, some of them totally unfit for any military service, some blind, some extremely old and others merely colts." As an old dragoon, Buford was so incensed at the lack of proper care given this regiment's mounts—which he found crowded together in a filthy stable, irregularly fed, never groomed—that he wrote a scathing letter to General Buell, which got desired results in a matter of days.

After inspecting the troops in southern Indiana, Buford recrossed the river to Louisville, where he spent much of December evaluating regiments recently arrived at Buell's headquarters. When not critiquing military performance, he continued to dispense such advice and information as he thought proper, and he made careful note of deficiencies in clothing, arms, and supplies. Four days before Christmas he appears to have left the Ohio River, probably for a holiday reunion with his family. He was back on the job at Louisville on 28 December, completed his work in the first week of the new year, and made the long journey back to Washington.[11]

He may not have travelled alone. At some point during Buford's stint as assistant inspector general, his family came to live with him in Washington. It is possible that on the occasion of his return to the capital from Louisville he was accompanied by wife, son, and daughter. If so, the family would have remained in Washington—with occasional visits to the home of Pattie's parents in Georgetown, Kentucky—throughout his war career. Their presence near the area of operations in Virginia would have been comforting to him, and he would see them in the city whenever he could get leave.[12]

* * *

Over the next several months Buford alternated his inspection duties between the capital and far-flung outposts. Among assignments he performed other administrative chores such as mustering in volunteer regiments recently arrived at Washington. By the spring of 1862 he seems to have grown restless, dissatisfied with these and other non-combat duties. He was performing work of importance to the army and the war effort, but it failed to engage his imagination or challenge his abilities. Furthermore, the war to reunite the nation was proceeding too slowly, too sloppily, to suit him. In the West, soldiers like those he had inspected in Kentucky and Indiana were winning battles for the Union under emerging commanders such as Ulysses S. Grant, William T. Sherman, George H. Thomas, and John Pope. Federal fortunes in the East were less bright, although late in March McClellan finally led his vast host against the Confederates in Virginia. The general's amphibious movement down the coast to Fort Monroe and then up the Peninsula toward Richmond had barely gotten underway, but newspapers were already predicting that the "Little Napoleon" would succeed where the army humiliated at Bull Run had failed.[13]

In reviewing the course of the war's first year, Buford must have been depressed by the realization that he remained on the sidelines of the conflict while so many other former Regulars who had left the army years ago were holding positions of power, authority, and respect. It almost seemed as if he were being punished for remaining in the ranks through the lean years of the 1850s while so many others had pursued the rewards of civilian life.

Another former Regular on whom fortune was smiling was Buford's half-brother. Since resigning his commission in 1835, Napoleon Bonaparte Buford had taught school, run a mercantile business in Rock Island, established an iron foundry and other businesses in partnership with John's brothers, opened a bank, and become director of one Illinois railroad and president of another. As though bored by prosperity, N.B. had joined the volunteer ranks at war's outset, commanding an infantry regiment under Grant. Now, though well past his fiftieth birthday, he stood on the brink of appointment to brigadier general of volunteers.[14]

While proud of his sibling's accomplishments, John Buford must have envied N.B.'s ascension to command and his ability to win the confidence of a government that looked skeptically upon officers born in the South. While Napoleon and hundreds of others like him were prospering in the volunteer ranks, John Buford was toiling in obscurity as a small wheel in the machine known as the War Department. The nature of such work failed to satisfy an ambition for field command that the assistant inspector general could no longer repress.

Not until late June, after returning to Washington from an assignment in Cairo, Illinois (which probably included a side-trip to visit his brothers and their families in Rock Island), did his fortunes improve. In the capital he chanced to meet one of those rising stars of the volunteer army, John Pope, recently come east to accept command of an army now organizing in north-central Virginia. The beneficiary of several small but highly publicized victories along the Mississippi River late in '61 and early this year, Pope was viewed by the Lincoln administration as a savior, a leader who would erase the memory of defeat-prone predecessors.[15]

Although the forty-year-old Pope was an arrogant egotist whose competence was overshadowed by his capacity for self-delusion and a tendency to bluster and boast, he and Buford had some things in common. Both were native Kentuckians transplanted to Illinois in early youth (as was Abraham Lincoln, to whom Pope was related by marriage). As a back-home neighbor, Pope knew Buford's family; as a prewar colleague, he was familiar with Buford's exemplary record in the Old Army. Then, too, one of Pope's brigade commanders during the recent operations on the Mississippi—Napoleon Bonaparte Buford—may have put in a good word for his half-brother with the army leader. Any of these factors may have persuaded Pope to seek the younger Buford for his staff. It is also possible that Buford petitioned the Inspector General's Office to detail him to the Army of Virginia. The latter may well have been the case, for in his postwar writings Pope implied that he did not know of Buford's availability for a staff position until he "reported to me for duty as inspector."

When Buford arrived at army headquarters, Pope was surprised to find him still a major sixteen months into the fighting. The army leader recalled asking him "how he could possibly remain in such a position while a great war was going on, and what objections he could have (if he had any) to being placed in command in the field." Pope noted that Buford "seemed hurt to think I could have even a doubt of his wish to take the field, and told me that he had tried to get a command, but was without influence enough to accomplish it." Pope mentally filed away Buford's desire for a field appointment; should a vacancy occur, he would give his fellow Northwesterner serious consideration.[16]

A vacancy opened more quickly than Pope could have anticipated. By mid-July George B. McClellan's much-ballyhooed attempt to seize Richmond had failed. Defeated in several clashes along the Peninsula, the Little Napoleon now lay along the James River a dozen miles southeast of his unattainable prize. To relieve the pressure being exerted on McClellan by General Robert Edward Lee's Army of Northern Virginia, the War Office had ordered Pope's 47,000-man command to operate along the eastern fringes of the Blue Ridge Mountains. Specifically, Pope was to attack the railroads that supplied Lee's forces and enhanced his mobility.

This action would prevent Lee from making a move northward against Pope while McClellan lay inactive.[17]

Pope, who placed great faith in the raiding abilities of his cavalry, assigned the railroad mission to one of his three horse brigades, that attached to Major General Nathaniel P. Banks's II Army Corps. On the morning of 17 July a couple thousand troopers under Brigadier General John P. Hatch marched from army headquarters at Culpeper Court House, between the Rappahannock and Rapidan Rivers, toward Gordonsville, about twenty-two miles to the south. After cutting the Orange & Alexandria Railroad near Gordonsville the cavalry was to proceed to the college town of Charlottesville, doing additional damage near the point where the O & A joined the Virginia Central.

To Pope's surprise and chagrin, Hatch failed to complete the mission. In violation of his instructions he loaded down his raiding column with infantry and a wagon train. Thus encumbered, he marched so slowly that by the time he reached Orange Court House, some half-dozen miles short of his objective, he learned that Lee had already marched out of Richmond. Scouts reported that elements of Major General Richard S. Ewell's division of Stonewall Jackson's command had occupied Gordonsville and points westward. Unwilling to engage foot troops even though he had some of his own, Hatch turned about and retreated. An angry Pope ordered him to try again, and Hatch did a week later. The second effort, however, was a larger failure than the first; this time the cavalry stopped almost twenty miles short of Gordonsville before turning back—a move necessitated, Hatch claimed, by poor roads and exhausted horses.[18]

Hatch's bungling discouraged his troopers and lowered their morale. One of them wrote home on 25 July that the past ten days had been filled with "fatigue, hunger, and wretchedness." He kept his account of that period "as brief as possible, for I dont like to dwell upon it." The cavalry's failure absolutely infuriated the man who had ordered it; upon Hatch's return from the second mission Pope relieved him from command and tabbed John Buford to replace him. Buford's appointment as a brigadier general came through two days later.[19]

Buford's ascension to high rank, while long overdue, was so sudden and unexpected that it must have caught him off-guard. Although ample precedent existed for such a promotion, he would not have anticipated jumping from major in the regular service to a brigadier of volunteers; it is doubtful that his hopes had risen higher than battalion or regimental command.

If the promotion surprised him, it did not stagger him. Buford had seen enough of volunteer cavalry to know that even after a year in the field the typical trooper—officer and enlisted man alike—had not mastered the duties and tactics peculiar to his arm of the service. While Buford had not exercised active command of a mounted unit in almost eight months, he had no doubt he could teach the still-raw recruits some worthwhile lessons.

Trouble was, with an active campaign underway he would have to devote himself to getting acquainted with brigade personnel; he had no time to school anyone in tactics. Upon reviewing some of his new troops, his inspector's eye told him that the men and their mounts had seen better days. Careful handling would be necessary to restore their stamina and remove the stigma of failure attached to them.

In terms of size, Buford's command was a substantial force. Perhaps 2,000 strong, it consisted of the First Michigan, under Colonel Thornton F. Brodhead; the Fifth New York, Colonel Othneil De Forest; Colonel Charles H. Tompkins's First Vermont; and Lieutenant Colonel Nathaniel P. Richmond's First Virginia (Union) Cavalry. While none of the regimental commanders struck Buford as a martial giant, each stood head and shoulders above the officers he had critiqued in Kentucky, Indiana, and Illinois. Despite their checkered past, the colonels' regiments appeared to be composed of promising material. The private soldiers, the non-coms, and the company- and battalion-level officers were perhaps half-way through the training period that drillmasters considered necessary to make seasoned cavalrymen out of volunteers; Buford had no reason to suppose his men were slow learners, and he believed he could expedite the educational process. He would gain a better appreciation of their capabilities as the present campaign unfolded.[20]

The job of getting acquainted with strangers was a two-way process. Few if any of General Banks's horsemen knew who Buford was; lacking an operational background, he was an unknown quantity. In letters home, some troopers misspelled his name; others thought he had come over from the artillery or the infantry. Newspapers, caught unawares by his rise to command, also lacked information on him. In presenting a lengthy biography, the 2 September issue of the *New York Herald* confused him with his older sibling; according to the *Herald* account, Napoleon Bonaparte Buford had been transferred from Tennessee to lead Pope's horsemen.[21]

Such an error would have neither surprised nor disappointed John Buford. The last thing he craved was newspaper publicity, for he had come to regard journalists—at least those who travelled with and reported on the army—as hacks, toadies to the high command, and meddlers in military affairs. In another sense, however, the *Herald* article would have disturbed and frustrated him. It told him that after a dozen years of advancing in his profession and earning a reputation of some note, he had returned to obscurity.[22]

CHAPTER V

Field Command

Not till 3 August could Buford turn over his inspector's work to his successor and take the field at the head of his brigade. It is difficult to say what sort of initial impression he made on his men. Presumably, some would have been intrigued by his appearance, which a staff officer later described as both ordinary and striking. Buford's medium height, tanned complexion, and tawny moustache would have turned few heads, but others who studied his expression might have characterized it, as the aide did, as "determined, not to say sinister"—the look of a man "not to be trifled with."

The troopers would have been impressed by Buford's raiment. In contrast to well-tailored commanders such as Pope, given to strutting and preening, Buford's habitual field garb consisted of a Kentucky hunting shirt—a well-worn, dark blue blouse "ornamented with holes," which he sometimes wore under, sometimes in place of, his general officer's tunic. The staff officer noted that "from one pocket thereof peeps a huge pipe, while the other is fat with a tobacco pouch." The remainder of his attire included "ancient" corduroy pants, "tucked into a pair of ordinary cowhide boots," and a small black felt hat, the type anyone might wear.[1]

The uniform suggested that its owner was a man not of show but of substance—and one willing to admit, as most of his colleagues were not, that officers were not so much different from the soldiers they led. One trooper, sizing up Buford, wrote home admiringly: "He don't put on so much style as most officers." Even infantrymen appreciated Buford's appearance. They could tell he was different from the rest of those dandyish fellows on horseback, who acted as though every soldier with mud on his shoes smelled of something terrible.[2]

Madison Court House

When Buford took command, his brigade was posted near Madison Court House, between Culpeper and the Rapidan River, keeping watch over Confederate movements out of Gordonsville. Its picket line extended to the river and ran westward from Barnett's Ford, just above Orange Court House, toward the Blue Ridge Mountains. At Barnett's the picket line connected with the right flank of a five-regiment brigade of horsemen attached to the III Corps, Army of Virginia, the latter under Major General Irvin McDowell (who happened to be not only the loser at First Bull Run but also a relative of Buford's by marriage). McDowell's pickets extended eastward from Barnett's Ford to Raccoon Ford at the confluence of the Rapidan and Robertson's River. Although Confederate cavalry lined the opposite bank of the Rapidan with sizable bodies of infantry close behind, Buford felt fairly comfortable in his present position. His men were posted so as to give timely warning of an enemy advance,

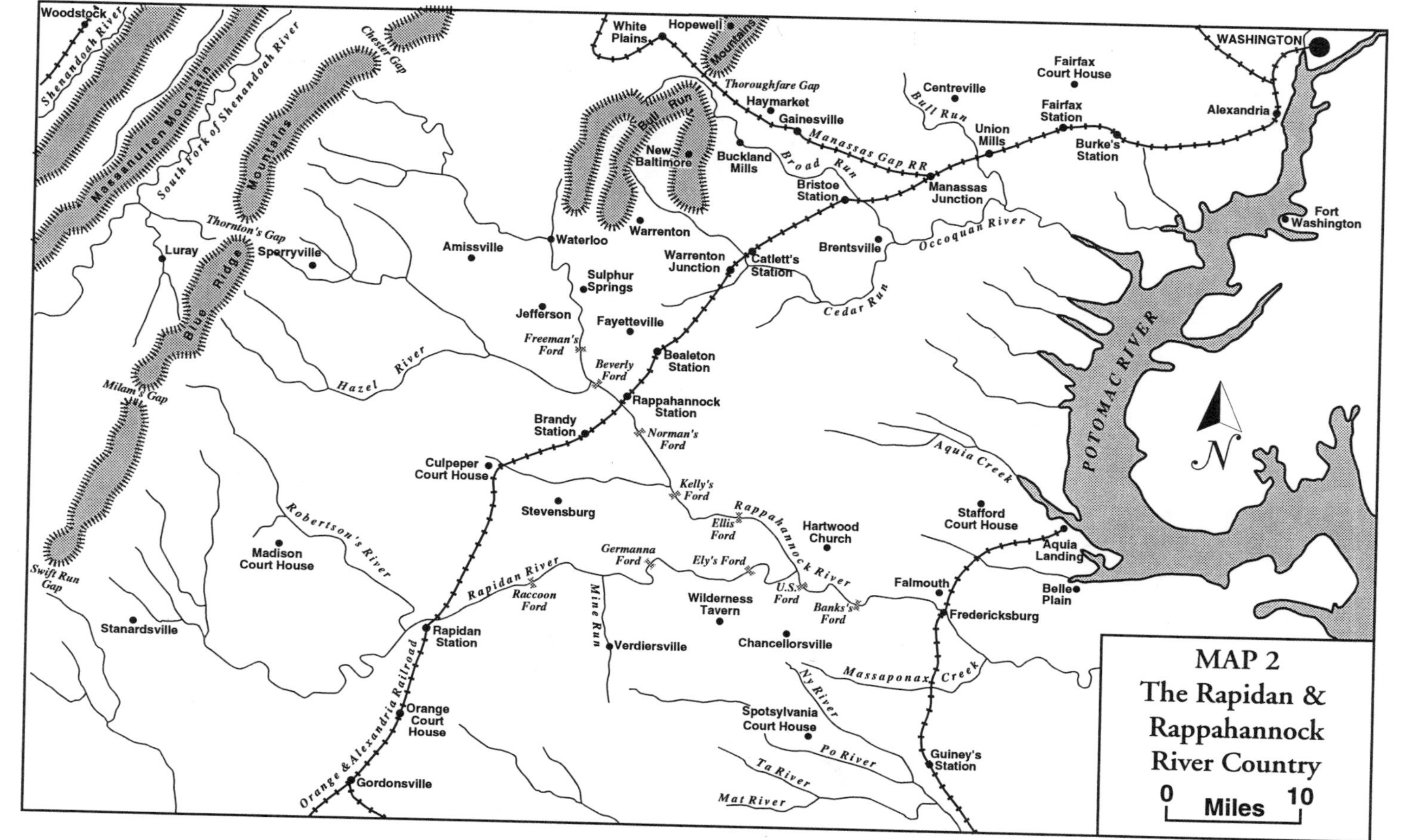
MAP 2
The Rapidan & Rappahannock River Country
0 Miles 10
N
Woodstock
Shenandoah River
Massanutten Mountain
South Fork of Shenandoah River
Mountains
Chester Gap
Thornton's Gap
Luray
Blue Ridge
Sperryville
Milam's Gap
Swift Run Gap
Stanardsville
Madison Court House
Robertson's River
Hazel River
Amissville
Waterloo
Warrenton
New Baltimore
Bull Run
White Plains
Hopewell
Mountains
Thoroughfare Gap
Haymarket
Gainesville
Buckland Mills
Broad Run
Manassas Gap RR
Bristoe Station
Manassas Junction
Centreville
Bull Run
Union Mills
Fairfax Court House
Fairfax Station
Burke's Station
WASHINGTON
Alexandria
Fort Washington
Occoquan River
Brentsville
Cedar Run
Warrenton Junction
Catlett's Station
Sulphur Springs
Jefferson
Fayetteville
Freeman's Ford
Beverly Ford
Bealeton Station
Rappahannock Station
Brandy Station
Norman's Ford
Culpeper Court House
Stevensburg
Kelly's Ford
Ellis Ford
Rappahannock River
Hartwood Church
Stafford Court House
Aquia Creek
POTOMAC RIVER
Aquia Landing
Belle Plain
Falmouth
Fredericksburg
Germanna Ford
Ely's Ford
U.S. Ford
Banks's Ford
Rapidan River
Raccoon Ford
Mine Run
Wilderness Tavern
Chancellorsville
Verdiersville
Rapidan Station
Orange Court House
Orange & Alexandria Railroad
Gordonsville
Massaponax Creek
Ny River
Spotsylvania Court House
Po River
Ta River
Mat River
Guiney's Station

and he thought highly enough of McDowell's cavalry commander, Brigadier General George D. Bayard—West Point Class of 1856 and formerly a leading light of the First United States Cavalry—that he considered his left flank secure.[3]

Only four days after reaching Madison Court House, however, Buford had to reevaluate his situation. Late on the seventh he was examining the western flank of his picket line amid the foothills of the Blue Ridge when an officer and a six-man escort from Bayard's headquarters galloped up, carrying a dispatch from their general. The message reported that Stonewall Jackson's troops had crossed the Rapidan, driving in Bayard's pickets and threatening his entire line. The officer added his superior's warning that unless Buford moved at once to his support "the line could not be held."

Buford understood the consequences of inaction: should Bayard fall back, Buford's perimeter would never hold. Even before Pope's headquarters directed him to assist Bayard, he sent a heavy detachment to the threatened sector and stood by to offer additional aid as requested. As he hastened back to Madison Court House he directed his pickets to eye their own stretch of the river with renewed vigilance.[4]

Next morning, the general heard rumors that despite his support Bayard's men had been driven away from the river. Though out of touch with Bayard, Buford learned from Pope that Jackson's troops had secured a foothold on the north bank and were massing along the road to Culpeper. Pope wished Buford to "feel down cautiously" toward Barnett's Ford, locate the nearest Rebels, and, if possible, strike them in flank and rear. To stiffen his advance Buford could call on one of General Banks's infantry brigades, positioned some distance in his rear.[5]

Short of Madison Court House, Buford realized that he had no hope of carrying out Pope's instructions. After muscling their way across Barnett's Ford the Confederates had fanned out to north and west, overrunning Buford's old headquarters and driving toward Sperryville, above Culpeper. Scouts quickly brought word that gray columns were moving along both of Buford's flanks as well as in his rear along the river. Although he must have abhorred the idea of retreating from his first encounter with the enemy, the brigadier made plans to do just that: he had no alternative.

While sending detachments to skirmish with the Rebels at the river, holding them in place, Buford directed the rest of the brigade to clear out. As most of his troopers headed north, those sent to buy time—augmented by some of Bayard's people, left behind when their comrades withdrew—gave a spirited account of themselves. Fighting and falling back in the face of Jackson's formidable column, they delayed the enemy by the quick and telling fire of their breechloading carbines. Even when finally forced to retire, their steadfastness had a residual effect: through the rest of the day the Confederates moved slowly, warily, toward the north. For fear of encountering the Union horsemen at unexpected points, Jackson divided his cavalry to protect his flanks, detailed a large infantry force to guard his trains, and left infantry pickets along his route as lookouts to discourage hit-and-run assaults. One historian notes that "Buford and Bayard would have been delighted with their impact, had they known."[6]

To avoid being overtaken by the Rebels heading for Sperryville and points north, Buford made a crosscountry circuit that carried his main body to the hamlet of Woodville, fifteen miles west of Culpeper. By hard riding, he slipped the trap; a few troopers captured in the rear constituted the extent of his loss. He did well to avoid further damage. A *New York Times* correspondent lauded the new general "for the very able manner in which he extricated his command from such a perilous condition." A few more such feats and the subject of this compliment would achieve something he professed to scorn: a newspaper reputation.[7]

* * *

Buford's roundabout route to the west prevented him from taking part in a major engagement fought on 9 August below Culpeper. The reports he and Bayard had sent Pope about the swiftness of the enemy advance prompted the army leader to push General Banks, with two infantry divisions, south of the courthouse village to bar Jackson's path. The opposing forces collided near Cedar (or Slaughter) Mountain, about eight miles below Pope's headquarters. An all-day slugging match under a blistering sun took a heavy toll of both sides including Bayard's cavalry, which guarded the Union right. Due to critical errors by the opposing commanders the fighting ended in stalemate, followed two days later by Jackson's withdrawal to the line of the Rapidan.[8]

On the evening following the battle, Buford reestablished contact with Pope's main army near Culpeper. Late the next day, having ascertained that Jackson had fallen back from Cedar Mountain, the Kentuckian turned southward with his four regiments and four pieces of horse artillery and joined General Bayard in a spirited pursuit. Against opposition from Jackson's rear guard the troopers pressed the Confederates to—and on the morning of the twelfth, across—the Rapidan.

After collecting dozens of stragglers and hundreds of badly wounded troops left behind by Jackson, the cavalry took up substantially the same line it had abandoned five days before. Buford was pleased by the hard-driving pursuit his troopers had mounted, especially the efforts of the First Vermont and First Virginia, whose men boldly forded rain-swollen streams near Thoroughfare Mountain. In his report of the action the brigadier noted that "the flight of the enemy ...was most precipitate and in great confusion." He could take much of the credit for that outcome.[9]

In the cavalry's rear, Pope's infantry and artillery lumbered down to the river. By the fourteenth, most of the army was in place just north of the Rapidan, with Major General Franz Sigel's I Corps on the right along Robertson's River, McDowell's corps in the center astride the flanks of Cedar Mountain, and Major General Jesse Reno's division of the IX Corps holding the left flank near Raccoon Ford.[10]

Reno's appearance signalled a War Department effort to strengthen Pope substantially. Not only was the rest of the IX Corps—recently based in North Carolina—being sent to augment the Army of Virginia, steps were underway to transfer McClellan's army from the James to the Rapidan. Reinforcements of this magnitude should enable Pope to make good on his oft-repeated boast to thrash Lee's army and seize the capital of that nation of traitors known as the Confederacy.[11]

The bumptious commander had no inkling that Lee had also decided to evacuate the line of the James. On the tenth, the Virginian launched preliminary operations aimed at sending the balance of his army, under Lieutenant General James Longstreet, to link with Jackson near Gordonsville. Given his interior lines of communication, the Confederate commander could concentrate against Pope more quickly than McClellan could reinforce him. Lee hoped to isolate and defeat the Army of Virginia, then turn on McClellan to give him yet another beating.[12]

The Verdiersville Raid

While awaiting McClellan's arrival, which would take several days, Pope determined to "operate with my cavalry upon the enemy's communications with Richmond." Buford complied admirably with these instructions. On the sixteenth, backed by Reno's infantry, he crossed the river near Rapidan Station, passed around Jackson's right, and, after a sharp engagement, occupied Orange Court House, ten miles inside Rebel territory. While Buford held the place, he sent his senior regimental leader, Colonel Brodhead, with detachments of his own First Michigan and the Fifth New York, southeastward toward Louisa Court House, along the railroad route to the enemy capital.

Reaching Verdiersville, north of Louisa, late on the seventeenth, the Michiganders and New Yorkers bore down on what they took to be a party of Rebel stragglers. Their quarry turned out to be Major General James Ewell Brown Stuart, the recently appointed commander of the cavalry division of the Army of Northern Virginia, and his staff. Although Stuart and most of his aides evaded capture by scant minutes, the "Beau Sabreur of the Confederacy" left behind several personal items including his scarlet-lined cloak and ostrich-plumed hat.[13]

Buford must have been pleased that the illustrious Stuart had been routed and embarrassed. Although a skillful opponent, the Rebel cavalier was everything Buford despised: flamboyant, foppish, enamored of newspaper publicity, a ladies' man. Yet Buford was more excited by the capture of Stuart's adjutant, Major Norman Fitzhugh, and the file of papers he had been trying to dispose of when nabbed. One document, a copy of an order from Lee to Stuart, revealed that Longstreet had joined Jackson below the Rapidan. Of greater import, Lee's reunited army was about to cross the river to squeeze the unsuspecting Pope in a giant pincers; the multi-pronged movement was to begin the next day.

First Brandy Station and Stevensburg

Buford rushed the intelligence—a brilliant coup for any field commander, let alone a spanking-new one—to Pope's headquarters. The army leader, horrified to learn of his precarious position, pulled north that same day; Buford's troopers, recently returned to the upper bank of the Rapidan, helped cover the withdrawal. By late on the nineteenth Pope had placed the more formidable Rappahannock River between his main body and his frustrated enemy.[14]

Seething over his lost opportunity, Lee pursued his quarry, Stuart riding in the advance, seeking revenge. On the twentieth the Southern troopers overtook Bayard's brigade at Brandy Station, a depot on the Orange & Alexandria Railroad a few miles above Culpeper. While the horsemen shot and slashed at each other, Buford's men played the role of spectators. Although ordered to concentrate his brigade opposite Kelly's Ford on the Rappahannock, within easy supporting distance of his fellow brigadier, Buford was prevented from fighting by orders to cover General Reno's headquarters at the ford. Despite his inactive status, he helped Bayard by supporting a horse battery that had unlimbered near Kelly's Ford.[15]

Once Bayard disengaged and led his battered regiments across the Rappahannock, Buford helped cover his withdrawal. Even after Bayard's departure, however, the Kentuckian remained south of the river, on the twenty-first reconnoitering south of Brandy Station, bolstered by three of Reno's regiments and a light battery. Encountering a detachment of Longstreet's infantry near Stevensburg, Buford dismounted his men and initiated what Reno called "a lively little skirmish" that ended with the Rebels taking refuge in a woods from which they dared not reemerge. In the fight Buford suffered ten casualties; enemy losses were not tabulated.

The morning after the Stevensburg mission, Pope recalled Buford and Reno to the north bank, ending the opening phase of what would become the Second Bull Run Campaign. Pope had decided to remain on the upper bank of the Rappahannock until McClellan's army and the remainder of the IX Corps could reach him. The leader of the Army of Virginia had been made to retreat from his forward position, but while his cherished offensive had been deferred it had not been terminated. As soon as he was at peak strength, he would unleash the full fury of his power against his unsuspecting foe.[16]

* * *

For the next three days, Buford's brigade operated on the western reaches of Pope's line, beyond the right flank of General Sigel's corps. Along a perimeter that ran from Fayetteville west to Sulphur Springs and then north to Warrenton, the troopers guarded infantry camps and probed southward to determine if Lee were moving to circumvent the Union left. On 24 August a part of Buford's force, backed by foot soldiers, advanced toward Waterloo, a village along the Rappahannock at the base of Carter Mountain. After burning the bridge at that point to prevent an enemy crossing, Buford lingered in the vicinity, awaiting orders. In the interim, he tried to minister to the tired troopers and played-out horses of a brigade that for several weeks had been kept almost constantly in motion. The high brigade was well aware of this undesirable situation; in his campaign report Pope admitted that "our cavalry numbered on paper about 4,000 men, but their horses were completely broken down and there were not 500 men, all told, capable of doing such service as should be expected from cavalry."[17]

Salem and White Plains

Broken down or not, much service was required of both mounts and riders. Early on the twenty-sixth—with the vanguard of the III and V Corps, Army of the Potomac, about to link with him via Alexandria—Pope learned that Lee had already landed the second blow of their long-delayed encounter. Four days before, J.E.B. Stuart, still seething over his near-capture at Verdiersville, had sneaked around Pope's right and into his rear, capturing and burning the Union supply depot at Catlett Station on the Orange & Alexandria. Now Pope learned that Jackson's "foot cavalry" had made a turning movement of their own around the same flank; via Thoroughfare Gap in the Bull Run Mountains they had joined Stuart at Gainesville, on the edge of the old Bull Run battlefield. For the second time in little over a week Pope headed north in response to an unexpected threat. He directed the widely separated elements of his army to converge toward Gainesville and Manassas Junction, where the Manassas Gap Railroad met the O & A.

What Pope did not know was that by the twenty-sixth Longstreet, thirty-six hours' march behind Jackson, was also moving by a circuitous route toward the Bull Run Mountains. Pope was so intent on bagging Jackson's 24,000 troops, who by late on the twenty-seventh had massed at Groveton, northwest of Manassas Junction, that he failed to pay due attention to Longstreet's flank column, some 26,000 strong, Lee at its head.[18]

Buford did detect Longstreet's approach; ultimately, however, his discovery did the Union cause no good. Early on the twenty-sixth, after Pope got an inkling that Rebel forces were passing through Thoroughfare Gap but before he learned of Jackson's menacing presence in his rear, the army leader ordered his ranking subordinate, Irvin McDowell, commander of the III Army Corps, to send Buford's brigade along the western side of the mountains. The brigadier was to scout the route the enemy was suspected of having taken. He was to report on the heading of the gray column, discern its intentions if possible, and contest its advance.

As he confessed to McDowell, Buford did not relish a long march that might involve his "almost disorganized" brigade in combat. While he was compelled to move, his implied complaint had an effect: on the morning of the twenty-seventh, just before starting out, his tired command was reinforced by most of the four-regiment, one-battalion brigade of cavalry attached to Sigel's corps, under Colonel John Beardsley. Beardsley's additions gave Buford as many as 2,500 troopers, although the poor condition of their horses meant that Buford's effective force was far smaller. Even so, the augmentees gave Buford some assurance that in any encounter with enemy infantry he would not be instantly overwhelmed.[19]

Early on the twenty-seventh Buford departed Waterloo, looped around the base of the mountains, and headed north through a picturesque valley toward the villages of Orleans, Salem, and White Plains. Immediately he noted signs that troops had recently passed this way. By the time he reached Salem, about midday, he had gathered up numerous stragglers from Jackson's column; they disclosed that Jackson's main body had passed on to Thoroughfare Gap. This, then, was the force Pope had discovered skulking behind his back.[20]

At about the same time that he learned of Jackson's advance toward and through the gap, Buford discovered a heavy Rebel force—Longstreet's—moving toward Salem in his rear. Only minutes after the cavalry moved north to White Plains, the newcomers occupied Salem, exchanging shots with Buford's rear-guard. Unable to move through Thoroughfare Gap due to Jackson's assumed proximity but aware that he must inform McDowell of Longstreet's coming as quickly as possible, Buford turned south along a road that led through the mountains to Warrenton, McDowell's recent headquarters.[21]

Buford had already done a good day's work, but he was not through. As the head of his column countermarched, he dismounted his rear guard and had it contest Longstreet's advance, slowing the Confederates' progress to a shuffle. At several points between Salem and White Plains, Longstreet's column halted and deployed in line of battle as Buford's carbineers fired on it, fell back, and fired again. Each time the Rebel advance would shudder to a halt, return the fire, then lurch forward. The delay meant that for some hours longer than Lee had anticipated, Pope would have the luxury of battling an unsupported Jackson.

The Union troopers were so aggressive in challenging their opponents that they bagged fifty prisoners. They nearly bagged fifty-one: General Lee barely escaped from the cavalry's clutches while occupying an exposed vantage point on the outskirts of Salem.[22]

En route to Warrenton, Buford rushed word to General McDowell that Longstreet was nearing Thoroughfare Gap. McDowell, bound by Pope's order to hasten to Gainesville, realized that despite Buford's obstructionism the Rebels would debouch from the pass early on the twenty-eighth. Aware of the consternation Longstreet could create if he moved unmolested behind Pope's main body, the III Corps commander disobeyed orders. Instead of joining Pope with his entire corps, McDowell sent one of his divisions, under Brigadier General James B. Ricketts, augmented by Bayard's cavalry, to Thoroughfare Gap in the small hours of the twenty-eighth.[23]

McDowell's instincts were good but his plan was faulty. A few brigades of infantry and one of cavalry could not stop more than 25,000 Confederates supported by artillery and horsemen of their own. Reaching the gap in advance of the enemy (thanks partially to Buford's delaying action), Bayard's troopers barricaded its mouth with felled trees, heavy boulders, lumber, and other natural and manmade obstacles. The barriers kept Longstreet back for several hours but by early evening flanking parties sent through narrower gaps on either side of Thoroughfare had rendered Ricketts's and Bayard's position untenable. No support coming from Pope, foot soldiers and horsemen withdrew dejectedly from the mountain and headed southeastward to rejoin Pope. To their rear, Longstreet's troops began to pour through the gorge just as General McDowell had foreseen.[24]

A myth has grown up in recent years (given new life by Shaara's *Killer Angels* and its film version, "Gettysburg") that Buford and his troopers shared the fate of Ricketts's and Bayard's men, holding valiantly at the gap for several hours, vainly calling for help from Pope, until overwhelmed and forced to retreat. In actuality, Buford's column did not come within ten miles of Thoroughfare Gap on the twenty-eighth. Rather, Buford led his two brigades through the mountains to Warrenton, worn-out horses dropping by the wayside, many of them dying. One of Buford's subordinates reported that the survivors reached their destination at nine P. M. where they "rested in the high road without forage for horses until daylight, the other troops of the corps having left [with McDowell] during the preceding day."[25]

After guarding the evacuated headquarters throughout the night, Buford led what remained of his command up the Warrenton Turnpike toward Gainesville, seeking to overtake McDowell's column. Thus the horsemen passed well to the east of the day's fighting at Thoroughfare Gap, while also missing the more sanguinary action at the other end of the turnpike, where, late that day, Jackson's troops at Groveton attacked one of the converging wings of Pope's army.

Reconnaissance at Haymarket

Although not committed to battle on the twenty-eighth, Buford rendered valuable service by giving Irvin McDowell timely word of Longstreet's progress in passing Thoroughfare Gap and closing up on Jackson. After bivouacking below Gainesville, Buford pulled his troopers off the turnpike on the morning of the twenty-ninth and led them northward to the crossroads village of Haymarket. From above that town the brigadier enjoyed a sweeping view of the road from Thoroughfare Gap, which passed through Haymarket before meeting the pike at Gainesville. By now the road was free of Ricketts's and Bayard's troops, they having proceeded southeastward toward Bristoe Station on the Orange & Alexandria to rejoin McDowell's corps. Their absence permitted Longstreet's men to advance toward Gainesville with a full head of steam. Urging them on were sounds of heavy fighting echoing from the area watered by Bull Run, where a general engagement was underway between Jackson and Pope.[26]

The first Rebels to reach Buford's line of sight were so intent on hastening eastward they paid scant notice to the horsemen watching them from above. For a time undetected, Buford took careful note of the enemy column as it route-stepped through Gainesville. By nine o'clock he had counted seventeen infantry regiments, five hundred cavalry, and a battery. In that force there may have been more regiments than he thought—Buford estimated each to consist of 800 men, an inflated figure—but his estimate should have sufficiently alerted his superiors to Jackson's imminent and substantial reinforcing. Buford's only other failing was his refusal to specify the origins of the Confederate force. Too far away to make an exact identification, he must have suspected that the troops were Longstreet's, but the possibility existed that they were members of Jackson's rear-guard.[27]

By about ten A.M., having finished enumerating his foe and anxious to clear harm's way, Buford prepared to head for Bristoe Station. Along that route he could cover the rear of Ricketts's division, to which he had been temporarily attached, rounding up stragglers in danger of falling into enemy hands. As he made ready to depart, he dispatched couriers to carry the information he had gleaned to both Ricketts and McDowell.

Ricketts's response to the intelligence is not known, but when his corps commander received the news, some time before noon, McDowell reacted curiously. He immediately shared its contents with Major General Fitz John Porter, whose recently arrived V Corps, Army of the Potomac, held the far left of Pope's enlarged army. Later that day Buford's dispatch would play a major role in persuading Porter not to attack Jackson, as Pope had directed, for fear of encountering Stonewall's fast-approaching reinforcements.

For some inexplicable reason, McDowell failed to forward Buford's dispatch to Pope himself. The army commander, by now obsessed with his vision of crushing an isolated Jackson, continued to lack an appreciation of Longstreet's rapid approach in the direction of the Union left. Later McDowell excused his omission by claiming that he had been unable to tell from Buford's message whether the troops flooding through Gainesville were in fact Longstreet's. Given McDowell's earlier prediction of Longstreet's rapid advance through Thoroughfare Gap, his explanation raises more questions than it answers. Buford had submitted an intelligence report that, properly exploited, would have enabled Pope to hold the major forces of his enemy apart long enough to defeat each in turn. But the Union high command appeared determined to make the least of the advantage Buford had handed it.[28]

Closing up on Manassas

As expected, in riding with his advance guard from Haymarket to Bristoe Station, Buford encountered straggling troops from Ricketts's column lounging by the roadside, rubbing sore feet or boiling coffee, oblivious to the threat of pursuit. Spying a band of Confederate cavalry coming up from the east along a trail that intersected the road he and the stragglers were taking, Buford reined in beside a group of loungers and called them to attention. One of the tired men heard Buford address him and his comrades "in a voice and tone that was not to be disobeyed," ordering them into the line of battle.

When the foot troops got to their feet, they stared pop-eyed at the enemy horsemen charging toward them. Hastily loading their rifles, at Buford's command they unleashed a ragged volley at the riders, by now only a few rods away. Most of the Confederates weathered the barrage and spurred forward before their assailants could reload. At Buford's cry of "run for your lives or the rebs will have you!" the stragglers took off down the road at a frantic pace, tripping over one another in their haste to escape. One can imagine Buford smiling at their discomfiture, before turning the carbines of his brigade on the enemy and putting them to flight.[29]

After clearing the road, Buford continued on to Bristoe Station. Discovering that the scene of action had shifted north, he moved up the railroad to the battle site near Bull Run. Early in the afternoon he took up a position on the far left of Pope's army along the meandering waters of Dawkins's Branch about two miles from Manassas Junction.[30]

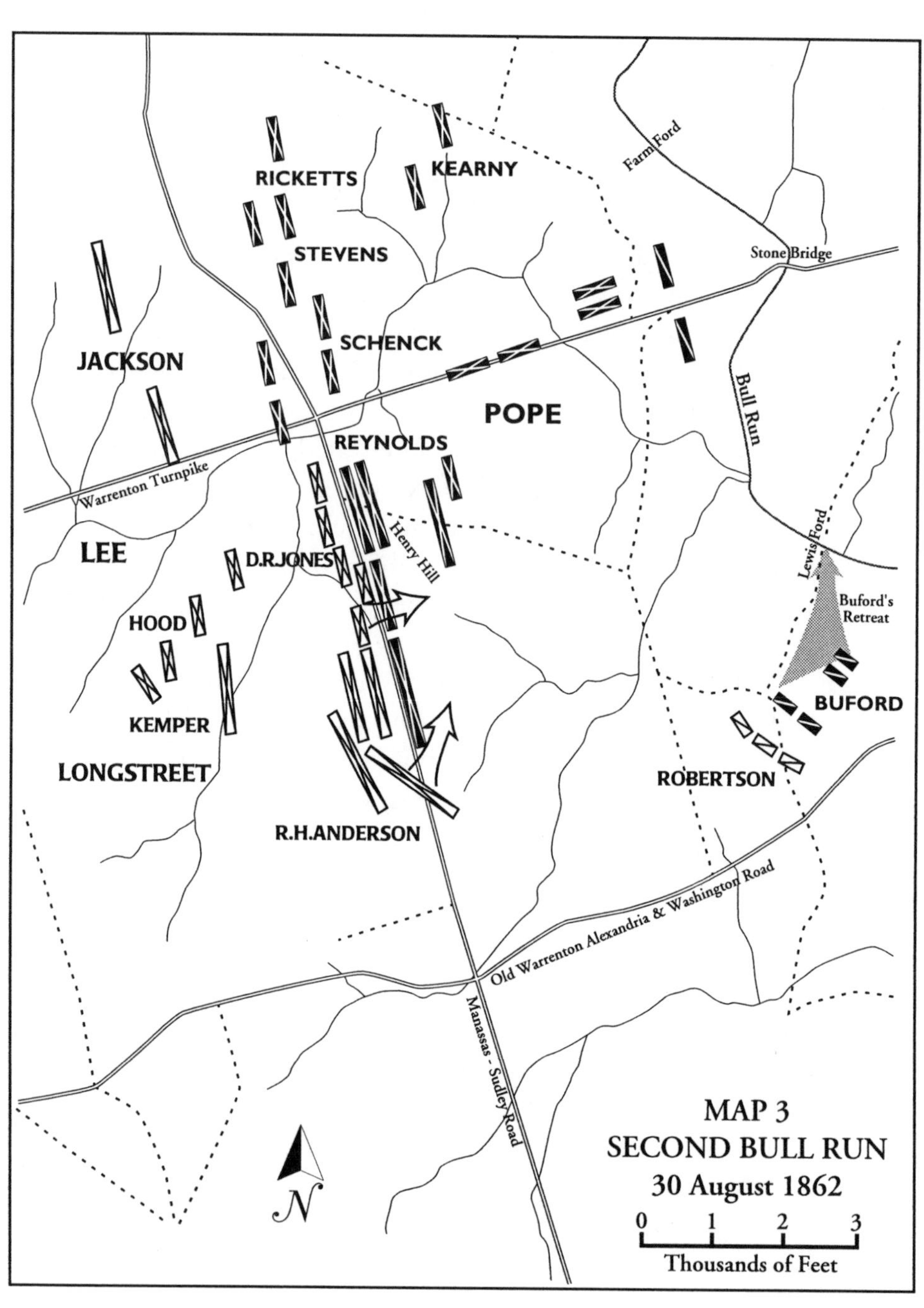
RICKETTS
KEARNY
Farm Ford
STEVENS
Stone Bridge
SCHENCK
JACKSON
Bull Run
POPE
REYNOLDS
Warrenton Turnpike
Henry Hill
LEE
D.R.JONES
Lewis Ford
Buford's Retreat
HOOD
BUFORD
KEMPER
LONGSTREET
ROBERTSON
R.H.ANDERSON
Old Warrenton Alexandria & Washington Road
Manassas - Sudley Road
MAP 3
SECOND BULL RUN
30 August 1862
0
1
2
3
Thousands of Feet
N

Seeking information on the progress of the battle, Buford learned that the previous day's combat had been fierce but inconclusive. Under a sweltering sun, Pope had attacked above Groveton in a daylong series of waves that might have crushed a lesser command, but not Jackson's. Stonewall was determined to hold his ground until Lee and Longstreet came up to aid him.

That event was imminent when Buford reached the battlefield, although neither he nor his commander knew it. Ignorant of Longstreet's approach along the Warrenton Turnpike—refusing to read the portents of impending calamity—Pope had resumed his assaults on Jackson's position. By throwing the infantry on his left, including the troops of his reluctant reinforcement Fitz John Porter, across the pike, Pope was offering up that part of his army as a sacrifice to Jackson's friends.[31]

Lewis Ford

For much of the afternoon, Buford had an easy time of it, patrolling the Warrenton-Alexandria-Washington Road where he experienced what an observer called "severe but somewhat spasmodic and localized fighting." Only a portion of Buford's command—now reduced to three regiments by the return of Beardsley's brigade to Sigel's corps and by the detaching of the Fifth New York to escort duty at Pope's headquarters—participated in this action. The tempo of Buford's work increased dramatically, however, when, shortly after four P.M., Longstreet's long delayed assault swept forward, overpowering everything in its path. In minutes, the Federal left cracked and collapsed. Reacting swiftly, Buford yanked his brigade toward the rear, where he could better assess the changed situation. By perhaps five-thirty his men had withdrawn to a point near Lewis Ford, where the road to Washington crossed Bull Run.[32]

Buford's fall-back, a natural reaction to Longstreet's assault, invited a countermove. While he regrouped behind a low ridge perhaps 700 yards in front of the ford, Buford received a message from the commander of Beardsley's Fourth New York, stationed nearby: a force of Rebel cavalry, at least two regiments strong, supported by a battery, was marching toward Buford's ridge. Well to the rear, one of Longstreet's columns was heading the same way.[33]

At once Buford prepared his lead regiment, Colonel Brodhead's First Michigan, to launch a saber charge. Behind the Wolverines he placed the mounted Fourth New York, which he had appropriated as a replacement for the Fifth. Farther to the rear he positioned the First Vermont and First Virginia to provide dismounted support to the chargers.[34]

The enemy force—five Virginia regiments under Buford's ex-comrade in the Second Dragoons, now-Brigadier General Beverly Robertson of the Confederate Cavalry—continued toward what it took to be a band of stragglers, the only Union troops not concealed behind the ridge. Without reconnoitering the ground in front, Robertson elected to charge and scatter the stragglers before continuing into the enemy's rear. Scorning to commit a large segment of his force, he dispatched a single regiment, Colonel Thomas T. Munford's Second Virginia, to clear the way. For his part, Munford assigned the task to a small detachment under his second-in-command.[35]

When this unit chased its quarry toward the crest of the ridge, Buford signalled Brodhead's men forward. Unwilling to miss a rare experience, the general had placed himself at the head of the regiment; now he began to shout commands. A trooper in the ranks recalled the upshot: "The order came, 'By fours front into line!' The men came up in fine style, and then came the order, 'By platoons, right about wheel! Draw sabres!' The rebel battery and cavalry were in front of us. I held my breath for a moment.... The bugle sounded the charge, and away we went...." Buford spurred forward, perhaps five hundred screaming troopers close behind, sabers twirling, pistols cracking, pounding at full speed toward the enemy.[36]

The attack dumbfounded the detachment of the Second Virginia, which turned and raced back to its starting-point, frenzied Michiganders, backed by equally excited New Yorkers, on its heels. En route to the rear the fugitives met the balance of their regiment, under Colonel Munford, heading the other way. Caught off-balance, knowing no alternative, Munford had resolved to commit his main body to a counterattack.[37]

Seconds later, the two forces collided with a sickening thud in the fields between the lines. Dozens of men went down on both sides, including Colonel Brodhead, who took buckshot through both lungs and fell, mortally wounded, into the hands of his enemy. With no time to regret the colonel's loss, Buford led his survivors in slashing their way through Munford's overmatched force. After several minutes of swordplay and small arms' fire, the Virginians turned about and made their way to Robertson's main body with haste verging on panic.[38]

Enraged and embarrassed by Munford's overthrow, General Robertson threw the next regiments in his column, the Twelfth and Seventh Virginia, at the triumphal Federals. Carving a path through unhorsed members of Munford's regiment, the fresh troops bore down on the re-formed First Michigan and Fourth New York. The attackers were astonished to find their enemy "facing us and halted as if on parade," an attitude of coolness bordering on arrogance.

Someone had instilled a sense of style and pride, as well as a combative spirit, in these Yankees.

Since most of the Federals were stationary, they made good targets. The charging troopers butted into them, bowling over horses and riders, cutting down other men with carbines and pistols. After a brief effort to hold their ground, Buford's people hastened back to the ridge, all semblance of formation lost. "From that time on," a Michigan trooper reported, the Union regiments fused together in "one mixed mass of ...men dismounted and horses without riders ...all trying to get away."[39]

A classic cavalry encounter consists of a succession of attack waves, each causing the previous wave to recede, counterattack repulsing attack and victory going to the antagonist with uncommitted reserves. The success achieved by the Twelfth and Seventh Virginia should have been temporary, cancelled out by the next attack. But the next attack never materialized. Through some error, Buford's First Vermont and First Virginia did not remount and charge in support of their comrades. The fault could not have been Buford's, for he was riding in the vanguard; a subordinate left in the rear must have failed to commit the fresh troops at the critical time.[40]

Ordinarily Buford might have rectified the problem and renewed the attack, but he was *hors de combat.* At the height of the melee he had taken a glancing but painful and disabling blow to the knee from a spent bullet. Unable to grip saddle leather, he drifted out of the fight as his men tried desperately to stave off defeat.[41]

It could not be done; without immediate support, they were at the mercy of Robertson's larger numbers. After several minutes of futile effort, the four regiments fought their way across Lewis Ford, leaving behind almost 300 comrades, dead, wounded, or captured. The casualties included the

wounding of every member of Buford's staff including a pair of "dashing, gallant and daring" aides-de-camp assigned him by General Pope, Captains Myles Keogh and Joseph O'Keeffe.

Once on the far side of Bull Run the survivors of the vicious little battle were safe. Showing a timidity that would color his later performances, General Robertson decided to forgo a close pursuit. Appreciative of the favor, John Buford painfully departed the scene of temporary success, missed opportunity, and ultimate defeat.[42]

CHAPTER VI

Missing in Action

The general's wound was more painful than serious. It would slow him for weeks, causing him to hobble about in obvious discomfort; it would not, however, cripple him. Perhaps confusing his injury with Colonel Brodhead's, some newspapers printed the erroneous story that the injury was life-threatening; in its 2 September editions, the *New York Herald* reported Buford killed. Latter-day historians, influenced by these accounts, would perpetuate the falsehood that Buford nearly died as a result of a severe wound received on 30 August.[1]

In actuality, damage would have been slight. A blow from a spent bullet would not have cracked the patella or done severe damage to the knee joint. The lack of a penetrating wound rules out infection, a serious threat to quick recovery. The most likely results of the injury would have been a prominent bruise and swelling in the soft tissue around the joint, symptoms Buford would have tolerated without great effort.

One indication that the injury was not serious was that

the patient was on inactive service for only a few days. After falling back across Bull Run, he felt well enough to remain with his command as it covered the retreat of three army corps. Buford's troopers, though all but "completely broken down" by their heavy workload in recent weeks, did their part in clearing a path of withdrawal toward Washington via Chantilly and Fairfax Court House—a path that neither Jackson nor Longstreet, despite repeated attempts and the advantage of momentum, could cut off.[2] Buford's good work in this critical capacity capped a campaign filled with able and occasionally inspired service. To his credit, John Pope recognized and appreciated the cavalry leader's contributions as well as those of George Bayard. Although critical of the performance of numerous subordinates, especially General Porter, in his after-action report Pope noted that "from the first to the last day of the campaign, scarcely a day passed that these officers did not render service which entitles them to the gratitude of the Government."[3]

Under the weary but watchful eyes of Buford's and Bayard's troopers, the flotsam of Pope's army floated back inside the defenses of Alexandria throughout the last day of the month and the first days of September. On 2 September the defeated and discredited Pope was superseded in command by George McClellan and left the main theater of the war forever. At about the same time John Buford left the field as well—albeit temporarily, to seek medical treatment and bed rest.[4]

While Buford lay abed in his rented house, ministered to by Pattie, waited on by his children, the dispirited survivors of Second Bull Run tried to recover from the physical and emotional shock of their defeat and to prepare for a new outing against Lee. Many found it difficult to overcome the pain and humiliation they had suffered under Pope. The vast majority held the army commander, whom they considered a gross incompetent, personally responsible for the debacle along the Warrenton Pike. Numerous survivors indicted Irvin McDowell for conspicuous complicity in the defeat. A surprising number gave credence to a rumor that McDowell had manipulated the defeat through covert allegiance to the Confederacy.

Nowhere were the denunciations and recriminations more severe than among the cavalry. On his deathbed Thornton Brodhead dictated a letter given wide circulation by the Northern press in the wake of the defeat; in the missive the colonel attributed his fate to the fact that "Gen. Pope has been outwitted, and that McDowell is a traitor. Had they done their duty as I did mine, and had [they] led as I led," victory would have been assured. Meanwhile, a cavalry surgeon from Indiana, Dr. Elias W. Beck, wailed that "we were badly out Generaled—they beat us to death...I would resign today—if not for pure shame when we are so badly beaten." The good doctor added that "Pope is sunk lower than Hell—where he belongs—McDowell had showed himself a Traitor & murdered his own men...." Even General Bayard, who rarely gave vent to base emotions, sprinkled vehement denunciations of both generals throughout the letters he wrote to his father.[5]

While everyone else suffered, Buford healed. His convalescence lasted less than three days; by 4 September he had rejoined his brigade, which in his absence had massed near Upton's Hill on the road between Falls Church and the District of Columbia. On that day he received a message from now-General Marcy, whose son-in-law had not only regained command of the Army of the Potomac but had added Pope's survivors to it. Marcy notified the Kentuckian that he and General Bayard would be responsible for picketing the country in the army's front, Bayard to operate north of Falls Church, Buford southward as far as Fort Lyon, below

Alexandria. They were to detect and block any attempt by Lee to pursue his beaten foe to the banks of the Potomac. Meanwhile, those troopers who had long been part of the Army of the Potomac would ready themselves for renewed campaigning against J.E.B. Stuart.[6]

The new assignment probably irked Buford. In its debilitated condition neither his brigade nor Bayard's was fit for battle service. But by the same token, neither were they fit to conduct the scouting and picket duty McClellan was thrusting upon them (Bayard complained that the idea of trying to patrol such an extensive area with exhausted troopers was "d——d nonsense"). Nor was Buford convinced the duty was necessary: if Lee intended to pursue his beaten enemy to Washington, would he not have shown up by now?[7]

Buford must have envied the leader of the cavalry sent to fight Stuart—field service was always preferable to picket duty. That man was Alfred Pleasonton, Buford's comrade in the Second Dragoons and his companion during the Sioux campaign of '55. Pleasonton, whose appointment as a brigadier general of volunteers predated Buford's by ten days, had recently received field command of McClellan's cavalry, five brigades strong, almost 7,000 officers and men.[8]

Buford's plight endured for only three days. On the evening of the seventh, by which time his brigade was probing along the Little River Turnpike toward the Orange & Alexandria Railroad, General Marcy contacted him again, this time with happier news. Buford was to turn over his command to his ranking subordinate and report to McClellan's headquarters in the capital. In response to reports that Lee had begun to range into western Maryland, the army leader was about to transfer his headquarters to Rockville, but Marcy would wait in the city until Buford's arrival. Obviously, something important was afoot.

Leaving his field headquarters along the Alexandria Road,

Buford painfully cantered up the pike to the District line, crossed Long Bridge into the heart of the city, and sought out Marcy, whom he found in the process of decamping for parts north. Marcy told his visitor to gather up his staff and follow him to Rockville: McClellan had appointed Buford chief of cavalry of the Army of the Potomac.[9]

* * *

On paper, Buford's new job—which may have stemmed from a recommendation by Pleasonton or by Buford's predecessor and West Point friend, George Stoneman—was a highly responsible one, vested with wide-ranging authority. In actuality, the post was an anomalous nonentity. Pleasonton would retain control of McClellan's horsemen where that control counted—in the field—while Buford would exercise titular command.

Buford's basic role was that of a conduit between army headquarters and the field units, relaying messages from McClellan to Pleasonton and his lieutenants. A profusion of other thankless, non-operational tasks became his responsibility as well: inspecting, clothing, equipping, feeding, mounting, and transporting cavalry units scattered throughout the area of operations. In sum, he was stuck with the drudgery, while Pleasonton reaped whatever glory accrued from field operations under McClellan. Buford was well aware that McClellan and other generals in the Army of the Potomac nourished a bitter animosity toward John Pope. Was his close association with that discredited general responsible for this thankless and overly demanding position? Or had his untimely wounding restricted him to inactive duty?

The Antietam Campaign

Trying hard to avoid resentment, Buford served faithfully

and well during the pursuit of Lee through western Maryland, which on 17 September culminated in the war's bloodiest day of battle along Antietam Creek outside the village of Sharpsburg. Throughout the week leading up to the climactic encounter, while Buford served as behind-the-scenes liaison between McClellan and Pleasonton, the latter led the army's advance, winning special notice on the fourteenth at South Mountain, where he commanded infantry and artillery as well as horsemen. According to Captain Keogh, in that battle Buford had charge of the mounted forces on the flanks of the army, although he served inconspicuously enough to escape official attention.[10]

Three days later, neither commander won recognition on a field all but devoid of mounted combat. Pleasonton's participation was limited to supporting the II Corps of Major General Edwin Sumner (former commander of the First Dragoons) along the right-center of the Union line. The field leader achieved a minor feat when, about midday, he advanced cavalry skirmishers, supported by the most famous unit of horse artillery in the old army—Battery A, Second United States, under Buford's West Point classmate, Captain John Tidball—and gained possession of Middle Bridge along the Boonsboro Turnpike. The position thus won enabled Pleasonton to bring up the rest of his horse batteries, easing the pressure of a crossfire that Sumner had been absorbing.

Beyond a spirited cannonade, the rest of the battle in Pleasonton's sector passed uneventfully. After the desperate fighting characteristic of other parts of the field died down, the cavalry remained essentially where it stood hours before; it had not been able to expand its foothold west of the creek or funnel more than a handful of troopers into the flow of the action. Pleasonton's casualties—fewer than thirty, all told—indicated the limited nature of cavalry's participation in the battle, a tactical stalemate that gained a measure of strategic significance when Lee recrossed the Potomac on the nineteenth, ending his first foray into what was considered Northern territory.[11]

The Army of the Potomac pursued its opponent only as far as the river whose name it had borrowed. For weeks a self-satisfied McClellan lolled in camp on the north bank as though deserving of a vacation. President Lincoln could not fathom his general's complacency but knew no way to overcome it.

While the greater portion of the infantry waged a static campaign, the cavalry nominally under Buford's control was active on a daily basis, crossing and recrossing the river, scouting Lee's new position, and skirmishing with Stuart's division. In time the overworked horsemen grew disgusted with the idleness of their comrades in the main army. Surgeon Beck of the Third Indiana asked himself: "Might we not have decimated them [the Confederates] in following up our victory—or will you let the man you knock down rise & get away? Now they are on Va Soil & we shall probably have to follow them to Richmond."[12]

The burden the cavalry carried after Antietam was especially onerous in view of the exhausted condition of the arm. Like Pope before him, McClellan wailed to Washington that his army was "wholly deficient in cavalry," but he could offer no solution. Buford, who had the primary responsibility of refurbishing the command, found himself all but powerless to improve its condition. The basic problem was the virtual impossibility of refitting a force that was constantly on the move. Throughout the Antietam Campaign, the cavalry had been shuttled from one operational area to another, frustrating Buford's efforts to provide it with rations and forage on a regular basis. After Lee's recrossing of the Potomac, the cavalry's plight eased somewhat, for in its fixed camps along the river, not far from the line of the Baltimore & Ohio

Railroad, it could be more easily provided with salt pork and hardtack, hay and oats.[13]

Even after finally being resupplied, the cavalry had a long way to go to regain its pre-Antietam strength. Its continuing weakness was a major factor in Pleasonton's failure to curtail the 9-13 October raid by Stuart's cavalry through Maryland into southern Pennsylvania. That expedition, which culminated in the sack of government warehouses outside Chambersburg, proved a great embarrassment to McClellan's cavalry by revealing its weakness in a defensive role.

Given his position and title, Buford received part of the blame for Stuart's dramatic exploit. Blame, however, was not rightfully his. From army headquarters, well in rear of the raid, he had worked strenuously to coordinate an effective pursuit. He dispatched units to scour the countryside for word of the raiders' whereabouts; he tried to keep Pleasonton's men apprised of Stuart's changing route; and he blocked all major roads leading south from Pennsylvania. Still, he could not overcome the timidity, the lethargy, and the ineptitude of those leading the chase, who allowed Stuart to slip through their outstretched hands.[14]

Stuart's ride around the Army of the Potomac—his second in four months, the first having occurred at the height of the Peninsula Campaign—had long-lasting effects. It helped persuade Lincoln that McClellan was not, nor would ever be, the man to run the enemies of the Union to earth. On 26 October, almost six weeks after Lee returned to Virginia, McClellan finally crossed the Potomac in pursuit. Lincoln was hopeful that Little Mac would make amends for his chronic lassitude, but when the commanding general moved sluggishly and erratically, as though without purpose, the president relieved him of command on the fifth of November.[15]

* * *

When his superior was deposed, Buford suspected that he would be relieved as well. But when McClellan's senior subordinate was chosen to replace him, Buford found himself serving under a friend from West Point, Major General Ambrose E. Burnside, former commander of the IX Corps. When Burnside took over, the army was grouped around Warrenton, its enemy on the opposite bank of the Rappahannock at and near Culpeper Court House. Having replaced a general guilty of inactivity, Burnside felt constrained to launch an offensive south of the river without delay. With a major operation imminent, he was not about to make staff changes, especially when, in Buford's case, he enjoyed the services of a trusted officer long familiar to him. Despite the many headaches his position entailed and the few compensations it offered, Buford—good soldier and good friend—agreed to serve "Old Burn" for as long as needed.[16]

The Fredericksburg Campaign

He soon discovered that under the new regime his job was, if anything, more frustrating than ever. Only a week after Burnside's assumption of command, the army was on the move toward Fredericksburg, jumping-off point for a swift descent upon Richmond. As always, cavalry screened the front, flanks, and rear of the army as it marched, while probing toward the enemy and in turn fending off Stuart's probes. The speed with which the new commander pushed southeastward enabled his army to reach the Rappahannock crossings opposite Fredericksburg in advance of General Lee. But it also played hob with the still-fragile health of cavalrymen and cavalry horses.

When crimps developed in Burnside's plan—including a lengthy delay in obtaining pontoons, crucial to crossing the bridgeless river—the army had to halt on the upper bank near Falmouth. By 20 November, three days after Burnside reached Falmouth, Lee's army had occupied Fredericksburg and the Federals' advantages of timing and position no longer existed.[17]

Stubborn Burnside refused to relinquish his vision of battering Lee into submission on open ground. Long after he had lost the strategic initiative, he lingered along the river, skirmishing intermittently in preparation for a forced crossing. As before, most of the army's foot troops enjoyed a long stretch under canvas, but the horsemen of Pleasonton, Bayard (who had recently joined the main army), and Brigadier General William Woods Averell were kept almost constantly on the move, scouting, demonstrating, and patrolling miles of picket line.

As the army dallied, winter drew near. A deadly combination of frost and thaw, rain, snow, and mud aggravated the effects of overwork and neglect common to extended field service. The result was a rash of equine diseases including glanders, "scratches," "hoof-rot," and "greased heel." Mounts by the dozen went lame; hundreds had to be shot. Others succumbed to malnutrition or tainted forage. Some regiments resorted to expedients to secure good grain for their animals; Buford reprimanded more than a few for stealing hay from the local populace or from other outfits.[18]

Due to its infirmities, the cavalry occupied an uncertain place in Burnside's plans during the balance of the campaign. By 9 December, as he prepared to cross the river on his recently arrived pontoons and challenge Lee beyond Fredericksburg, Burnside confided to General Averell that he was still "unsettled as to what should be done with his horsemen." His only thought was that the cavalry attached to each of the army's Grand Divisions (a grouping of two or more army corps) should follow their commands to the lower bank, guarding its flanks and rear, their subsequent movements to be dictated by events. When Averell suggested that a battle would be well advanced, perhaps finished, by the time the cavalry reached Fredericksburg, Burnside sharply asked him if he had a better idea.[19]

Burnside's inability to devise a meaningful strategy for his cavalry was symptomatic of his overall approach to fighting Lee. On the eleventh he led his 122,000-man army across the river and marched it through the ruins of a city shattered by artillery fire. The next day, while the crossing concluded, he positioned Major General William B. Franklin's Left Grand Division for an assault against Lee's right flank, which occupied alarmingly high ground that had been fortified and improved over the past several days. Burnside's vague plan also called for an offensive farther north against even taller, more formidable ground by Sumner's Right Grand Division, backed by the Center Grand Division of Major General Joseph Hooker.[20]

Once the infantry went forward, Burnside hoped to find something useful for his horse soldiers to do. Until then, they would serve in rear of the battlelines. Buford would serve even farther back, at army headquarters. From there, his superior must have assumed, he would be able to coordinate mounted operations on all parts of the field.

Burnside began the battle at about eight-thirty on the thirteenth by launching Franklin against Stonewall Jackson's position. Segments of Franklin's I and VI Corps, especially the divisions of George Gordon Meade and John Gibbon, achieved initial gains, penetrating sections of the Rebel line on the west side of the railroad to Richmond. Their assaults finally ran out of energy, however, and counterattacks regained the ground Jackson had lost. Meanwhile, to the north, Sumner and Hooker experienced a worse fate, wave after wave of assault troops breaking on the Confederate defenses atop Marye's Heights and receding in a bloody froth. Refusing to admit a mistake or concede defeat, Burnside kept the attacks coming until well after dark. By then thousands of his men lay heaped upon the frozen ground between the lines.[21]

With its ringing note of futility, Burnside's debacle drowned out even Pope's disaster at Bull Run. Like everyone else watching from the rear, Buford was appalled by the loss of life, which gained the army no advantage whatever. The best he could have said of the battle was that the troopers under his nominal authority played virtually no part in it and thus suffered minimal casualties. The most significant loss had occurred in Bayard's brigade, whose young and talented commander had been mortally wounded by a shell. While Bayard's command had seen some action, by Burnside's order only two detachments of Pleasonton's brigade, and none from Averell's, had crossed the river; the majority of the men remained beside their saddled mounts, ready for action but denied it. As one of Averell's officers commented, "evidently a terrible battle was going on, but with what result we could only guess, for we ...did not see an enemy or hear the whir-r-r of a single shot."[22]

After 13 December, Buford could not have been keen on serving under Ambrose Burnside. He must have been shocked by his friend's deadly ineptitude, his dogged insistence on turning defeat into nightmare. Nor would Buford have appreciated the continuing impotence of his position as chief of cavalry. In the aftermath of the battle, he was reduced to coordinating scouting reports and stockpiling supplies for use during the weather-aborted offensive known as the "Mud March." Toward year's close, when Burnside and Averell discussed a large-scale expedition across the Rapidan to break enemy communications toward Richmond and

Petersburg (a project ultimately scrapped), Buford was not even consulted on the matter.[23]

All things considered, Buford must have been relieved to detach himself from the army and travel to Washington in the last week of the year. The visit was for the purpose of providing sworn testimony at the court-martial of Fitz John Porter. The former corps commander had been brought up on charges preferred by Pope's inspector-general but framed by Pope himself: disobedience of certain orders during the campaign of Second Bull Run and slow and inadequate execution of others.

Buford's 31 December appearance at the trial, held in a public building off Pennsylvania Avenue, took only a few minutes. His testimony concerned the events surrounding his 29 August scouting report of enemy forces passing through Gainesville, which had prompted Porter to withhold a blow that Pope had ordered him to strike. Whatever the effect of Buford's contribution, in January the court convicted Porter on all charges and sentenced him to be dismissed from the service.

While doubtless uneasy about providing testimony potentially damaging to a brother officer (and a fellow Democrat), Buford was happy about the family reunion the trip made possible. He was able to see not only Pattie and the children but also his half-brother. Brigadier General Napoleon Bonaparte Buford had come east with his wife, Mary, to recover from a debilitating illness contracted in Mississippi; late in November Secretary of War Edwin McMasters Stanton had selected him to serve as one of the members of Porter's tribunal.[24]

When the leave that had brought him to Washington ran out, Buford returned to army headquarters but without enthusiasm. He disliked the thought of resuming a staff position under a commander who had been as much discredited by Fredericksburg as Pope had been by Second Bull Run. In fact, the ill-considered Mud March, then in progress in Virginia, would constitute Burnside's last effort in army command. The criticisms of politicians, editors, and subordinates including Hooker and Franklin had rendered his relief a foregone conclusion.[25]

Buford's return to Virginia lasted only a few weeks. On 2 February, he returned to a Washington courtroom to repeat his testimony about Gainesville, this time before a panel examining General McDowell's conduct at Second Bull Run. Immediately afterward Buford went from witness stand to judges' table, serving a stint of court-martial duty that kept him in the capital for several weeks.[26]

While in Washington two job offers came his way. Major General Robert C. Schenck, newly installed commander of the Middle Department and the VIII Army Corps at Baltimore, petitioned the War Department for Buford's services. Apparently, Schenck's choice let it be known that such a position did not interest him and the assignment was not made. Then Buford learned that opportunity beckoned along the Rappahannock. Maneuvered into offering his resignation, which the White House accepted with a show of regret, Ambrose Burnside had finally left the Army of the Potomac. On 26 January President Lincoln had replaced him with one of his most insidious enemies, General Hooker. "Fighting Joe" began immediately to reorganize the army, jettisoning many of his predecessor's subordinates and casting about for talented, battle-tested replacements. John Buford seemed to fill the bill very nicely.[27]

The cavalryman may have hesitated to accept the assignment. Although intelligent and personally brave, Hooker was an unscrupulous opportunist known neither for his ethics nor his strategic expertise. The prospect of active duty was a powerful lure, however, especially after Buford learned that the army's cavalry would be grouped under George Stoneman. Rumors led Buford to "take it for granted" that he would be offered a command under his old friend.

His only concern was that his absence from Virginia would hurt his prospects for an assignment. As he wrote Stoneman during a break in his court-martial duties, "I am a little afraid that the different brigade commanders being on the ground may succeed in getting the fighting regiments, leaving me the less desirable ones." His preference was to command all the Regular cavalry in the army. Given his long association with professional soldiers, "I believe they would prefer me to . . . the other Cavalry Commanders." Stoneman agreed; he made plans to grant Buford's wish.[28]

Buford's imminent return to the field coincided with the dawning of a new day for the cavalry of the Army of the Potomac. Joe Hooker was determined that under his regime the oft-misused horsemen would enjoy an independence they had not experienced under McClellan, Pope, or Burnside. He planned to group Stoneman's troopers into a full-sized army corps, a move that would keep them from the clutches of infantry commanders who cared nothing about the special abilities and needs of the arm.[29]

Once his new assignment came through, Buford must have wished to be free of his court-martial responsibilities as soon as possible. Hooker tried, but failed, to get him excused from that onerous assignment. Not till 7 March could Buford pry himself loose from duty and family and head south to assume his first operational command in six months.[30]

General William S. Harney (National Archives)

General Philip St. George Cooke (National Archives)

Captain John Buford, ca. 1861 (Library of Congress)

General George B. McClellan (Library of Congress)

General John Pope (Library of Congress)

General George Stoneman (Library of Congress)

General J.E.B. Stuart, C.S.A. (Library of Congress)

Stoneman's Raiders, 1863 (Library of Congress)

General Wesley Merritt (Library of Congress)

General Joseph Hooker (Library of Congress)

General Ambrose E. Burnside (standing—third from right) and subordinates, 1862: Brigadier General John Buford (seated—far right) (Library of Congress)

General Alfred Pleasonton (Library of Congress)

Brigadier General John Buford (seated) and staff, 1863: Captain Myles Keogh (far left) (Library of Congress)

neral George G. Meade (third from left) and subordinates, 1863 (Library of Congress)

Brigadier General John Buford (standing—left), ca. 1863; Colonel Delos Sacket (seated—center) (Library of Congress)

General Buford's grave and monument in the U.S. Military Academy cemetery, West Point, N.Y. (Photograph by Mary Dabrowski)

CHAPTER VII

Leader of the Reserves

The Reserve Cavalry Brigade of the Army of the Potomac had been conceived of as a source of professionalism from which the volunteer troopers might learn and upon which General Hooker and his commander of horse might rely in a crisis. A hybrid organization, it was composed of four Regular outfits, the First, Second, Fifth, and Sixth United States Cavalry, plus the Sixth Pennsylvania—the latter still known as "Rush's Lancers" for the anachronistic weaponry its men had lugged about for the past two years.

For the first six weeks of Buford's tenure the Pennsylvanians served apart from the Regulars, operating under the "special instructions" of corps and army headquarters. When they finally became a permanent component of the brigade, however, they did not dilute its operational effectiveness. In deportment, discipline, and combat capability the erstwhile lancers would become so like their new comrades that Buford would come to refer to them as "my Seventh Regulars."[1]

Now that the War Department had reversed its earlier policy, numerous Regular officers had been able to transfer to the volunteer service, thus gaining higher rank and authority. Even so, a number of familiar faces stared back at Buford from the ranks of the Reserves. Only one face was conspicuously absent: Colonel Cooke's. The loyal Virginian, from whom Buford had learned so many aspects of the military art, had preceded Buford at the head of the Regular Brigade, only to lose his command (along with much of his reputation) through a disastrous mistake. At the battle of Gaines's Mill the previous June, Cooke had led 250 Regulars in an ill-advised saber charge against a large force of Confederate infantry. Attacking across a long stretch of open ground, the troopers made such inviting targets that 150 went down killed or wounded before they even reached their target. In their headlong retreat, the survivors disrupted the withdrawal of artillery and infantry forces they had been assigned to protect, turning an orderly retreat into a chaotic rout.[2]

Among old acquaintances who remained in the Regulars, Buford would have been most pleased to see now-Captain Wesley Merritt, his executive officer in Company B of the Second Dragoons. He quickly refamiliarized himself with other officers who had remained in the regular service, some of whom were enlisted men the last time he saw them. One officer he knew not as an old colleague but as a nephew: twenty-nine-year-old Second Lieutenant Temple Buford, N.B. Buford's eldest child and one of the most recent additions to the Fifth United States Cavalry.[3]

Buford knew little about his regimental commanders, including Major Charles Jarvis Whiting, senior officer of the Second Cavalry, who had transferred to Buford's old regiment only four months ago. The rank of the other regimental leaders indicated how badly the officer strength of the standing army had been depleted: Captain Richard S. C. Lord, First Cavalry; Captain James E. Harrison, Fifth Cavalry; and Captain George C. Cram, Sixth Cavalry. Unknown faces they might be, but Buford could be confident of their abilities; each had spent years coming up through promotion channels, during which he would have learned every nuance of command.[4]

Despite the numerical weakness of his command—a disadvantage that Regular Army skill and efficiency would help to overcome—Buford must have been highly pleased to have landed the Reserve Brigade. He knew he would not have to spend long hours tutoring officers and men in the intricacies of tactics, as he would have felt constrained to do had he remained with the volunteers he led at Second Bull Run. Nor would he have to lose valuable time worrying where to obtain equipment and remounts for his command, for on these and other counts the cavalry had undergone a revival since Hooker took over the army.

As promised, Fighting Joe had improved virtually every aspect of mounted service. He had streamlined the supply process by increasing the number of quartermasters detailed to the arm and by closely overseeing their work. He had tightened up the cavalry inspection system to certify that deficiencies in arms, ammunition, and horseflesh were rectified as quickly as possible. He had increased the frequency of drills and reviews, not only to sharpen readiness but to raise *esprit de corps*. Hooker had reopened the discontinued network of schools of instruction for commissioned and noncommissioned officers. Examining boards under his supervision were weeding out unfit officers and recommending promotions for deserving ones. He had also instituted a furlough system to ensure that only the most efficient, best disciplined regiments could benefit from the issuance of leaves.[5]

These and other reforms had gone far to raise morale from the depths to which it had sunk after Second Bull Run and

Fredericksburg. A New York trooper, writing at about the time Hooker replaced Burnside, observed that "the tide of military life has possibly reached its lowest ebb, and the signs of the times are ominous of ill." By the time Buford returned from Washington, this man's confidence had been completely restored, and he was looking forward to an early resumption of campaigning. In mid-March, an officer in an Illinois regiment informed his sister that "Gen Hooker took this army in the gloomiest moment, when discouragement prevailed, when demoralization was apparent to any one, when no one thought it could be rescued from being disbanded ...and by unceasing toil, by severity and kindness, he has rebuilt its foundation, extracted the rotten beams and replaced them by sound ones...."[6]

Of Hooker's many reforms, the one that had the most beneficial long-term effect on the mounted arm was his decision to remove it from the control of infantry leaders and give it a corps organization of its own. On 5 February the Cavalry Corps of the Army of the Potomac—an organization that even the most optimistic trooper probably doubted he would live to see—formally came into existence. The command consisted of three divisions, each comprising two brigades, with Buford's Regulars theoretically forming a separate command. In practice, however, the Reserves would be attached to the First Division so often as to constitute one of its components. The initial strength of the corps topped 11,000 officers and men present for duty, a force of horsemen the size of which had never been seen before in Virginia.[7]

The combat potential of so many horse soldiers grouped into a cohesive organization provided another spur to morale, as did the heightened sense of identity lent the cavalry by its independence from outside authority. One of those who appreciated the new order, Lieutenant George B. Sanford of

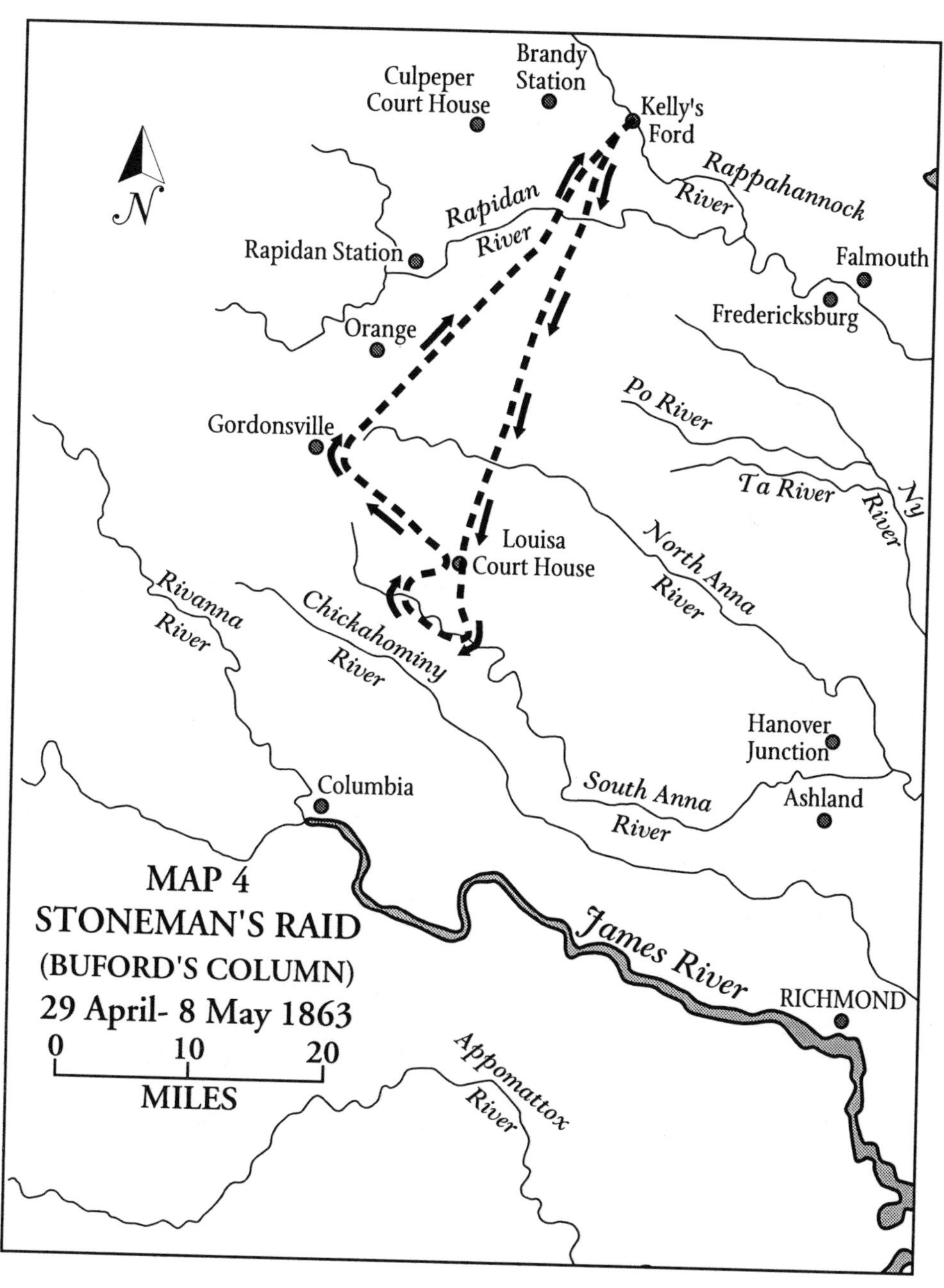
Brandy Station
Culpeper Court House
Kelly's Ford
Rappahannock River
Rapidan River
Rapidan Station
Falmouth
Fredericksburg
Orange
Po River
Gordonsville
Ta River
Ny River
Louisa Court House
North Anna River
Rivanna River
Chickahominy River
Hanover Junction
Columbia
South Anna River
Ashland
MAP 4
STONEMAN'S RAID
(BUFORD'S COLUMN)
29 April- 8 May 1863
0
10
20
MILES
James River
RICHMOND
Appomattox River
N

Buford's First United States, declared that the cavalry "owes to Gen. Hooker a debt of gratitude, which it would be difficult to repay." Doubtless Sanford's general would have agreed.[8]

* * *

Buford's attitude toward his place in the circle of command is unknown but can be surmised. He would have had no reservations about Hooker's choice for corps commander, although he must have envied the fact that unlike his own role under Burnside, Stoneman's position combined administrative and field command. Buford regarded George Stoneman as a courageous and dedicated officer of iron-ribbed integrity and of at least average ability. Out of long acquaintance with him, Buford was inclined to overlook Stoneman's occasional eccentricities (when the corps was formed, for example, Stoneman had toyed with the notion of outfitting it in bright red jackets and caps and pea-green trousers). Buford would have been less concerned with Stoneman's quirks of personality than with his physical health, since the corps leader was known to be suffering from a chronic hemorrhoid condition that depleted his stamina.[9]

Buford might well have felt slighted by his exclusion from the next level of command, especially in light of the qualifications of those officers who received divisions under Stoneman. Long a fixture of the cavalry of the Army of the Potomac, Alfred Pleasonton was a logical choice to take the First Division, and Buford would have had no quarrel with his selection. Pleasonton, like Hooker, was an opportunist, an inveterate politician and intriguer, a seeker of promotion and preference. He was also a publicity-hound; one of his officers complained that the brigadier "does nothing save with a view to a newspaper paragraph."

Such qualities, added to Pleasonton's dandyish ways and

epicurean habits, would have been off-putting to John Buford. More troubling to Buford was Pleasonton's sometimes lax leadership and especially his frequent failure to separate wild rumor, baseless speculation, and hard intelligence. Still, Buford would have made some allowance for a colleague with whom he had long been on good terms. Moreover, he appreciated the deference that Pleasonton had shown toward him ever since Antietam and Fredericksburg when he had been the older man's nominal superior.[10]

Stoneman's other ranking subordinates might have raised Buford's hackles. General Averell, assigned to command the Second Cavalry Division, had flashes of competence but in the main was a plodder, and not overly bright; his forte appears to have been brigade or perhaps regimental command. Like Pleasonton, however, Averell had been conspicuous in mounted campaigning since the opening of the war—his original command, the Third Pennsylvania, had been the first volunteer cavalry regiment to take the field in Virginia—and this distinction appears to have conferred on him a form of seniority.[11]

The commander of the Third Division was a more worthy figure, Brigadier General David McMurtrie Gregg, prewar mainstay of the First United States Dragoons and handpicked successor to George Bayard. Known throughout the army for his polished professionalism, Gregg hid a tragic secret beneath his dignified exterior: he feared a violent death in battle. Although he gave the impression of inherent courage, it appears to have been an artifice, a pose that took a great effort of will to maintain. Some of his colleagues saw through his disguise and called him—behind his back, of course—a coward. According to his division surgeon, Gregg used that term to describe himself when, in late 1864, his nerve finally gave way and he resigned his commission.[12]

Evidently Hooker, not Stoneman, was responsible for the

appointments to the Cavalry Corps; Stoneman would not have chosen Alfred Pleasonton, whom he disliked and distrusted, for his ranking lieutenant unless Hooker had demanded it. After the war, Hooker regretted his failure to give Buford a higher command than he received, one more commensurate with his abilities. He excused himself by blaming Buford's low rank. Since Pleasonton, Averell, and Gregg wore no more stars than Buford, Hooker must have been referring to the issue of seniority. That explanation does not hold up, however, for while Pleasonton was senior to Buford by a few days (and had been Buford's senior in the Second Dragoons), Buford's appointment as brigadier antedated Averell's by two months and Gregg's by four; he had also been senior to both men—by several years—in the Old Army.

Buford's relatively low status in the Cavalry Corps—the other brigade leaders, each a colonel, commanded more troops than he—may have resulted from his long absence from field duty. It may have stemmed from the residual effects of his perceived closeness to three deposed commanders. Or it may have reflected his inability to compete with colleagues with substantial political support. Averell enjoyed the backing of legislators from both Pennsylvania and New York, his native state, while Gregg was the cousin of the North's most powerful war governor, Andrew G. Curtin of Pennsylvania. Whatever the reason, Hooker's regret over not elevating Buford to higher station appears to have been a postwar lament rather than a contemporary sentiment.[13]

* * *

Although Hooker's organizational actions and administrative reforms made him appear a patron of the cavalry, he was cynical about the mounted arm's ability to contribute effectively to the operations of the main army. It seemed to him that too often the cavalry had failed to carry its share of the burden in field campaigning. Cavalry's casualty rates, always low in comparison to infantry losses, seemed to confirm this belief; the contrast lay behind Hooker's celebrated jest that no one ever saw a dead cavalryman.

With the Army of the Potomac under new management, Hooker expected the picture to change, quickly and dramatically. By March 1863 he had gone to great lengths to ensure that his horsemen lacked nothing to prove themselves a worthy component of what he termed the ablest fighting force on the planet. Now he wanted results, a tangible return on his investment in cavalry's future.[14]

An event that took place during the middle of that month offered some encouraging signs, and Buford's command played a role in it. Angered by successful Rebel assaults on his cavalry's picket lines, Hooker ordered General Averell across the Rappahannock at Kelly's Ford to rout a mounted force that had been assembling near Culpeper Court House under J.E.B. Stuart's most trusted subordinate, Major General Fitzhugh Lee. Dutifully, Averell marched down on the ford with two brigades, led by Colonels Alfred N. Duffie and John B. McIntosh, plus the greater part of Buford's First and Fifth United States under Captain Marcus Reno of the First.

The Federals captured a picket post on the upper bank, then slowly forced a crossing in the face of moderate resistance. On the far shore, McIntosh's brigade mixed with two Virginia regiments and eventually forced them into retreat. On McIntosh's left, Duffie's people tangled with three other Virginia outfits. Supported by a successful saber charge by Reno and two squadrons of the Fifth United States, Duffie forced the Virginians to disengage and re-form. Then, with the battle fairly begun, Averell ordered everyone back across the river. In his after-action report he attributed the retreat to the exhaustion of his horses and the feared proximity of Confederate infantry.[15]

All in all, Averell's accomplishments had been overshadowed by his failures. He had taken too long to cross the river, had withdrawn prematurely, and had inflicted only a modest number of casualties (one of them J.E.B. Stuart's brilliant young chief of horse artillery, Major John Pelham, mortally wounded at the height of the action). But the very fact that Union horsemen had attacked, surprised, and gotten the advantage of Stuart's heralded cavaliers was news throughout the Army of the Potomac and another boost to cavalry's morale. The following day an officer in Averell's old Third Pennsylvania boasted to his father that "we are more than ever *sure* that on a fair field the Rebel Cavalry can't stand [up to] us."[16]

Stoneman's Chancellorsville Raid

Hooker saw Kelly's Ford as a promising tune-up to larger, more significant operations. By early April, following a conference at Falmouth with President Lincoln—who lauded Stoneman's troopers as they paraded past him on review—the army commander stood ready to lead his 130,000-man army out of winter quarters against Robert E. Lee's 60,000 Confederates.[17]

From the first, Hooker projected a major role for the rejuvenated cavalry. Stoneman's horsemen would initiate the campaign by sweeping northwestward along the Rappahannock, crossing above Lee's positions outside Fredericksburg, then heading south to rampage in the Confederate rear near Hanover Junction, eighteen miles above Richmond. At Hanover, where the Virginia Central Railroad crossed the Richmond, Fredericksburg & Potomac, Stoneman would sit astride Lee's main line of communications. His troopers were to inflict as much damage as possible to railroad track, rolling stock, and supply houses.

Unable to abide a large enemy presence in so critical an area, Lee would turn about to strike Stoneman with troops of all arms. Thus distracted, he would be ripe for defeat when Hooker attacked him in front. Dislodged outside Fredericksburg, Lee must retreat toward his capital. When he broke and ran, Stoneman was to "fall upon his flanks, attack his artillery and trains, and harass and delay him until he is exhausted and out of supplies." Hooker left no doubt as to what he expected of his cavalry leader: "Let your watchword be fight, and let all your orders be fight, fight, fight...."[18]

Early on 13 April, after days of preparation and planning, Stoneman led his men and horses out of the camps around Falmouth and for the first time placed a column of horsemen 10,000 strong in motion. Buford rode jauntily at the head of the Reserve Brigade, brimming with pride at the soldierly bearing of his four regiments of Regulars. As he expected, his men held up well on the first day of the march, which covered more than twenty miles along the north fork of the Rappahannock—a good distance considering the column's inherent impediment, a long horse- and mule-drawn supply train that Stoneman had seen fit to take. The Reserve Brigade bivouacked that night at Morrisville, within easy reach of the designated river crossings, nearly eight miles upriver from the site of Averell's qualified victory on 17 March.[19]

On the morning of the fourteenth, the greater part of Stoneman's column—Averell's division, followed by Gregg's—was expected to cross at Beverly Ford. Buford would cover the operation, before sweeping south to ford near the O & A Railroad bridge. On the far bank the Reserve Brigade would be responsible for protecting the left flank of the larger column—the same role that Reno's detachment had played in the fracas at Kelly's Ford.

At an early hour, however, complications disarranged Stoneman's plans. First, he encountered a heavier force than expected opposite Kelly's Ford. The enemy had artillery, which caused the Federals to scramble for cover; more than a dozen shells struck Buford's position. He replied with Lieutenant Samuel S. Elder's Battery E, Fourth United States Artillery, which had reported for duty with the Reserves the previous day. Buford, who had a great admiration for the artilleryman's art, was pleased to note that Elder quickly "drove the rebel guns out of sight." The Confederates shifted their defense to a series of rifle-pits along the river, from which they peppered Averell's and Buford's commands, doing "no damage" to the latter beyond wounding a few horses. Averell had enough troops that he might have forced a crossing and overwhelmed the opposition, but he chose not to, and Stoneman chose to let him be.[20]

Averell's failure to bull his way across had major repercussions. Early that evening it began to rain; the storm grew steadily worse and continued for several hours, inundating the countryside for miles around and making miserable the lives of everyone in the raiding column. By dawn of the fifteenth, when Stoneman ordered him to cross near Rappahannock Bridge, Buford could not: "the ford was swimming" and the ground leading to it flowed "like a sea." Then the rain turned to hail that, according to a trooper in Colonel Benjamin F. ("Grimes") Davis's brigade of Averell's column, "came down as large [as] hen's eggs. Our horses jumped and kicked like fun...."[21]

The ferocity of the storm meant that the cavalry would remain north of the quickly rising river for an indefinite period. The delay aggravated Stoneman but it positively infuriated General Hooker, who unnecessarily reminded his cavalry leader that until he advanced the army was doomed to immobility. Stoneman's predicament also bothered Abraham Lincoln, who had taken a personal interest in the raid. Late on the fifteenth the president expressed his concern in a telegram to Hooker: "General S. is not moving rapidly enough to make the expedition come to anything.... I do not know that any better can be done, but I greatly fear it is another failure already...."[22]

On the sixteenth Buford's Regulars abruptly quit the river. Swimming their horses across Marsh Creek, they returned to Morrisville, where they guarded the column's supply train until relieved of that burdensome duty on the eighteenth. On that date the river was still too high to ford and the weather had yet to clear, so the disgruntled troopers moved up the railroad to bivouack at Bealton Station. For the next eleven days they picketed the swollen river, breaking up the monotony of that duty with short marches in the direction of Warrenton Junction. The Regulars were not the only troops kept moving in an attempt to ward off inertia and discouragement; but in no case did the activity have the desired effect. An officer in the First Massachusetts remarked that the entire corps "changed camp frequently, grew weary with marching and countermarching, used up its supplies, and became always less confident and able." For Buford's brigade, the only bright moment in this bleak period was the arrival of the Sixth Pennsylvania—minus its hallmark lances, recently exchanged for carbines.[23]

By 22 April the impatient General Hooker could stand the delay no longer. Certain that the element of surprise had been irretrievably lost, the army commander gave his cavalry leader a new set of instructions. Stoneman would no longer be responsible for turning Lee out of his position; the army's infantry, screened by a single brigade under Alfred Pleasonton, would handle that chore. Stoneman would still head south as soon as possible to cut the Confederate line of supply. Hooker recommended that the expedition operate in detachments that would "dash off to the right and left, and inflict a vast deal of mischief, and at the same time bewilder the enemy as to the course and intentions of the main body."[24]

Not until the twenty-ninth did the river fall enough to permit a large-scale fording. That morning—sixteen days behind schedule and with Hooker's main army already in motion toward the Confederate left—Stoneman pushed his way across at Kelly's against greatly diminished opposition. On the far shore, he made final preparations for carrying out his revamped orders. When the march resumed at about midday, the cavalry curved westward in two columns, Averell's division trotting down the railroad toward Culpeper and Rapidan Station, Gregg and Buford turning farther south. The southerly column, which Stoneman accompanied, would cross the Rapidan River at Raccoon Ford, make for Louisa Court House and other points along the Virginia Central, then move to Hanover Junction, striking the R, F & P in the direction of Richmond.[25]

Although Averell made early contact with the enemy, Gregg and Buford had an uneventful first day. That evening, at Stoneman's direction, Buford sent two squadrons of the Fifth Cavalry, under Captain Thomas Drummond, to Brandy Station to communicate with the upper column. Near the depot the squadrons found Averell's troopers in such close contact with the enemy—a couple of cavalry regiments under General Lee's son, Brigadier General "Rooney" Lee—that Drummond could offer the division leader no help; without delay, he returned to his brigade via a night march, always a dangerous feat when undertaken in enemy territory. Though his mission accomplished little except to fix Averell's position, Buford praised the "most handsome manner" in which the captain had managed his units.[26]

On the thirtieth Buford's brigade, leading Stoneman's march, reached the Rapidan at Mitchell's Ford, found the crossing site impassable, and swung west to Morton's Ford, where the column splashed across. It did so with the aid of an advance detachment of the Fifth Cavalry, under Lieutenant Peter Penn Gaskell of Buford's staff, which surprised the enemy's pickets and drove them away from the crossing site. The brigade bivouacked that night near Raccoon Ford, Gregg's division in its rear.

The raiders gained an added dividend from their contested crossing. Captives taken at the river reported that Stuart's main body—whose suspected presence in Lee's rear was a nagging concern to Stoneman—had passed through the Rapidan River country that morning heading for Fredericksburg in response to Hooker's advance. At first Stoneman was skeptical, but when Stuart failed to show himself the following day the raiding leader rejoiced that his march to the railroads would be unimpeded.[27]

With Rooney Lee's brigade and other detachments of Rebel horsemen known to be operating south of the Rapidan, Buford may not have shared his superior's confidence. Even so, he found the next three days free of large-scale opposition. On the first day of May his command marched unmolested to the North Anna River via Verdiersville, scene of Stuart's near-capture at Buford's hands the previous July. On the second, he made a leisurely march in rear of Gregg's division, which had gone ahead to occupy Louisa Court House near the line of the Virginia Central. There the work of destruction began. As Gregg's men torched warehouses, downed telegraph wires, and ripped up track near the courthouse, Buford sent Captain Lord and the First Cavalry down the tracks toward Richmond, where they inflicted the same kind of damage at Tolersville and Frederick's Hall Station. Lord's regiment also burned a North Anna bridge leading toward Fredericksburg.

Side-expeditions by detachments of the Fifth Cavalry marked Buford's march on 3 May, which ended with the Reserves in bivouac at Thompson's Cross Roads on the South Anna River. By now the raiders had penetrated forty-five miles into the Confederacy without encountering serious resistance or incurring heavy loss, while tearing up almost twenty miles' worth of precious railroad track. But they had farther to go and more to do. From Thompson's, detachments scoured the area for spoils. One band, under the dashing Captain Keogh, overtook and burned a mule train of fifteen supply wagons. In a move perhaps appreciated by his comrades, perhaps not, the staff officer distributed the captured mules to troopers whose horses had gone lame.[28]

The Federals' joyride ended on Monday, 4 May. That morning a force of perhaps 1,000 Rebels—Rooney Lee's troopers, reinforced since breaking off their engagement with Averell at Brandy Station—chased down Captain Harrison, whom Buford had dispatched at the head of a 109-man demolition party to Flemmings's Cross Roads. Despite making a "determined stand" against ten-to-one odds, the little band lost thirty-two casualties, all as prisoners of war, in fighting its way back to Buford. One of the captives—a casualty in the first engagement of his military career—was Lieutenant Temple Buford. Paroled and exchanged several weeks later (quite possibly through his uncle's intercession), the youngster would resign his Regular Army commission and return to Kentucky to finish out the war as a private soldier in a volunteer infantry regiment.[29]

While Buford scouted the countryside around Thompson's Cross Roads, numerous elements of his brigade and Gregg's division were heading to far-off points. All were doing their part to fulfill Stoneman's desire that the raiders act "like a shell" bursting "in every direction," scattering damage along as wide an arc as possible. Buford's role in this plan was to lead a picked force of 650 men, aboard the strongest horses, in recrossing the South Anna and laying waste to untouched regions below the axis of the Virginia Central.

Impenetrable pine forests and impassable roads forced the brigade leader to revamp his intended route and backtrack to Louisa Court House, where his men cut telegraph cable that had been restrung since their first visit. Passing up the tracks toward Gordonsville, the Regulars and Pennsylvanians lay waste to rails, water towers, and hand-cars as well as trackside stores of weapons, ammunition, and rations. Near Gordonsville late that day Buford's advance guard detected an enemy force of unknown size laying in wait; opting for discretion over valor, Buford bypassed the village to the north and by daylight on the sixth put the North Anna between his men and any pursuers.[30]

Later that morning he was joined at Orange Springs, north of the river, by the balance of the Reserve Brigade as well as by General Stoneman and the majority of Gregg's reunited division. Two raiding columns, under Colonels Judson Kilpatrick and Hasbrouck Davis, had ridden to damage distant sections of the Richmond, Fredericksburg & Potomac, including Hanover Junction; cut off from Gregg's main body, they would not rejoin it for days or even weeks. Those parties and the others dispatched by Buford and Gregg had already done a vast amount of destruction to Lee's communication lines, especially the Virginia Central, but they had also picked up rumors of a Union setback below the Rappahannock. The reports worried Stoneman, who feared to tarry much longer so far from Hooker's main force.

Resuming their march in the early hours of 7 May, the raiders crossed the Rapidan at Raccoon Ford and pushed

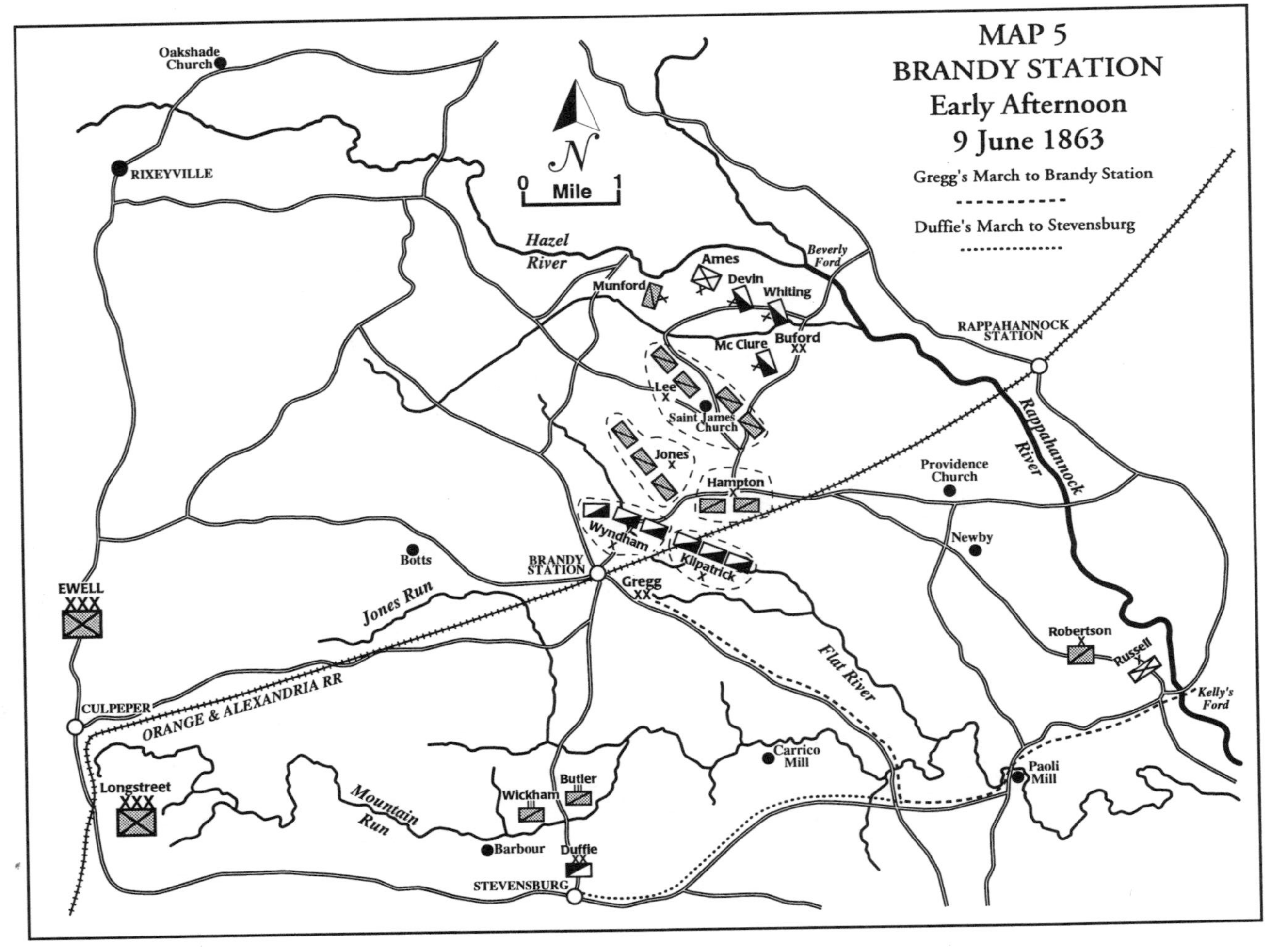
MAP 5
BRANDY STATION
Early Afternoon
9 June 1863
Gregg's March to Brandy Station
Duffie's March to Stevensburg
0 Mile 1
Oakshade Church
RIXEYVILLE
Hazel River
Munford
Ames
Devin
Whiting
Beverly Ford
Mc Clure
Buford
RAPPAHANNOCK STATION
Rappahannock River
Lee
Saint James Church
Jones
Hampton
Providence Church
Wyndham
Kilpatrick
Newby
Botts
BRANDY STATION
Gregg
EWELL
Jones Run
Flat River
Robertson
Russell
Kelly's Ford
CULPEPER
ORANGE & ALEXANDRIA RR
Carrico Mill
Paoli Mill
Longstreet
Butler
Wickham
Mountain Run
Barbour
Duffie
STEVENSBURG

north at a steady pace, spurred by what Buford called "the first reliable information that General Hooker had recrossed the Rappahannock." Reaching Kelly's Ford—still "swimming" from the recent rains—in the middle of the night, the raiders stood to horse until dawn, when they made a slow and difficult crossing, "effected," Buford noted proudly, "without losing a man." On the far shore, the raiders unsaddled for the first time in several days and drew forage. By the ninth they were at Bealton Station on the O & A, within the protective embrace of Hooker's infantry pickets.[31]

Buford's service over the past three and a half weeks had been an ordeal such as he had never experienced. "From the time that the brigade struck the river at Rappahannock Bridge on the 15th," he wrote in his campaign report, "...it seemed as though the elements were combined against our advance.... During the whole expedition the roads were in a worse condition than I could have supposed to be possible, and the command was called upon to endure much severe discomfiture. The men's rations were destroyed [by the weather] almost as soon as issued. No fires could be lighted to cook or dry by, and the dark, cold, wet nights that the men were compelled to march wore them out; but all, without exception, were full of enthusiasm, ready for any emergency, and did their duty with hearty good-will. I have not heard of a complaint or murmur...."[32]

Buford's men—the great majority of them—were Regulars, and Regulars were supposed to endure hardships without a complaint or murmur. Nevertheless, the conditions had been such that they deserved the kind of praise Buford bestowed on them. The officers and men of the Reserve Brigade had done their commander proud.

CHAPTER VIII

Toward Gettysburg

After refitting at Bealton, Buford's Reserves took up the time-honored task of picketing for the main army. As the vedettes at Falmouth ranged up and down the north fork of the Rappahannock, their comrades indulged in a lengthy round of finger-pointing and recrimination, the legacy of their recent failure against Lee. Joe Hooker's boldly planned, carefully executed effort to outflank the Rebels below the river had come undone almost at the last minute. While on the verge of sneaking into Lee's rear, Hooker had permitted his enemy to rush up and stop him in the Virginia Wilderness, causing him to lose his nerve, his bearings, his advantage of surprise, and 17,000 of his men. Throttled into virtual helplessness by faster, more aggressive forces under Stonewall Jackson (who fell mortally wounded during the action of 2 May), Hooker had hung on among the pines and thickets near a crossroads named Chancellorsville through four inconclusive days of combat before giving up his offensive and returning to Falmouth in disgrace.[1]

The defeated commander was too much the egotist to

accept full blame for what happened below the river. Casting about for scapegoats, he landed hard on the cavalry. He fired William Averell, who had returned to the army after his fight with Rooney Lee, his mission of thrashing Rebel cavalry along the Rapidan unaccomplished. The inept Averell deserved his fate; but then Hooker began to rant and rave in the direction of George Stoneman. The newspapers were filled with stories of the vast damage Stoneman's raiders had inflicted between Fredericksburg and Richmond, but Hooker realized that since the main army had failed, torn-up railroad track and burned warehouses counted for nothing. The Confederate commander had foreseen as much: to ensure Hooker's downfall, Lee had allowed Stoneman to wreak all the havoc his heart desired. By ignoring the raid, Lee had been able to keep Stuart's main force close to his side during the critical period of Hooker's advance. Freed of the opposition it would have encountered had Stoneman not gone raiding, the Southern cavalry made a substantial contribution to Lee's counteroffensive, especially to the 2 May turning-movement around the Union left that had sealed Hooker's fate.[2]

Lashing out in a blind rage—conveniently forgetting that he himself had mapped the cavalry's role in the recent campaign—Hooker declared Stoneman's raid a farce, a misguided indulgence that had served no useful purpose. Devising an excuse to disguise his intentions, two weeks after the raiders' return Hooker sent Stoneman to Washington for treatment of his hemorrhoids. At once he announced Alfred Pleasonton as Stoneman's "temporary" replacement. Pleasonton, who had been campaigning for Stoneman's job as openly as Hooker had intrigued against Ambrose Burnside, was overjoyed; command of a corps would bring him the promotion to major general he had long craved.[3]

Many troopers expressed dismay at the brigadier's promotion; a Massachusetts officer explained that "Stoneman we believe in.... Pleasonton ...is pure and simple a newspaper humbug." A Pennsylvania captain complained that "this being under Pleasanton [sic] is very demoralizing, though, and we sincerely trust the Government will ...promote him to a Maj General of New York Home Guard, or something in the sinecure way that we may be rid of him."[4]

For his part, John Buford must have regretted the whole affair. He would work well with Pleasonton; more than likely, he was Pleasonton's choice to take the now-leaderless First Division. But Buford undoubtedly mourned the downfall of Stoneman, who deserved better than to be tossed into the discard for a failure not of his own making.

* * *

By mid-May the War Department had been overtaken by fears that Stuart's cavalry, if not Lee's army in its entirety, was on the verge of invading Northern territory. Buford's and Gregg's pickets were instructed to be alert to signs of an enemy concentration south of the Rappahannock and to unexplained movements by elements of Lee's army. For a time, however, Buford's brigade—composed of what its commander called "pretty well used up" horses and "pretty tired" men—was granted a respite from this watch. Early on the seventeenth, the Reserves were relieved along the river and sent to the rear to resupply. At the vast complex of supply depots along Potomac Creek, northeast of Fredericksburg, the troopers spent some days resting, taking on new equipment, and replenishing ammunition. Apparently, however, they lacked the opportunity to exchange their worn-out plugs for fresh stock, for by the twenty-seventh Pleasonton was complaining to army headquarters that the Reserve Brigade had fewer than 900 horses fit for duty and required nearly 1,400 remounts to be "in readiness for service in the field."[5]

New horseflesh would have come in handy, for the high command levied a demanding assignment on Buford as soon as he resumed picket duty. On 28 May Hooker reacted sharply to a report out of General Gregg's headquarters at Bealton that Rebel cavalry had crossed the Rappahannock, taking position in the Federal rear around Warrenton and Sulphur Springs. Next day Pleasonton directed Buford to determine the validity of the report, which was based on a recent but perhaps hasty reconnaissance. Buford's instructions recognized his seniority and displayed Pleasonton's confidence in him: on the mission, he would command Gregg's division as well as his own brigade.[6]

Buford validated Pleasonton's trust by doing an exceptionally thorough job of combing the countryside. His reconnaissance of the thirty-first, which ranged as far south as Waterloo, as far west as Orleans, and as far north as Gainesville, turned up no enemy troopers near those far-flung points or anywhere among them "save those who have been here all winter."[7]

This finding should have calmed Hooker's fears, but the army leader appeared obsessed that large bodies of Rebels were skulking about on some nefarious errand. Only two days after Buford's scouting mission, army headquarters asked him to check out rumors that three brigades of Confederate horse had marched from the Rappahannock basin to the Shenandoah Valley. No one seemed to know the meaning of such a move, if underway, but Hooker feared it meant an upcoming raid—somewhere.

Hooker's tasking seemed to indicate that his overheated imagination had gotten the better of him. And yet, on 3 June, one day after Fighting Joe petitioned Buford to scout toward the Shenandoah, elements of Lee's army took to the roads leading west from Fredericksburg. Their advance, which ended more than six months of occupation duty across from Falmouth, ushered in Lee's second invasion of Northern territory, this one fated to carry his army into the Pennsylvania countryside.[8]

Although Lee's movement was screened from Union view, the day it began enemy activity increased in front of the cavalry's picket lines. Colonel Duffie, who had succeeded to the command of Averell's division, reported a "considerable force" of the enemy crossing the Rappahannock at Sulphur Springs. While the Rebels did not confront their counterparts, Buford took pains to discover what was going on. By the fifth he was certain that the rumors of Rebel movements toward the Valley were nothing more than idle talk—at least as of that date. But he was also able to inform Pleasonton that "all the available cavalry force of the Confederacy [in Virginia] is in Culpeper County." Loyal Virginians had relayed to Buford's headquarters at Warrenton Junction word that as many as 20,000 troopers—Stuart's organic command, plus three newly attached brigades—had gathered around Culpeper Court House. The purpose of this concentration was unclear, but more than one informant used the attention-getting word "raid." Buford relayed the suggestion to Pleasonton, who gladly passed it on to Hooker, knowing it would confirm his suspicions.[9]

This was all the army leader needed to hear. By 6 June Buford was instructed to send his wagons and pack-mules to the rear and clear for action. Two days later he was moving in concert with Gregg and Duffie toward the Rappahannock fords, prepared to cross and give battle. Hooker had sent Pleasonton explicit instructions: he was to attack and defeat Stuart and kill his plans for a foray into the North.[10]

Hooker had given his cavalry enough tools to do a thorough job of smashing things; these included a goodly portion of Major General George Gordon Meade's V Army Corps, which had been helping the horsemen patrol the

Rappahannock. The brigade of Brigadier General Adelbert Ames, some 1,300 strong, would accompany Pleasonton and Buford across the river at Beverly Ford. Brigadier General David A. Russell's slightly larger brigade of foot troops would follow Duffie's and Gregg's column, which would cross at Kelly's Ford, eight miles below Beverly. According to Pleasonton's plan, the columns would group at Brandy Station before waking Stuart from his slumbers at Culpeper.[11]

The only trouble was that Stuart was no longer slumbering around the courthouse. The day before, the Southern leader had moved his troopers into the fields around Brandy Station, close to the point at which he proposed to cross the river on 10 June to begin screening Lee's northward advance. Thus the Federal wings were expecting to link in the midst of their enemy's camp.

It was an ominous note on which to commence a critical battle for supremacy with the Southern cavalry. From war's outset, the troopers of the Army of the Potomac had been consistently bested by Stuart's celebrated cavaliers. Now, however, the blue riders were feeling the effects of two long, grueling years of training, experience-gathering, and trial and error. Their apprenticeship had ended and they were on the verge of demonstrating whether they were worth the outlandish cost the United States government was paying for their upkeep. The answer lay across the Rappahannock, where throughout 9 June 1863 Pleasonton's men would engage Stuart's in the largest, longest, and most significant cavalry battle ever waged in the western hemisphere.

* * *

Some time after dawn—Pleasonton put the time at four-thirty A. M., other participants about an hour later—Buford led his new command across Beverly Ford. As his troops trotted past on the way to the river, the general sat his favorite charger, Grey Eagle, along the road from the Bowen mansion, one and a half miles southeast of the ford. There he had bivouacked the First Division—campfires forbidden, horses saddled, men trying to sleep with reins looped around their wrists—for the past several hours.[12]

Riding up, one of Pleasonton's staff officers observed Buford, wreathed in the morning mist, as he reviewed the passing column "with his usual smile." The officer liked the fact that Buford was puffing on his pipe as though without a care: "It was always reassuring to see him in the saddle when there was any chance of a fight."[13]

There was more than the chance of a fight this morning, as indicated by the slapping sounds of carbine- and pistol-fire that had begun to echo from across the stream. As the first glow of dawn painted the sky, Buford's leading brigade, under Alabama-born "Grimes" Davis—an Old Army acquaintance whose spit-and-polish demeanor and love for combat Buford admired—splashed through water that lapped at the men's saddle-skirts. Only when reaching dry ground did the stealthy column alert the nearest picket post, manned by troops under Brigadier General William E. ("Grumble") Jones, one of those brigades recently given Stuart for the invasion. To Buford's approval, Davis burst through the gray cordon, scattering sleepy Rebels in all directions.[14]

His path quickly clear, Davis led his three units—the Eighth New York, Eighth Illinois, and Third Indiana (the latter only six companies strong)—along a southwestward-leading trail toward St. James Church, a prominent landmark in that heavily forested area north of Brandy Station. In rear of Davis's column, Buford's Second Brigade began to surge across the Rappahannock: the Sixth and Ninth New York, the Seventeenth Pennsylvania, and two companies of the Third West Virginia Cavalry. At the head of this force rode an officer until recently unknown to Buford but one in whom the general already reposed confidence: Colonel Thomas C. Devin, a balding, ruddy-faced Irishman from New York City. Though never a professional soldier, Devin possessed so much militia experience and book knowledge that no less an authority than Assistant Inspector General Delos Sacket had pronounced Devin's grasp of tactics superior to his own.[15]

Beyond Devin a truncated edition of the Reserve Brigade, which Buford had entrusted to Major Whiting, waited its turn to cross. Whiting's force this day consisted of his own regiment, Captain Mason's Fifth and Captain Cram's Sixth United States, and the Sixth Pennsylvania of Major Robert Morris, Jr. Captain Lord's First Cavalry had been detailed to detached service, an untimely loss in strength and expertise to Buford's column. Even farther to the rear were General Ames's foot soldiers, waiting with unconcealed boredom for the cavalry to finish fording so that the real soldiers could get moving.[16]

Beverly Ford

Generals Buford and Pleasonton were conferring along the road to the ford when word reached them of the first snag—a substantial one—in their plans. An increase in the volume of rifle-fire from the far shore had already alerted Buford that reinforcements were en route from the area around the St. James Church to challenge Davis. Now Buford learned the upshot: the colonel was dead, felled by a pistol-wielding Virginian whom he had confronted with only a saber.[17]

The brisk pace of the advance died as Davis's lead regiment, the Eighth New York, milled about in confusion under a deadly fire. One trooper, given to time-honored similes, observed that "like hail the balls whized [sic] by my head by the hundreds." After several minutes of such treatment, the uncertain New Yorkers withdrew toward the river. Although the regiment's retreat was a limited one, conducted in good order, it stymied the next regiment in the column, the Eighth Illinois. As Buford crossed the river and pushed to the front to try to get the attack rolling again, his troopers dismounted and sought cover against the fast-arriving regiments of Grumble Jones's brigade, the Sixth and Seventh Virginia Cavalry.[18] For a time confusion held sway along Buford's front. Finally the general located Davis's successor, Major William McClure of the Third Indiana. McClure slowly untangled the New Yorkers and Illinoisans and led them, along with his own half-regiment, to the left of the road, where he grouped them in column of squadrons, many among woodlots. Meanwhile, Buford led some of Devin's regiments, followed by the few under Major Whiting, along a westward-running road branching off of the road to St. James Church.[19]

More and more of Jones's men came up to fight, backed now by cannon from the horse artillery brigade of Major Robert F. Beckham as well as by four Virginia regiments and one from North Carolina, originally camped farther north under Rooney Lee and three regiments from the Carolinas and three smaller "legions" from Georgia and Mississippi under Brigadier General Wade Hampton, placed near Brandy Station. As resistance stiffened, Buford explained to Pleasonton that he could no longer force his way forward with any hope of success. With the enemy positioned much closer to the river than expected, the game appeared to be in the opposition's hands and all bets were off.

Buford finally persuaded his superior to approve new strategy. Deciding to dig in short of St. James Church, he dismounted the majority of Devin's men and placed them behind cover: trees, farm fences, stone walls. Whiting's regiments he hauled forward but kept mounted for use if a saber charge appeared in order. At about the same time, he brought up a battery from the horse artillery brigade of Captain James M. Robertson, while directing Ames's foot troops to wade the river; their hour of battle was at hand. As Buford completed his dispositions, Pleasonton sent staff officers south to confer with Duffie and Gregg, both of whom he hoped to bring in against the flank and rear of Buford's opponents.[20]

Despite Buford's best efforts, by midmorning the situation on his front appeared to be deteriorating. No contact had been established with the lower column; the First Division remained dependent upon its own resources. Beckham's gunners had gotten the range of Robertson's pieces, chasing some of them from forest clearings. And Hampton and Rooney Lee, under J.E.B. Stuart's personal supervision, were putting heavy pressure on Buford's flanks. To recapture the initiative, the division leader turned to the Reserve Brigade and called for a mounted charge, perhaps mindful of how well that tactic had worked—initially, at least—at Second Bull Run.[21]

This time, however, the opposition was not a single mounted regiment but dismounted as well as saddled troopers, supported by a bank of artillery and sharpshooters concealed behind trees. Undaunted, the first regiment in Whiting's column started forward. Covered by skirmishers from the Second Cavalry and the same battery that had accompanied the Reserve Brigade on Stoneman's Raid, five companies of the Sixth Pennsylvania galloped across a wide clearing in column of squadrons, men riding knee-to-knee, elements of the Sixth United States racing along both flanks.

The charging troops thundered 800 yards across the plain, "yelling like demons." They managed to evade downed men and horses, tree stumps, and a series of ditches—only to be blasted to a standstill short of their target by artillery- and carbine-fire. Major Morris having been unhorsed and captured, the Pennsylvanians and their supports raced back to their starting-point, their effort apparently wasted.

The charge, however, had taken the edge off Stuart's momentum; fearing more attacks, both Lee and Hampton pulled back from their advanced position on the flanks. By noon the fighting on Buford's front had degenerated into an extended, defensive contest, dismounted men and cannoneers blasting away from less-than-advantageous positions, neither side able to achieve a breakthrough.[22]

Some time after noon Buford's prospects appeared to improve. Word came from the front that many more Confederates had pulled back. At about the same time, the roar of battle from the south indicated that General Gregg had entered the fight at last. Having detoured around a small blocking force near Kelly's Ford under the yet-timid Beverly Robertson, the Third Cavalry Division had belatedly charged into Brandy Station. Alerted to the danger in his rear, Stuart had galloped to the depot at the head of most of Hampton's and Jones's troopers, leaving only a handful from both brigades to help Rooney Lee hold Buford in check.[23]

Unable to determine the scope of Stuart's pull-back—and perhaps sobered by the losses suffered by the Sixth Pennsylvania and Sixth United States—Buford failed to press ahead, as he might have, with McClure's and Devin's troopers. He did confront Rooney Lee, however, with his infantry supports, for General Ames sent forward his Second Massachusetts and Third Wisconsin. The foot troops were not used to doing the bidding of cavalry officers but—impressed by Buford's businesslike attitude and "commanding presence"—moved forward to gouge some pesky sharpshooters out of good cover opposite Devin's position.

But even as part of Lee's line began to waver, several squadrons of mounted Confederates appeared in its rear, ready to launch a charge of their own. Buford responded by returning to the fight the survivors of the Sixth Pennsylvania, backed by the Second Regulars, dismounted members of Devin's brigade, and more of Ames's infantry. Thus bolstered, the former lancers bounded forward—this time to collide head-on with the Ninth Virginia under Rooney Lee's personal command. In the fracas, dozens of men on both sides went down dead or wounded—Robert E. Lee's son among the latter—and the fighting hung in the balance for several minutes. Finally, Lee's successor, Colonel John R. Chambliss, Jr., sent in the Second North Carolina and Tenth Virginia. In desperate hand-to-hand fighting, the supports gradually overwhelmed the Federals. In the frenzied struggle, Captain Merritt of the Second Cavalry lost his hat, and nearly his head as well, to a sabre blow from a powerful assailant.[24]

When the antagonists at last broke free of their deadly tangle, both sides withdrew in haste, urged back to their lines by carbine balls, exploding shell, and canister. Made cautious by the heavy casualties thus far incurred, neither Buford nor Chambliss launched another attack. The balance of the afternoon was given over to slow advances by dismounted troopers, corresponding retreats, and long-range skirmishing.

One reason that Buford remained on the defensive was the inhibiting presence of General Pleasonton, who had been considering a withdrawal since shortly after noon. He was strengthened in his attitude when General Gregg rode up from Brandy Station to report that his advance had bogged down against opposition from the troops Stuart had led down from St. James Church. After returning to his command, Gregg made a final effort to push through to Buford but could not pull it off. Then, late in the afternoon, Fitzhugh Lee's brigade of five Virginia regiments (today under Tom Munford, whom Buford had not met since Second Bull Run) moved south from Welford's Ford to reinforce Chambliss, leading Pleasonton to table a plan to have Buford fight his way to Gregg's sector. At about this same time, Pleasonton became attuned to vague but troubling reports that Confederate infantry—the North Carolina brigade of Brigadier General Junius Daniel—had arrived from Culpeper to back Stuart.[25]

These influences, added to the fact that the Union troopers had been fighting under a hot sun for several hours, convinced Pleasonton, about five P.M., to order a fighting retreat. Retrieving his forward units, Buford slowly disengaged, remounted, and, once under the protective cover of Ames's infantry, pulled back to Beverly Ford. At the same time, Gregg crossed lower down at Rappahannock Ford, his rear covered by Duffie, just returned from an ill-considered foray to Stevensburg that had effectively taken his men out of the battle.[26]

The exhausted Confederates did not contest the withdrawal beyond shelling it from afar. By seven o'clock, almost fourteen hours after the day's combat had begun, Buford's division was back on the north bank of the Rappahannock. Despite leaving the field in Stuart's hands and although they had suffered more heavily than their opponents—866 casualties to fewer than 500 for Stuart—Pleasonton's sweaty, grimy troopers were in high spirits. For days they would brag to anyone in earshot that they had surprised, jolted, and embarrassed the cream of the Southern cavalry, fighting Stuart to a standstill for half the day and coming within an ace of routing him utterly.[27]

Buford's command, although unable to make the upper jaw of the Union pincers close on its enemy, had performed ably throughout the day. Its battle losses—500 troopers killed, wounded, or missing—attested to its heavy involvement and its determined resistance to efforts by Stuart to sweep it into the Rappahannock. Despite plans gone awry, despite having to fight on ground not of its choosing, it had pressured its enemy on all quarters of the field, had maintained the offensive for much of the fight, and had retreated of its own accord, not through coercion. Buford's men might not have routed and dispersed Stuart as Hooker had demanded of Pleasonton, but they had served notice of a subtle shift in the balance of power. From now on the Union cavalry would be a force to be reckoned with rather than the plaything of its opponents.

Unsurprisingly, John Buford had done well in his first battle as director of a division. He had deftly coordinated operations among his three brigades. He had made effective use of his infantry support without treating it as a crutch. He had adapted his tactics to geography and the nature of the opposition, fighting mostly on foot due to the broken terrain and the abundance of cover but twice employing mounted attacks to destabilize the enemy and preempt an incipient offensive.

Perhaps most important of all, he had not been cowed by fluctuating fortunes; throughout the fight he rode slowly along lines of mounted and dismounted troopers, dispensing orders, advice, and encouragement, while enjoying his pipe. His equanimity impressed not only infantrymen unused to taking orders from a cavalry officer but also the men of his new command, who quickly came to accept him as their boss. By day's end troopers who did not know John Buford's name or face at battle's start spoke as though he had been leading them skillfully, and they following him confidently, for years.[28]

* * *

The day after the battle, Pleasonton's reunited corps went into camp in the vicinity of Warrenton Junction, where it remained for five days. Along the railroad it could repair the damage suffered at Brandy Station, while dispatching the badly wounded to hospitals in Washington and absorbing returning detachments and reinforcements. During this period Buford's command neared full strength upon the return of the First Cavalry as well as four companies of the Twelfth Illinois, which had finally completed their part in Stoneman's Raid. On the fourteenth the division's firepower increased with the attachment of Battery A, Second U. S. Artillery, Captain Tidball's old unit, whose six 3-inch ordnance rifles were now commanded by Lieutenant John H. Calef. At about this same time, Buford welcomed two new brigade commanders—both former non-coms in dragoon outfits—to Warrenton Junction. Colonel William Gamble, the bewhiskered, excitable, oft-wounded commander of the Eighth Illinois, arrived to replace Grimes Davis at the head of the First Brigade. Meanwhile, another of Buford's comrades in the Old Army, Colonel "Paddy" Starr, just back from a two-year stint as commander of a New Jersey infantry regiment, superseded Major Whiting as senior officer of the Reserve Brigade.[29]

While most of Buford's command resupplied in the rear, it contributed a force to the ubiquitous picket line along the Rappahannock. As established by Pleasonton, that line ran for many miles along the north fork of the river. Even so, it did not stretch far enough to detect the 10 June resumption of General Ewell's advance. On that morning Rebel foot troops passed around the cavalry's right flank via Sperryville and Gaines's Cross Roads and made for the Shenandoah Valley, a major corridor to the Mason-Dixon Line.[30]

Although he heard disturbing reports of enemy movements far upriver, Alfred Pleasonton refused to believe them. Aware that Stuart's battered division was salving its wounds near Brandy Station, the Union commander doubted that Lee's main army would march north on its own. He was wrong. On the fourteenth General Hooker learned by telegraph from Winchester that Ewell's advance was overrunning Union garrisons in the Shenandoah. Angry that his foe had stolen a march on him, Hooker ordered the army northward to counter Lee's moves. As he pulled out of Falmouth, the rest of the Army of Northern Virginia continued its shift from Fredericksburg and Culpeper, preparing to follow Ewell down the Valley.[31]

Guarding Hooker's withdrawal along the line of the Orange & Alexandria to Fairfax Station, the First Cavalry Division (to the command of which Buford had officially been appointed three days before) found itself at Bristoe Station on the fifteenth and Manassas Junction the following day. At the latter place the refit begun in the immediate aftermath of Brandy Station concluded with a wholesale issuance of firearms. The great majority of the command turned in older, less reliable weaponry and drew in return Sharps 52-calibre, single-shot breechloading carbines, highly prized for their accuracy and rapid reloading capability.[32]

Early on 17 June, with Stuart's horsemen known to be moving north, screening Lee's flanks and rear, Hooker ordered Pleasonton to seek out and shred that screen, exposing the position of the Confederate army. With Gregg's newly renumbered Second Division in advance, Buford's First Division following (Duffie's command had been broken up and its regiments assigned to Gregg following its misuse at Brandy Station), Pleasonton led the command northwestward toward the Loudoun Valley and beyond the Blue Ridge, whose rocky walls concealed the eastern flank of Lee's invasion force. Throughout the day the corps ranged across territory quite familiar to Buford, passing north of Thoroughfare Gap in the Bull Run Mountains. Then the column turned west, pushed through Aldie Gap, and closed up on the village of that same name, just inside the valley. That afternoon Gregg's advance, under Judson Kilpatrick, had a sharp but indecisive four-hour encounter outside Aldie with part of Stuart's command. Meanwhile, a few miles to the west, Colonel Duffie, having been reduced to command of a single regiment, tangled with many times as many Rebels at Middleburg, losing most of his force in killed, wounded, and captured, leading bands of survivors to safety via Thoroughfare Gap.[33]

Philomont and Union

Next day, with Stuart's counterreconnaissance barrier still intact, Pleasonton sent out scouting parties, including two from Buford's division—one to search for the remnants of Duffie's outfit, the other to search for Lee. That morning Devin's brigade ranged south to Thoroughfare Gap, near which it remained, unsuccessfully combing the country for Duffie's survivors, for the next two days. At the same time, Gamble's brigade and Calef's battery trotted toward Snicker's Gap in the Blue Ridge, a promising venue for reconnaissance. The promise was not fulfilled, however, because Colonel Gamble found his path blocked along Goose Creek, short of the mountains, by Thomas Munford, fresh from the fighting at Aldie. Crossing the creek bridge, Gamble and Calef uprooted Munford's skirmishers and sent them whirling through the town of Philomont. Beyond that point, however, resistance stiffened, and after long but inconclusive skirmishing Gamble headed back to camp. Despite the colonel's inability to reach the gap—which lay only a few miles east of Robert E. Lee's new headquarters in the Shenandoah Valley—Buford expressed "great delight" at the hard fighting the men of his First Brigade had done outside Philomont, for which he "complimented them highly."[34]

On the nineteenth, as the cavalry continued its campaign to push around or through Stuart, Gregg forged westward to Middleburg. Meeting Rebel cavalry in that vicinity, the division commander tangled with Stuart's legions for much of the morning and half the afternoon. Although minus Devin's brigade, still guarding Thoroughfare Gap, Buford attempted to support Gregg, but without great success. Soon after the Second Division made contact with the enemy outside Middleburg, Gamble's troopers and Calef's cannoneers marched north toward Union, from that vantage point hoping to flank Gregg's opponents and gain their rear. Instead, General Stuart sent a Virginia regiment of Munford's command, backed by a portion of William Jones's brigade, to block Gamble's path. Three miles south of Union the two sides clashed inside fenced-in fields of clover; dismounted fighting continued until late afternoon with neither side gaining the advantage. Still, at the end of the fight Gamble held his position, having repulsed a succession of attacks. That position placed him within striking distance of Ashby's Gap, which Stuart must bar to the Federals for at least a few more days, till Lee's advance had progressed so far that detection would not upset his plans.[35]

Upperville

One more engagement—Buford's fiercest fight since Brandy Station—closed out his participation in the Loudoun Valley campaign. Two days after Gregg's engagement at Middleburg, Pleasonton advanced the Second Division toward Stuart's new line of defense in front of, and above, Upperville. This day, as on 9 June, Gregg was closely supported by an infantry force—in this case, a full division from Meade's corps—a tactic that Pleasonton considered critical to landing the knockout punch that General Hooker wished Stuart to receive. While the infantry held Stuart's right flank in place, Gregg was to plow ahead against the Confederate center.[36]

Meanwhile, the upper flank of Stuart's line would be the target of Buford's now-reunited division (Devin had returned from Thoroughfare Gap the previous day). Buford was to move north of the pike that led to Upperville, veer westward just below the bed of Goose Creek and, once he cleared Stuart's left, cut behind the flank, striking in rear just before Gregg attacked in front—the same maneuver Gamble had been unable to execute two days before.[37]

The plan failed again on the twenty-first, primarily because of Pleasonton's lax intelligence-gathering. That morning, when Buford's brigades moved north, struck the creek, and pushed west, they expected to find open, unobstructed country, as Pleasonton had assured them would be the case. Instead, they bogged down on trails made muddy by a recent thunderstorm, then ran hard aground against Jones's brigade, which had gone into position to prolong Stuart's flank above Upperville. Unable to make further headway south of the creek and aware that he must try again, and quickly, to find the end of Stuart's line, Buford turned his column about and countermarched until he found an unobstructed ford. Crossing the creek about noon against a long-range skirmish fire, he turned west once again, hoping for better results this time.[38]

Against mounting opposition—Rebels were continually arriving from points south to slow his march—Buford pressed on to Millville, planning to recross the creek near that village. To his extreme frustration, when he reached Millville he found more of Jones's Virginians, backed by elements of Colonel Chambliss's brigade.

Realizing that he was now so far from Upperville that he would accomplish little even if he found Stuart's flank, Buford sent a courier to Pleasonton explaining his lack of progress. He followed with a thoughtful gesture, sending Major Starr and the Reserve Brigade to Gregg's assistance in the belief that the Second Division should delay its attack no longer. Buford then turned south onto a farm road and led Gamble, Devin, and Calef toward Upperville. The going was slow, thanks to the boggy consistency of the trail; soon Buford began to doubt that his main body would reach Gregg in time to do him any good at all.[39]

The only agreeable feature of the march was that Jones's and Chambliss's opposition had diminished, both brigades having been recalled to Stuart's field headquarters. As he moved to comply with this order, Jones started his supply train southwestward toward Ashby's Gap in the Blue Ridge. Alerted to the wagons' proximity, Buford abruptly turned in the same direction and started off in pursuit.

A mile and a half of rapid, bumpy travel brought him to the tag end of the column. He was on the verge of overhauling it when he suddenly found himself "engaged with a superior force"—Jones's main body, which had reversed course to keep Buford apart from his quarry. A Virginia battery attached to Jones's brigade shelled the Federals into a brief withdrawal, whereupon Buford dismounted Gamble's brigade, placed it behind stone walls, and had it level such a fusillade at the battery that its cannoneers abandoned their guns. A furious saber charge by one of Jones's regiments kept the Federals from capturing the pieces and put many of Gamble's men to flight. Only when Devin's brigade reached the scene, backed by the divisional artillery, did the Confederates—having saved both their wagons and their artillery—cease and desist.[40]

It had been a frustrating and largely unsuccessful day for Buford, but when Jones retreated toward the mountains it was nearly over. Farther to the south, the rest of the day's action—Gregg and the infantry versus Stuart's main force outside Upperville—was also ending badly for the Federals. Though he had kept Stuart on the defensive for much of the afternoon, Gregg had been unable to shake him loose from his position until, with evening approaching, the Beau Sabreur withdrew toward the mountains at a leisurely pace, battered but unbowed. Not even the addition of Starr's Regulars had enabled Gregg to control the battle. The Reserve Brigade's major contribution to the day's offensive—a long-distance saber charge by the Sixth Cavalry against Stuart's right flank—had fallen far short of its objective, due to broken terrain and blown horses.[41]

For John Buford, however, the day was not devoid of accomplishment. By following Jones toward the mountains at day's close, he managed to place some of his men within hailing distance of Ashby's Gap. While comrades distracted Stuart's pickets at the base of the mountain, several Federals scaled one of the slopes and in the fading light gained the summit. Peering into the valley beyond, they gazed upon a Confederate infantry encampment—tangible evidence at last of Lee's progress toward Maryland and Pennsylvania.[42]

* * *

Buford's latest intelligence feat—like those he had performed for the benefit of John Pope—failed to make an impact at army headquarters. As though unimpressed by word of his enemy's progress through the Shenandoah, General Hooker remained in the vicinity of Fairfax Station for five days after Buford's sighting. Not till late on the twenty-sixth did he start after the Confederate invasion force. Hooker's perceived disinterest in safeguarding Northern lives and property would play a part in his impending demise.[43]

To his credit, Fighting Joe had taken a few steps that suggested an intent to stage a pursuit of some vigor. On 25 June he had ordered to the Potomac River his senior subordinate, Major General John F. Reynolds, a highly regarded career soldier (and a native Pennsylvanian) whom he had designated commander of the left, or forward, wing of the army, its I, III, and XI Corps. At Reynolds's direction, two pontoon bridges were laid across the Potomac opposite Edwards Ferry, Maryland, to accommodate the passage of thousands of troops, horses, artillery units, and wagons. As soon as the bridges were operating, Reynolds began to cross his infantry onto Northern soil. Meanwhile, Major General Julius Stahel's cavalry division from the Washington defenses—which included the brigade Buford had led throughout the Second Bull Run Campaign—forded the Potomac not far from Reynolds's bridgehead and ranged toward strategic gaps in the Catoctin and South Mountain ranges. On 28 June part of Stahel's force, two Michigan regiments under Brigadier General Joseph T. Copeland, penetrated as far north as a crossroads village in south-central Pennsylvania named Gettysburg.[44]

When Hooker's main army trod the pontoons, Buford's men crossed with it and headed north in close support of the left wing. By the twenty-seventh—with the whole of Lee's army ensconced in the Keystone State, most of it near Chambersburg—the Army of the Potomac closed up on Frederick, Maryland. From that city emanated momentous news: Hooker was out, a victim of lethargy, poor relations with the War Department, and the residual effects of Chancellorsville. John Reynolds having made known his unwillingness to succeed to the position, army command passed to his friend and colleague, George Meade.[45]

A change of commanders on the verge of a showdown with Lee in Pennsylvania seemed to many in the army a major miscue by the Washington authorities. To the officers and men of the Cavalry Corps—especially to those who thought less than highly of Alfred Pleasonton—the shakeup had beneficial effects. Unlike Hooker, Meade desired to keep his mounted commander on a short leash; he immediately removed Pleasonton (who had received his cherished second star only five days before) from the field and made him a virtual prisoner at army headquarters.[46]

This was not unhappy news for Buford, who had felt rather uncomfortable at Brandy Station with Pleasonton on the scene, looking over his shoulder. Other aspects of the cavalry's reorganization, however, left Buford with mixed feelings. On the twenty-eighth he learned that the corps had assimilated the troopers of the Department of Washington. The command of this new Third Cavalry Division went to Judson Kilpatrick, a favorite of Pleasonton's, whose fighting spirit had been amply displayed at Brandy Station and Aldie but whose reputation for recklessness troubled Buford.

Another byproduct of Meade's succession to army command was the authority he gave Pleasonton to promote deserving officers over the heads of dozens of their superiors. This power resulted in one appointment Buford favored and perhaps recommended: Captain Wesley Merritt of the Second Cavalry was named a brigadier general of volunteers to lead the Reserve Brigade. Two other promotions did not sit as well with Buford: Captains Elon J. Farnsworth and George Armstrong Custer of Pleasonton's staff became brigadiers and brigade commanders under Kilpatrick, the latter replacing Copeland.[47]

It must have been galling to Buford, who had waited so long and worked so hard for a field command, to see officers many years his junior handed their stars as if on a platter. He vented his displeasure in a burst of pointed humor a few weeks later, after some suspected spies captured by his troopers were released by army headquarters. Obviously frustrated, he loudly declared that if he caught another spy he would "hang him and not send him up to be promoted to a Brigadier-General."[48]

CHAPTER IX

Rendezvous with Destiny

On 29 June General Pleasonton set in motion a chain of events that would culminate in enduring fame for John Buford. The cavalry commander decreed that the First Division, the advance element of the army, would move with any two of its brigades and a horse battery to Emmitsburg, Maryland. From Emmitsburg, keeping ahead of General Reynolds's infantry, the troopers and cannoneers would cross the Pennsylvania line to Gettysburg; near the crossroads town they were to locate Lee's army and discern its intentions. The third brigade of Buford's command, along with another battery and the divisional trains, would march farther east to Mechanicstown, Maryland, protecting Buford's right and rear and Reynolds's left flank.[1]

Buford did not have to wrack his brain to make the necessary assignments. Since he expected to meet the enemy in Pennsylvania, he would go there in company with his senior subordinates, Gamble and Devin, and Calef's experienced artillerymen. The newly minted General Merritt would escort the wagons, supported by Captain William M. Graham's Battery K, First U.S. Artillery.

The two columns split up at Middletown, Maryland, in the valley between South Mountain and the northern extension of Catoctin Mountain. Buford and the main body headed west via Turner's Gap to Boonsboro, then sharply northward through Cavetown toward Monterey Springs, Pennsylvania. Meanwhile, Merritt and the wagons trundled slowly up the valley toward the foothills of the Catoctins, the Reserve Brigade camping for the night about eight miles below the Pennsylvania border.[2]

Unencumbered by vehicles, Gamble's and Devin's brigades made better time, crossing into the Keystone State late that afternoon and bivouacking for part of the night at Fountaindale. At three A.M. on the thirtieth Buford shook the men out of their bedrolls and the march resumed to Fairfield, where the column had its first encounter with the invaders of Pennsylvania. Shortly after daylight Buford's advance guard stumbled upon a Confederate outpost, two infantry regiments and two cannon from the division of Major General Henry Heth, one of Buford's companions on the Sioux expedition. The meeting-engagement occurred because local townspeople—whom Buford had counted on for help in locating the enemy—failed to warn the approaching troopers, perhaps for fear of Rebel retaliation.[3]

Enjoined to hasten to Emmitsburg and Gettysburg, Buford feared being delayed en route. Therefore he dismounted one of Devin's regiments, which held the enemy in check while the rest of the column countermarched around the town, dropping back down into Maryland. By nine o'clock the men were trotting through the streets of Emmitsburg under the gaze of I Corps infantrymen. Although their meeting is not documented, undoubtedly Buford sought out General Reynolds and gave him a situation report, highlighting Heth's proximity to Gettysburg, where Reynolds was also bound. When the conference broke up, the cavalry leader rode to overtake the head of his column, which had regained its northward heading.[4]

Gamble's brigade, followed by Devin's men and the artillery, covered the ten miles to Gettysburg in something over two hours, entering the Adams County seat before eleven-thirty. Having learned of General Copeland's presence in Gettysburg a few days before, Buford expected to find the Michigan brigade in the vicinity. Copeland, however, had evacuated his advance post only a few hours after assuming it. The only people the First Cavalry Division encountered in Adams County were civilians.

In traversing Maryland Buford's troopers had found local residents "enthusiastic in their greetings and expressions of satisfaction at the approach of the Union army." No residents, however, were made happier by the cavalry's appearance than the citizens of Gettysburg, who thronged the streets, waving, shouting, and singing patriotic songs as Buford's advance passed through.[5]

The locals had seen rough times of late. Four days before, they had been scared out of their wits when a brigade of Confederate infantry, part of General Ewell's corps, paid an unannounced visit, routing local militia and ransacking stores and homes. Two days later, Copeland's horsemen had failed to remain in Gettysburg long enough to assuage the people's fears. And a few hours before Buford's entrance on 30 June, yet another invasion force—hard-bitten veterans of the corps of Lieutenant General A.P. Hill, some of whom still lingered west of town—had approached from South Mountain, pushing the residents toward panic once again. "No wonder," a member of Devin's Sixth New York recalled,

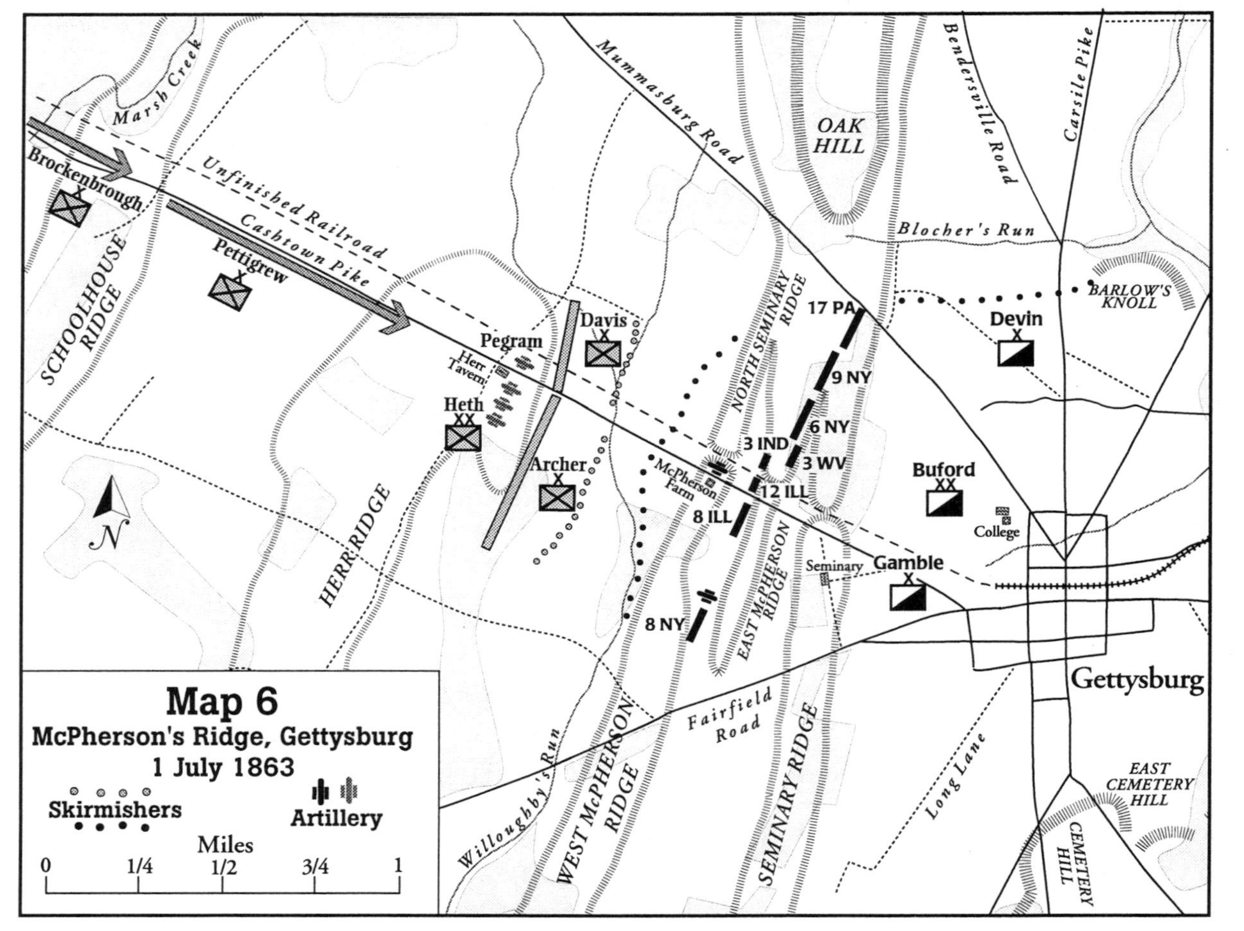
Map 6
McPherson's Ridge, Gettysburg
1 July 1863
Skirmishers
Artillery
Miles
0
1/4
1/2
3/4
1
Marsh Creek
Brockenbrough
SCHOOLHOUSE RIDGE
Unfinished Railroad
Cashtown Pike
Pettigrew
Pegram
Herr Tavern
Heth
Davis
Archer
HERR RIDGE
Mummasburg Road
OAK HILL
Bendersville Road
Carsile Pike
Blocher's Run
BARLOW'S KNOLL
Devin
17 PA
9 NY
6 NY
3 IND
3 WV
12 ILL
8 ILL
8 NY
NORTH SEMINARY RIDGE
McPherson Farm
EAST McPHERSON RIDGE
WEST McPHERSON RIDGE
SEMINARY RIDGE
Seminary
Gamble
Buford
College
Gettysburg
Fairfield Road
Willoughby's Run
Long Lane
EAST CEMETERY HILL
CEMETERY HILL

"that the people should manifest such extreme gladness and joy at our coming."[6]

While some of his troopers partook of an impromptu dinner served up by the citizens, Buford led Gamble's main body through the town via Washington Street, then out Chambersburg Street and its namesake turnpike toward the mountains. Buford halted his vanguard on the property of a prosperous farmer and politician named McPherson, about a mile and a half northwest of Gettysburg. On his approach, Hill's soldiers, who had drawn to within a few miles of Gettysburg, began to retire as though cowed by their adversaries. Buford knew better: the Rebels must be under orders, as he had been at Fairfield, to avoid a fight. They would return, with a good many comrades, when they felt like it—probably on the morrow.[7]

After dispatching Gamble's scouts toward South Mountain, Buford set Devin's troopers to scouring the ridges and fields north and east of Gettysburg. While marching through Maryland, Buford had heard reports of troop concentrations in those directions; the reports suggested that elements of Ewell's command were moving toward Gettysburg from York and Carlisle, as if aware that the Yankees were finally catching up to them. If Lee was concentrating in preparation for a fight, Gettysburg was the perfect setting. Even at a glance Buford could see that a dozen or more roads entered the town from as many directions like spokes meeting at the hub of a wheel. That made Gettysburg a magnet for the Army of the Potomac as well as for its opponent; those roads would draw together Meade's far-flung forces like no other town in that corner of Pennsylvania.[8]

The thought that his 3,000 troopers might soon be tangling with an enemy force many times as large would have staggered another general, but not John Buford. Astride Grey Eagle he rode along the outskirts of town in company with his brigade leaders, his scouts, and his staff including Lieutenant Aaron B. Jerome, his signal officer. Buford, puffing away on his pipe, peering through field-glasses, studied the road network and the lay of the land. He calculated distances to physical landmarks and tried to determine how long it would take those Confederates massing behind South Mountain to come within carbine range. All the while, he displayed a composure that impressed onlookers. A youth observed the general in the streets of Gettysburg that afternoon. Despite the swirl of activity and the ominous portents all about, "his calm demeanor and soldierly appearance . . . struck me forcibly."[9]

Slowly, almost imperceptibly, Buford began to develop a plan in which topography played a major role. The land west of town—from which direction he expected the initial, and perhaps the heaviest, opposition to come—rolled to the mountains in a series of ridges. Some of these were fringed by woods and skirted by streams and each was capable of serving as a defensive position: McPherson's Ridge and its northern and eastern crests, less than two miles outside Gettysburg; Herr Ridge, some 1,300 yards farther west, across Willoughby Run; and, farthest out, three miles from the heart of town, School House Ridge.

The longest of the elevated ranges west of town—that closest to Gettysburg—was known as Seminary Ridge for the Lutheran theological school athwart its upper reaches. Atop Seminary Ridge a force gouged out of the positions farther west might rally and make a stand. The high ground would furnish especially good vantage points for infantry and artillery, assuming that Reynolds's troops came up in time to relieve Buford.

Reynolds is usually given credit for realizing the strategic potential of yet another elevation, nearly a mile east of Seminary Ridge, directly below the town. Given his eye for commanding terrain, however, it is entirely possible that John Buford was the first to evaluate Cemetery Hill. This, the most northerly point of a two-mile-long ridgeline that ran parallel to Seminary Ridge, might serve Buford and his comrades as a last ditch rallying point. Together with the other positions farther west, Cemetery Hill could provide the Army of the Potomac with a critical advantage in a battle to curtail the invasion of Pennsylvania.[10]

By early evening, armed with reliable reports of enemy movements in the vicinity, Buford appears to have convinced himself that he could pull off something never achieved in this war: a defense in depth by dismounted cavalry against a large force of foot soldiers with full artillery support. Of course it would be a risky proposition: his scouts had informed Buford that not only would he face a good portion of Lee's army out of Chambersburg and Cashtown, he would also have to contend with veteran infantry along the roads from Carlisle and York. To oppose these several columns Buford could place perhaps 2,200 troopers on the firing line after subtracting from his aggregate force the one man in four who would serve as a horse-holder in the rear.

Against such odds, Buford could expect to hold his ground for a few hours at best. But would he have that much time? Although he was in contact with Reynolds and knew the wing commander would march for Gettysburg come morning, Buford could not say when the nearest elements of the army would reach him. By refusing to flee from Lee's path, by committing himself to fight in an advanced position however favorable, he risked not only his division's annihilation but the disarranging of General Meade's plans, which were predicated on a defensive struggle among the rolling hills of northern Maryland.[11]

Each of these considerations, and others that came to Buford's mind, carried its own argument against doing what he desired to do. Taking a long puff on his pipe, he considered each argument in turn, scrutinizing it from a variety of angles. Then he went back over his plan and matched each of its assumptions with an appropriate set of consequences. For a time he permitted the mixture of pros and cons to simmer. In the end, the strength of the defensive position he had selected for his army, as well as an irresistible enthusiasm for the calculated risk, overpowered whatever misgivings he might have entertained. Before sundown on that last day in June Buford had committed himself, in thought and in deed, to the greatest challenge of his career.

* * *

By late that evening he had made dispositions relevant to his situation. He had established his field headquarters adjacent to Colonel Gamble's camp, midway between McPherson's and Seminary Ridges. He had also set up a command post at the Blue Eagle Hotel, one block west of the center of Gettysburg. From both vantage points he could coordinate scouting reports, interview citizens who had useful information, and dispatch communiques to Reynolds's and Pleasonton's headquarters.[12]

He tried to post his field force as close to the scenes of anticipated action as possible. He encamped the body of Gamble's brigade between the Mummasburg Road and the road from Fairfield (also known as the Hagerstown Road). Farther north and east, Devin's men bivouacked between the Mummasburg and Harrisburg Roads. Astride the Chambersburg Pike (or Cashtown Road), in the midst of Gamble's bivouac, Lieutenant Calef unlimbered his six cannon, covering the most likely route of Confederate advance.

Picket posts from both brigades described a wide arc that covered the territory between the Fairfield Road and the York Pike. On Gamble's front, vedettes stretched beyond School

House Ridge toward Cashtown. The most advanced position, astride Marsh Run more than three miles west of Gettysburg, was manned by a detachment of the Eighth Illinois under Lieutenant Marcellus E. Jones. The most extended point on Devin's vedette line—held by three companies of the Seventeenth Pennsylvania—lay near Keckler's Hill, where the Herr's Ridge Road met the road from Carlisle five miles north of town.[13]

By midnight, Buford had sent several dispatches to his superiors, informing Reynolds (then at Moritz Tavern, five miles to the south), and Pleasonton (with Meade at Taneytown, Maryland) of the challenges morning would bring. Through the "untiring exertions of many different scouting parties," he had surmised that throughout 1 July Hill's corps—the divisions of Major Generals Heth, William Dorsey Pender, and Richard H. Anderson—would come sweeping in from Cashtown, while the better part of Lieutenant General Richard S. Ewell's corps, Major General Robert E. Rodes's division in advance, would troop in from points north and east. In providing his superiors with this information, Buford upheld his reputation as an expert gatherer of intelligence. As one historian observes, "this was cavalry scouting and reporting at their best, a model of precision and accuracy, with fact carefully separated from rumor."[14]

To oppose the enemy's hordes Buford must rely on "fagged out" troopers and horses, low on rations, forage, and horseshoes. Still, he made "arrangements . . . for entertaining" the enemy, determined to hold his carefully chosen ground until relieved. In so doing, he was demonstrating his faith in John Reynolds's ability to support him with Major General Abner Doubleday's I Corps, then with Reynolds at Moritz Tavern, and the XI Corps of Major General Oliver Otis Howard, which by the evening of the thirtieth was two miles below

Doubleday, at Emmitsburg. Still, Buford must have realized that circumstances beyond Reynolds's control might delay his march, forcing the First Cavalry Division to quit Gettysburg after taking heavy losses. With a twinge of pessimism, he wrote Reynolds at ten-thirty P.M.: "Should I have to fall back, advise me by what route."[15]

One of Buford's lieutenants would have none of that kind of talk. According to a well-worn account, around the campfire that evening Tom Devin tried to assure his commander that his brigade would easily handle whatever opposition it encountered over the next twenty-four hours. A prescient Buford supposedly replied: "No, you won't. They will attack you in the morning and they will come booming—skirmishers three deep. You will have to fight like the devil to hold your own until supports arrive. The enemy must know the importance of this position and will strain every nerve to secure it, and if we are able to hold it, we will do well." If Buford indeed made this little speech, he had a near-perfect grasp of his situation, for what happened the next morning fulfilled his prophecy.[16]

* * *

Although shots were exchanged just after dawn between Devin's vedettes on the Carlisle Road and advance parties of General Ewell's infantry, the first sustained fighting on 1 July took place along the Chambersburg Pike about three hours later. Harry Heth's division took to that road at five A.M. and his skirmishers drew within sight of Gamble's pickets just shy of seven-thirty. From his advanced position along Marsh Creek, Lieutenant Jones spied the head of Heth's column and, shrouded by the morning mist, snapped off a few long-range shots with a borrowed carbine. The invaders replied with musketry and, later, cannon-fire. Within minutes other segments of Gamble's vedette line became heavily engaged with Confederate skirmishers topping School House Ridge.[17]

Despite the steadily growing opposition in their front, Heth's troops pushed toward Gettysburg briskly, confidently, even nonchalantly. Their nonchalance was a product of ignorance. Heth, who lacked reconnaissance support, believed he was facing militia, home guards, Pennsylvania emergency troops, or at most a small detachment of observation. The division commander believed that the Army of the Potomac, still under Joe Hooker, remained miles away in Maryland, if not farther to the south in Virginia.

Not only Heth, but the greater portion of Lee's army, was moving blindly through unfamiliar territory thanks to J.E.B. Stuart's decision to lead most of his cavalry around Meade's flank. Armed with conditional permission from Lee, Stuart had left Salem, Virginia, on 24 June in advance of the main army's entrance into Pennsylvania. Via a rather hazy plan of cooperation, he intended to link with his infantry comrades in the Keystone State. Yet unexpected obstacles, delays, and other problems beyond an acceptable margin of error had conspired to keep the cavalry leader far apart from the divisions he should have been guiding toward Gettysburg. Stuart's flawed planning and ill luck would place the fortunes of the two most prominent cavalry leaders in the East in stark contrast. Even as the Beau Sabreur of the Confederacy was muddling through his least successful and most controversial operation, John Buford was approaching the zenith of a long and distinguished career.[18]

At the outset, however, Buford must have wondered if he were approaching a career-ending disaster. About a half-hour before skirmishing broke out along Marsh Creek the cavalry leader learned of Heth's advance from Lieutenant Jerome. The signal officer had established an observation perch in the cupola of the Lutheran seminary. Buford intermittently joined him in the tower, scanning the fields and roads in the murky light, waiting for the inevitable to occur. "He seemed anxious," Jerome later recalled, "even more so than I ever saw him."[19]

Buford's anxiety also prompted him to ride from one point to another, ensuring that preparations to meet the enemy were in place. Just before the firing started, he appears to have galloped back to his command post in Gettysburg for a final briefing from his scouts. He was conferring with a bevy of subordinates outside the Blue Eagle Hotel when a staff officer of the I Corps, who had come up from Moritz Tavern in advance of his command, reined in at the hostelry. Believing that the newcomer was on a nonessential errand, Buford advised him to return at once to his command. The officer was perplexed: "Why, what is the matter, General?" As if on cue, a Confederate cannon thundered in the near-distance, startling everyone but Buford. "That," he replied tersely, "is the matter."[20]

Spurring back to Seminary Ridge, Buford directed Gamble and Devin to establish a common line of battle. Some time after eight A.M., their regiments moved into position atop the main crest of McPherson's Ridge. They formed a discontinuous perimeter more than a mile long, their right flank anchored on the Mummasburg Road, their left resting perhaps 300 yards above the road to Fairfield. Running astride and below the Chambersburg Pike, Gamble's line consisted of, from right to left, six companies of the Third Indiana, four companies of the Twelfth Illinois, the Eighth Illinois, and the Eighth New York Cavalry. Devin's regiments extended the line north of the pike: from right to left, the Seventeenth Pennsylvania, the Ninth New York, the Sixth New York, and two companies of the Third West Virginia. Permitted to choose his own position, Calef moved up the turnpike to more commanding, more defensible ground. At

Buford's suggestion, the lieutenant spread his pieces wide apart to deceive the enemy into thinking his battery was actually two artillery units.[21]

While Buford built a line of defense, Colonel Gamble reinforced his advanced positions. The picket line of the Eighth Illinois near Marsh Creek had been augmented soon after the first shots were fired. Now Gamble dispatched a substantial force—several hundred strong, he claimed—to bolster the skirmishers along Herr Ridge and Willoughby Run.[22]

At first the reinforcements appeared to count for little. Soon after eight A.M. Buford received word that Gamble's pickets were being driven back to Herr Ridge by Heth's infantry, supported by the artillery battalion of Major William J. Pegram. Then, however, the weight of the Union defensive effort began to tell, rapid-firing carbines and the accurate shelling of Calef's three-inch rifles slowing the Rebel advance. Not until about nine o'clock could Heth's men shove their opponents back to McPherson's Ridge while securing the length of Herr Ridge.

The stiff resistance he had encountered told Harry Heth that he was not facing citizens-in-arms but well-disciplined regulars in some strength. The rapid fire of Buford's carbines and the lack of visible horse herds, however, made the Confederate commander suspect he had encountered infantry rather than cavalry. Heth, who entertained a high regard for the staying-power of foot troops, paused before continuing toward McPherson's Ridge.[23]

During the interval, he made a fateful decision. Rather than push ahead in skirmish formation, he formed line of battle. He spent over a half-hour deploying his leading brigade, under Brigadier General James J. Archer, and extending its left flank with the next brigade in line, that of Brigadier General Joseph R. Davis. In the meantime, he had some of Pegram's guns shell Yankee-infested woods in their front, while additional artillery units lumbered forward. It was some time after nine-thirty before the gray column resumed its advance. The delay enabled Buford to strengthen his grasp on McPherson's Ridge. It also gave John Reynolds additional time on his march from Moritz Tavern.[24]

Some historians, reviewing this phase of the action on 1 July, maintain that the delays Heth's men encountered between seven-thirty and nine-thirty were due less to their opponents' stubborn defense than to their commander's timidity and vacillation. This *non causa pro causa* argument ignores the reason for Heth's indecision: the fierce resistance he was meeting at the hands of troops he had originally expected to scatter like leaves in the wind.

* * *

When Heth forged eastward from Herr Ridge, Buford realized that his ability to stave off an irresistible onslaught was a matter of an hour or less—perhaps much less. Once they got up a proper head of steam Archer's brigade south of the pike could crush Gamble's men, while Davis's troops to the north flattened Devin's line. Buford desperately needed to hear that Reynolds was within supporting distance of him. By ten o'clock, however, he had an imperfect idea of the wing commander's whereabouts.[25] Reynolds and Doubleday had left Moritz Tavern at eight A.M. The I Corps was within three miles of its destination by about ten-fifteen when Reynolds, having ridden with his escort in advance of the corps, reached the battlefield. The traditional site of his meeting with Buford is the seminary building, whose cupola the latter had reoccupied. Noting Reynolds's arrival, Buford supposedly remarked, with a sense of profound relief: "Now we can hold the place." In one of two slightly different postwar accounts of the reunion, Lieutenant Jerome quotes the wing commander as shouting to Buford, "What's the matter, John?" and Buford, upon descending from the cupola, as answering, "The devil's to pay!" When the cavalry leader reached his side, Reynolds hoped aloud that "you can hold out until my [leading] corps comes up." To this Buford returned what Jerome called a "characteristic reply," laconic, matter-of-fact, yet full of determination: "I reckon I can."[26]

Conflicting with Jerome's story is the recollection of a Gettysburg citizen who claimed to have seen both generals that morning outside Buford's command post at the Blue Eagle; a now-lost postwar account by one of Buford's aides supposedly corroborates the citizen's remembrance. Then, too, the memoirs of the I Corps aide whom Buford advised to return to his command places Buford at the hotel a short time before Reynolds's arrival. It is therefore possible that the meeting between wing commander and cavalry leader occurred in the streets of Gettysburg rather than in the more dramatic and long-accepted setting of Seminary Ridge.[27]

Whatever the circumstances of their encounter, the generals proceeded to Buford's headquarters near the seminary, then rode out the Chambersburg Pike toward the firing lines. En route, Buford, shouting to make himself heard above the din, explained his defensive plan and pointed out the geographical advantages on which it was based. Nodding in approval, Reynolds endorsed his dispositions and promised that his infantry would arrive momentarily. The foot soldiers, and the staying-power they represented, were badly needed; as Reynolds drew abreast of the position of the First Cavalry Brigade, Colonel Gamble rushed up to report that his skirmish line was coming apart under pressure.[28]

Appreciating the urgency of Gamble's situation, Reynolds sent gallopers to urge the XI Corps to increase its pace and to inform Meade that two corps would soon be engaged at Gettysburg. Then the wing commander left Buford to ride south and escort the head of Doubleday's corps on the last mile of its double-quick march.

Some time after ten-thirty—only minutes before Buford's troopers could be outflanked and their positions overrun—Reynolds returned to Seminary Ridge at the head of the I Corps' vanguard, the division of Brigadier General James S. Wadsworth. He directed Wadsworth's Second Brigade, under Brigadier General Lysander Cutler, toward a railroad cut, there to stop the advance of Davis's Mississippians and North Carolinians. Reynolds then supervised Brigadier General Solomon Meredith's "Iron Brigade" as it relieved Gamble's troopers on McPherson's Ridge and opposed Archer's Tennesseans and Alabamians. Reynolds was helping steady a part of Meredith's line that showed signs of wavering when he toppled from his horse, mortally wounded by a sharpshooter's bullet.[29]

Had it come a short time earlier, Reynolds's death might have thrown the I Corps into a fatal confusion. Well before ten-thirty, however, enough of Doubleday's men had taken position on both sides of the Chambersburg Pike to avert an early retreat. Eventually, the infantry succeeded in blunting the advance of both of Heth's leading brigades, in the process capturing General Archer. Heth's setback forced him to call up his remaining brigades, under Colonel J.M. Brockenbrough and Brigadier General J. Johnston Pettigrew. And by eleven o'clock, Reynolds's ranking subordinate, the stolid but capable General Howard, had reached the field to assume wing leadership. Howard's corps, now under Major General Carl Schurz, was only a few miles short of the battlefield when the change of command occurred.[30]

The I Corps did not have to hold McPherson's Ridge and secure the railroad cut all by itself. On both sides of the turnpike the foot soldiers were aided by the carbineers they had rescued from possible annihilation. They were also supported by the incessant fire of Calef's guns, which occupied a dangerous position in advance of most of the foot troops.

Battery A was doing yeoman service this morning. A short time before Doubleday's men arrived, dwindling ammunition had forced the unit to quit its station along the Chambersburg Pike. It was an eventuality for which General Buford had prepared his artillery commander. In the thick of the early fighting Calef's superior had materialized at his side to impart some calm advice: "Our men are in a pretty hot pocket, but, my boy, we must hold this position until the infantry comes up. Then you withdraw your guns in each section by piece, fill up your limber chests from the caissons, and await my orders."[31]

Accordingly, at about ten o'clock Battery A pulled back to the Seminary grounds to replenish ammo chests. After the I Corps reached the field, however, Buford sent one of Calef's guns to oppose the Rebels near the railroad cut, and some time before noon General Wadsworth ordered four other pieces back to McPherson's Ridge to relieve a shattered battery of his own division. Calef's return to the front was greeted by such a shower of musket balls that he quickly lost a dozen men wounded and more than that many horses killed. The battery suffered so heavily that Buford prevailed on General Doubleday to relieve it with a fresh battery from the I Corps. By this time, Buford had been highly impressed by his artillery's performance. As he told Calef's survivors at day's end, "you have done splendidly. I never saw a battery served so well in my life."[32]

Just shy of noon, as General Heth positioned his rear brigades to renew the assault, and while Pender's division came up in Heth's rear, a lull settled over the battlefield. In the interval, Buford recalled Gamble's brigade and placed its tired, sweat-streaked men in a relatively quiet sector southwest of town. Only the Eighth Illinois, under Major John L. Beveridge, remained in close contact with the enemy. Gamble had left the regiment on McPherson's Ridge close to the Fairfield Road, from which point it could observe the right flank of Hill's still-arriving corps.[33]

* * *

As Pender's division came in from the west to bolster Heth, another Confederate command was approaching Gettysburg along a northerly route. Heralding the advance of General Ewell's corps, the division of Major General Robert Rodes trooped down the road from Carlisle. This sector was under the watchful eye of Devin's troopers, who had shifted farther to the north once Doubleday's corps had relieved them above the Chambersburg Pike.[34]

Rodes's skirmishers made contact with Devin's vedettes near Keckler's Hill at about eleven A.M. Thrusting the outnumbered pickets before them, the gray tide kept rolling toward Gettysburg until it struck Devin's skirmish line. During the intense fighting that resulted, the weight of Ewell's vanguard threatened to uproot Devin's men just as Gamble's had faced overthrow at the hands of Harry Heth.

The weight applied to Devin's line increased after noon when his vedettes encountered the advance contingent of Major General Jubal A. Early's division of Ewell's corps, coming down the road from Harrisburg. Spearheaded by the Ninth New York, dismounted members of the Second Brigade held back the newcomers as long as possible. Eventually, Devin was compelled to pull his troopers "by successive formations in line to the rear by the regiment." A member of the Seventeenth Pennsylvania wrote that his comrades "fought dismounted, with carbines, and when their ammunition for their deadly weapons was exhausted, and lines at points reached close quarters, they used their Colts' revolvers to the best advantage possible. While compelled to fall back from one position to another, as heavy lines of infantry pressed upon their front and flank . . . these troops yielded slowly and doggedly, answering every exulting Rebel yell with a ringing loyal cheer...."[35]

The pressure on Devin began to abate at about twelve-thirty, when the head of the XI Corps reached the front and formed on Doubleday's right. Through Devin, Buford was able to warn General Howard of Early's concentration beyond the XI Corps's flank. This timely intelligence enabled the XI Corps to shift to the right to counter the ever-increasing breadth of Ewell's approach. Again relieved by the infantry, Devin moved even farther to the right to guard its flank.

Although some of his skirmishers had been cut off by Rodes's advance and had retreated towards parts south and west, Devin led his main body almost a mile out along the York Pike. Suddenly a large portion of his command came under the fire of an XI Corps artillery unit. Mistaking the riders of the Second Brigade for Confederate cavalry, Captain Michael Wiedrich's battery, which had unlimbered on Cemetery Hill to protect the Union rear, did no harm to Devin's troopers but killed several of their mounts. When the friendly fire persisted, Devin shepherded his men into the streets of Gettysburg, thus uncovering Schurz's right.[36]

Even had the cavalry retained its original position, it could not have overcome enemy numerical superiority west, north, and northeast of Gettysburg. In early- and mid-afternoon, the Federals absorbed a succession of devastating blows ordered by the recently arrived Robert E. Lee. Supported by Pender's division and a portion of Rodes's, at about two-thirty General Heth launched a new offensive. After some initial difficulty, the drive succeeded in pushing the I Corps from McPherson's Ridge onto the rallying-point Buford had sized up the previous day, Seminary Ridge. About a half-hour after Heth went forward, and despite a spirited delaying action by Devin's main body near the Harrisburg Road, Early's fresh troops overran part of the XI Corps line. And within minutes of Early's success, one of Rodes's previously uncommitted brigades struck south from Oak Hill, carrying a sector on Doubleday's right near its connection with Schurz's left.

As Federal infantry began to recoil on all parts of the field, Lee and A.P. Hill directed a climactic effort aimed at prying their enemy loose from Seminary Ridge. Just short of four o'clock Hill sent in Pender's main body, 6,500 strong, off Heth's lower flank. From north to south in succession, the Carolina brigades of Brigadier General Alfred M. Scales, Colonel Abner Perrin, and Brigadier General James H. Lane struck the main line of Doubleday's battered, bloodied corps.[37]

The left of the line on Seminary Ridge was now held by the Union cavalry and horse artillery. Either on his own initiative or in response to a request from Doubleday, Buford had plucked Gamble and Calef from their resting-places near Gettysburg and had positioned them south of the Fairfield Road to anchor the infantry's lower flank. The majority of Gamble's men lay in wait, dismounted, behind a tree-shaded stone wall perpendicular to the path of Perrin's advance. The Eighth Illinois of Major Beveridge, deployed amid an orchard, a woodlot, and open ground farther to the south and west, occupied a similar position in relation to Lane's approach.

From their hiding places, the troopers and horse gunners did damage disproportionate to their numbers. As Perrin's right-flank regiments, the Twelfth and Thirteenth South Carolina, drew near Seminary Ridge, Gamble and Calef treated them to a murderous enfilade. "We went to popping at them," recalled a member of the Eighth New York. "...They fell like rain. The ground soon got covered with them. The front collumn [sic] broke and started to run but their rear collumn pressed...on."[38]

At first startled by the unexpected opposition, the assaulted regiments faced to the southeast and made for the stone wall under a "constant and withering fire." Although their second rank unleashed a volley that eventually displaced the cavalry, the Confederates found the going extremely tough. A trooper of the Third Indiana recalled that the enemy came "within less than 10 paces" of the stone wall "before we retired." When ordered to fall back, this man and many of his comrades wished, instead, to attack: "Could we have charged them they would have been routed...."[39]

While Buford led Gamble's main body eastward toward Cemetery Hill, the Eighth Illinois, from its detached position, lashed the right flank of Lane's brigade. To an even greater degree than their comrades in Gamble's main body, Major Beveridge's 400 men inflicted carnage and chaos at a critical time. Their fire not only staggered Lane's advance and caused it to drift south of Perrin's position, it brought Lane to a halt well short of Seminary Ridge.

The North Carolinians feared that if they continued their advance, worse was to come. Spying a large detachment of Beveridge's regiment saddled and waiting behind a fence, pistols and sabers in hand, General Lane ordered part of his command to form hollow squares, a proscribed maneuver to counter a mounted charge. For several minutes the North Carolinians remained immobile and thus unable to support Perrin in his contest with Gamble's main body. At last a flanking company of the Seventh North Carolina gained a position from which to force the troopers' retreat. But by then Lane's opportunity to flank the I Corps battle line on Seminary Ridge and prevent Doubleday's withdrawal to

Cemetery Hill—a feat that might have visited disaster on the Army of the Potomac—had faded out.[40]

* * *

Buford's determined stand on Doubleday's left helped prolong the I Corps's occupation of Seminary Ridge but could not save the command from ultimate defeat. Not long after four o'clock the bulk of Pender's division—Scales's brigade and the upper portion of Perrin's—began to overwhelm its opposition, making Doubleday's retreat a matter of time. Meanwhile, the combined battering of Early's and Rodes's divisions rendered Schurz's line north of town untenable.

To the last, General Howard hoped that reinforcements would arrive to enable him to hold on; as of midday the main elements of the III and XII Corps were less than eight miles from Gettysburg. But by four-ten Reynolds's successor could see that critical elements of both Doubleday's and Schurz's commands were giving way. Reluctantly, he ordered a full withdrawal to Cemetery Hill, already held by some XI Corps infantry and artillery. Within a half hour, the first elements of Schurz's corps were streaming south through Gettysburg and grouping on the heights below the town, closely followed by the initial arrivals of the I Corps. Howard formed the survivors of the XI Corps on the right of the Baltimore Pike, Doubleday's remnants on the left.[41]

Atop this rallying ground the troops came under the supervision of Major General Winfield Scott Hancock, commander of the II Corps, who had reached the battlefield *sans* his command. Upon learning of Reynolds's death, General Meade had sent Hancock, whom he trusted to act in his place, from Taneytown to Gettysburg. Hancock carried authority to supersede Howard, who, while senior to the newcomer, lacked Meade's full confidence.[42] John Buford may have been responsible in some degree for Hancock's assignment. Shortly before three-thirty the cavalryman had sent a communique to Pleasonton, who quickly passed it to Meade, complaining of a vacuum in Union command: "There seems to be no directing person. . . . We need help now." This comment may have dealt an unfair blow to General Howard, who had acted responsibly in withdrawing from Seminary Ridge and had skillfully initiated the defense of Cemetery Hill. Even so, Buford's concern for the well-being of his army ensured that an energetic, quick-thinking, confidence-inspiring officer would be on hand to sustain the buildup on the high ground south of town.[43]

Hancock knew that in performing his ordained duties he could count on support from Buford's bone-weary but still serviceable cavalrymen. The division leader had proved as much shortly before Hancock reached the field. At the outset of the pull-back to Cemetery Hill, General Doubleday had sent a staff officer to petition Howard for reinforcements. The latter had directed the man to Buford, who had grouped Gamble's remnants a short distance west of the hill. Doubleday's emissary found Buford as tired as his battle-scarred troopers. When apprised of Doubleday's request, the Kentuckian rose in his stirrups and exclaimed: "What in hell and damnation does he think I can do against those long lines of the enemy out there?" Taken aback, the aide replied that he was merely following orders, whereupon a mollified Buford remarked, "Very well. I will see what I can do."[44]

What he did was to remount Gamble's men and lead them an indeterminate distance west of the heights, "in plain view of the enemy" as well as of those foot soldiers still streaming toward Cemetery Hill. The retreating troops must have been heartened by this display of strength; certainly the newly arrived General Hancock was. In later years the corps commander called the spectacle "among the most inspiring sights" he had ever seen: hundreds of horsemen in a compact mass, pistols and carbines drawn, daring the occupiers of Seminary Ridge to venture within range of their arms. None accepted the challenge.[45]

The show of brawn and bravado was a fitting note on which to close a memorable day's work by the First Cavalry Division, Army of the Potomac. Soon after Buford's men moved forward from Cemetery Hill, the sun brushed the horizon; fleeting daylight cost the Confederates the chance to drive the harried Yankees from their final refuge. Between five and six o'clock advance elements of the III and XII Corps began to file into position along the ridge that ran south from the cemetery. Their arrival ensured that at least one more day of fighting would be needed to decide the outcome of the war's pivotal struggle. No one had made a greater contribution to this achievement than John Buford and his tenacious, triumphant command.[46]

After dusk, as both armies realigned their ranks and strengthened their positions, Buford moved to put his exhausted people to bed. Soon after Gamble ended his stand west of Cemetery Hill, Devin's troopers had come down from the lower environs of Gettysburg to augment the First Brigade. Now, with Hancock's approval, Buford led the combined force, plus Calef's battery, down the road to Emmitsburg and into bivouac near a peach orchard owned by a farmer named Sherfy.[47]

While troopers and cannoneers slumbered all around him, the cavalry leader remained awake long into the night, enjoying his pipe, wrapped in the blanket in which he usually slept, Indian fashion, around the campfire. He did not want to relax his grip on this day, the finest day of his career. Above all, he did not wish to lose the mental pictures that recalled the strength, the savvy, and the sacrifice his officers and men had displayed throughout the fight. Already he may have been framing the words he would not set to paper for another six weeks:

"The zeal, bravery, and good behavior of the officers and men on the night of June 30, and during July 1, was commendable in the extreme. A heavy task was before us; we were equal to it, and shall all remember with pride that at Gettysburg we did our country much service."[48]

CHAPTER X

In Warm Pursuit

After such a long, draining, damaging day, Buford's troopers deserved their rest. For many of them, however, morning came all too soon. Some time after five A.M. on 2 July, fighting flared up after Devin moved a skirmish line across the Emmitsburg Road to scout the enemy and met Confederate infantry engaged in the same work. The firefight thus begun lasted for several hours, taking a toll of both Devin's troopers and Calef's battery, which ably supported the Second Brigade although still sore from "the severe work of the 1st."[1]

Not until late in the morning were Devin's reinforced skirmishers relieved by the nearest infantry unit, part of Sickles's corps. Even after withdrawing most of his troops, Devin left a squadron of the Ninth New York in position off Sickles's left. The gesture was a timely one; just after noon that flank came under the fire of Rebels advancing from Seminary Ridge. The New Yorkers would remain with the III Corps until sundown.[2]

The thought that his battle-worn soldiers and their jaded

steeds would have to spend the day securing the flanks of the infantry troubled Buford a great deal. Such a dangerous job might entail even greater losses than the fighting of 1 July, which had cost him 139 officers and men killed, wounded, or captured. While the losses represented less than 6 percent of the troops engaged, the division's horses were in poor condition, as they had been for many days. Calef's battery had been so roughly handled that it lacked enough men to operate its full complement of guns. Then, too, Buford was concerned that his third brigade, and the supply train it guarded, remained many miles to the south.[3]

Haunted by painful memories—horses and men collapsing on the march from Salem and White Plains, winded mounts defeating the charge of the Regulars at Upperville—Buford hesitated to test his division further at Gettysburg, fearing that its continuing debility would make it impotent. Although the record is unclear, it appears likely that he petitioned Meade, who had arrived on the field during the night, to permit his men to go to the rear for a refit. In due course Meade's headquarters responded that the First and Second Brigades and Calef's battery should head to Taneytown, Maryland, four hours' march to the south, where the army's supply trains had been collected. From Taneytown Buford should convey the trains to the railhead supply base at Westminster, thirteen miles farther east. There his men could rest and replenish cartridge boxes and forage bags beyond reach of the enemy's guns.[4]

Buford wasted no time availing himself of this opportunity. Gamble's brigade, which had not seen action today beyond what Colonel George H. Chapman of the Third Indiana called "a little work between the skirmishers & an occasional shot from the artillery," started down the Taneytown Road past Meade's headquarters at about nine A.M. As soon as able to break contact with Sickles's opponents,

Devin's troopers and Calef's gunners followed. They reached the wagon park late that day, spent the night in Taneytown, and the next morning escorted the long column of vehicles eastward. Arriving at Westminster, where the roar of cannon was only a memory, the troopers and artillerymen settled down to their first lengthy respite since before Brandy Station.[5]

The troopers may have earned their vacation from war, but their leave-taking had far-reaching consequences for the army at Gettysburg. General Sickles, who held the southern end of Meade's line on Cemetery Ridge, considered himself in dire need of flank guards and mobile reconnaissance units; the single squadron of New Yorkers Devin had left appeared wholly inadequate to his needs.

Partially due to this perceived lack of cavalry support, Sickles in midafternoon made a fateful shift of position that he failed to clear with army headquarters. Moving west from Meade's line, Sickles stationed his infantry along elevated ground little more than a quarter-mile from Seminary Ridge. Instead of securing his position, however, the move left him vulnerable to an offensive launched some time after three o'clock by troops along Lee's right. The Rebels decimated the III Corps and came within minutes of seizing the critical sector Sickles had abandoned, before being stopped by Meade's desperate shifting of reinforcements to the threatened spot.[6]

It should be pointed out that Buford had ample permission to leave the battlefield; both Meade and Pleasonton shared his concern over the condition of his troops and considered his request justified. Neither general, however, had a right to remove from the front the army's only disposable cavalry without making provision for its replacing. Pleasonton, at least—and probably his superior as well—ought to have known that neither Gregg nor Kilpatrick was close enough to Gettysburg at that hour on 2 July to fill the gap Buford's departure created. Along with Buford himself, both commanders must share the blame for the near-disaster that befell the army at least partially due to the cavalry's ride to the rear.[7]

* * *

At Westminster, thirty miles from the field of battle, where Buford obtained critically needed rations, forage, and other supplies, all was serene for most of Friday, the third. About one P. M., however, distant thunder heralded the climactic event of the three-day struggle in lower Pennsylvania: the cannonade preceding the dramatic assault against Meade's center by infantry under Major Generals George Pickett and Isaac Trimble and Brigadier General Pettigrew.[8]

Details of this doomed offensive, which sealed Lee's defeat and prompted his withdrawal from the North, would come later; on 3 July, as Colonel Chapman noted in his diary, Buford's people could get "no reliable word from the battlefield." The following day, however, the colonel reported that intelligence of "a favorable aspect" had begun to filter down to Westminster, confirming hopes and confounding pessimism.

The early part of Independence Day was given over to resting, feeding, and reshoeing the division's horses—"slow work," as Chapman said. Toward evening, however, the command received word "rather unexpectedly" to move out in the direction of Frederick: Meade was anticipating a Confederate withdrawal and was determined to stage a vigorous pursuit through Maryland to the Potomac.[9]

At Buford's order, the men slung on their gear and got into motion; by six P.M. the column was wending its way southwestward. It progressed only five miles, however, before night persuaded Buford to go into bivouac. Next morning the march resumed at an early hour, halting at Frederick in the afternoon, where Buford received additional supplies. These came courtesy of the local commander, Major General William H. French, whose several thousand foot troops, recently stationed at Harpers Ferry, would soon join the Army of the Potomac, French replacing the severely wounded Dan Sickles in corps command.[10]

At Frederick, Gamble, Devin, and Calef were joined by Merritt's brigade and Graham's battery, fresh from Gettysburg and points nearby. Most of Merritt's troopers had seen hot action, but had achieved little success, late on 3 July. Under the orders of the impetuous Judson Kilpatrick, the Regulars and Pennsylvanians had attacked well-entrenched infantry along the Confederate right, with predictable results. While Merritt's main body was being repulsed at Gettysburg, Major Starr and the Sixth Cavalry were being slashed to pieces outside Fairfield, where Grumble Jones's brigade prevented the Regulars from overtaking a Confederate supply train and made casualties of Starr and 240 of his men.[11]

Aware that Merritt required a refit at least as extensive as Gamble's and Devin's, Buford spent the night a few miles west of Frederick tending to the Reserve Brigade's needs. While there he pondered the orders recently received from Meade's headquarters: to cross South Mountain and move up the banks of the Potomac to Williamsport and Falling Waters, where Lee was expected to try to cross back into Virginia. At Falling Waters and nearby Harpers Ferry the Confederates had laid pontoon bridges. Known to Buford but not to Lee, on 4 July cavalry from French's command had captured and destroyed the main bridge at Falling Waters; later, other horsemen would demolish the spans opposite Harpers Ferry. These acts of vandalism, added to recent rains that made the Potomac impassable, threatened to trap Lee on the north shore for an indefinite period.[12]

Williamsport

Whether or not he knew of the danger taking shape in his rear, in advance of his main army's retreat Lee had started a column of supply wagons and ambulances, fully seventeen miles long, toward Williamsport by a roundabout route beyond South Mountain. Though protected by a heavy force of artillery and two of General Stuart's brigades, this critically important train would be a ripe target if forced to idle along the river until new bridges could be laid. Buford's assignment was to overtake the caravan before it reached the river or to destroy it if he found it parked at Williamsport.[13]

Resolved to waste no time, Buford led the way out of Frederick and through Catoctin Mountain before dawn of the sixth. Thirteen hours of steady travel carried his reunited division from Middletown, through Turner's Gap in South Mountain, to Boonsboro. At Boonsboro, Buford was joined by General Kilpatrick, whose Third Cavalry Division had pushed southwest from Gettysburg early on the fourth in advance of Meade's infantry pursuit. With Gregg's division guarding the flanks of the army, Buford and Kilpatrick would share the responsibility for harassing Lee's retreat and stopping it short of Virginia.[14]

According to Kilpatrick, the generals compared assignments and capabilities and made a satisfactory division of labor. Buford would continue to Williamsport, attacking Lee's trains, while Kilpatrick moved north to Hagerstown, the reported location of Stuart's main body, occupying Stuart's attention and preventing him from interfering with the First Division.[15]

After Kilpatrick rode off, Buford put Boonsboro behind

him and by the middle of the afternoon began to close up on Williamsport. As soon as he encountered Confederate pickets east of the town, he saw that his quarry would be more of a challenge than he had supposed. The supply wagons and ambulances were under the command of Brigadier General John D. Imboden, a resourceful officer well equipped for his present task. Although the two horse brigades assigned him were some distance from the river, battling pursuers and guarding other approaches to the town, Imboden could call on not only twenty-two cannon but also his own brigade of cavalry and mounted infantry and a motley assortment of teamsters and ambulatory wounded. Imboden had placed much of his impressive array of artillery on the hills that surrounded the town and commanded all approaches to it, supporting them with dismounted horsemen. Further, he had massed his vehicles in such a way as to augment his defensive position, with each group of wagons commanded by a wounded line officer.[16]

The ragtag nature of Imboden's troops notwithstanding, his artillery lent him an early and major advantage. When Buford pushed his dismounted carbineers along the road from Boonsboro, they remained for a time beyond effective range of the guns. Thus they were able to drive Imboden's pickets to within a half-mile of the wagon park. At that point, however, the attackers met a tempest of roundshot, shell, and canister from four cannon posted to sweep the Boonsboro Road, supported by as many guns between the pike and the road to Hagerstown. Buford pulled back and formed a perimeter, Merritt's troopers and Graham's gunners on the right, Gamble and Calef on the left, Devin in reserve. Despite efforts by units on each part of his line, however, Buford's men were able to advance no farther toward their objective.[17]

They did repulse some limited offensives by Imboden, including one directed against Gamble, many of whose men remained well concealed behind shelter until the Rebels came within "short carbine range." Then the colonel's Sharps repeaters did "terrible execution," sending the enemy into headlong retreat. Later in the fight Colonel Chapman led the Third Indiana southward across the Downsville Road, where he destroyed an isolated segment of Imboden's train. Feats such as these prompted Buford to declare that with troops such as Gamble's "he could scale the walls of Hell." On the right, meanwhile, Merritt "most admirably foiled" a Rebel sortie, after which he and his opponents contented themselves with long-distance sharpshooter and artillery exchanges.[18]

Late in the afternoon Buford heard sounds of fighting from the direction of Hagerstown, where Kilpatrick had encountered not only Stuart's main body but Lee's infantry advance. At Buford's suggestion, Kilpatrick detached George Custer's brigade in order to connect with, and augment, Merritt. The link-up offered the prospect of a renewed offensive, but soon after Custer's arrival at Williamsport the rest of Kilpatrick's division—including most of the regiments Buford had led at Second Bull Run—gave way under mounting pressure and fled from Hagerstown, racing across Buford's rear and for a time disarranging his ranks. That ended all hope of a successful drive against Imboden.[19]

Some time after dark, a frustrated Buford broke off the fight. Deciding to retire to Boonsboro, where he could receive new orders, he marched eastward via Jones's Cross Roads. At that road junction he halted for the night, his rear well protected by Devin's troopers, and mulled over the day's events. The memory may have kept him from a good night's sleep. The failure to take Williamsport was a bitter experience for a proud commander who days before had outfought several times as many men as John Imboden commanded—and all of them able-bodied.

Despite his mortification, Buford offered no excuses and refused to shift the blame to anyone else (although he might, with some justification, have moved it in Kilpatrick's direction). Of his mission to destroy Lee's train, he would report, simply: "This, I regret to say, was not accomplished. The enemy was too strong for me...." Here was an admission that neither Kilpatrick, Pleasonton, nor Custer would have made in his most unguarded moment.[20]

* * *

By the morning of 7 July the Federals' chances of cutting off Lee's army from the Potomac had been reduced to zero. Although Meade's pursuit was moving slowly—not for another three days would all elements of the Union army be within striking range of the river—Lee's rear guard had constructed a line of defense between Hagerstown and Williamsport, while heavy works were going up along the still-impassable river, extending as far to the southeast as Downsville.

Boonsboro

While he might have aimed another blow at the Rebels before they could perfect their defenses, Buford spent the day on the retreat and on the defensive. His return march to Boonsboro, made in company with Kilpatrick's reunited division, was spasmodically contested by a mixed band of pursuers. The most serious clash occurred around eleven A.M. when, about two and a half miles out of Williamsport, Devin's rear guard formed a barrier across the road to Boonsboro until Gamble, Merritt, and Kilpatrick could cross Antietam Creek to safety.[21]

Devin's men did an inspired job of holding off the enemy—not only Stuart's troopers but a brigade of Georgia infantry, just down from Hagerstown. After ensuring their comrades' escape Devin crossed the Antietam under a torrent of rifle- and cannon-fire, Buford watching anxiously from the far side, happy to learn that the operation had not entailed heavy loss. Had the infantry pressed his flank and rear, Devin might have met disaster. Added to the terrible beating one of the Regular regiments had received early that day while reconnoitering toward Stuart's bailiwick at Hagerstown, Devin's narrow escape may have caused Buford to feel suddenly older than his thirty-seven years.[22]

He felt no younger the next day. Early that morning, the Federals' pursuers—four brigades under Stuart, supported on the flanks by infantry—approached Buford's new bivouac on the outskirts of Boonsboro, seeking a fight. Their job this day was to screen the passage of Lee's main army through Hagerstown to the river; Buford suspected, however, that the Rebels were moving to block the South Mountain passes east of Boonsboro against Meade's approaching army.[23]

To keep the gaps clear, Buford built a strong line of his own a mile or more west of the town. He placed Gamble and Calef to the north astride Stuart's approach from Hagerstown. To bar the infantry's path, Merritt took station in the center, on the Boonsboro Pike, and Devin went into line on the left, almost as far south as the road to Williamsport. To the rear, Buford positioned Kilpatrick's men as a reserve force.

Well before noon both of Buford's flanks came under heavy fire from carbines, rifles, and cannon. His cavalry opponents—most of them advancing on foot, a rare tactic for Stuart—pressed the north flank so stoutly that Gamble and Calef had to pull back to a new line closer to town. Stuart's infantry then managed to flank Devin's brigade via the Williamsport Road; running low on ammunition, the men of the Second Brigade also retreated.[24]

More than a few cavalry generals would have buckled under this much pressure, but Buford merely warmed to the challenge. At a critical point in the battle he committed Kilpatrick's reserves on both flanks. To the south, the Third Division covered Devin while mounting a counterattack that persuaded many of Stuart's people to withdraw to Williamsport. On the north flank, Gamble's men, urged on by Buford, returned to the fight when Kilpatrick's advance bogged down. After several minutes of prodding, the Confederate main body drew off sullenly toward Hagerstown, crossing the same creek over which they had driven Devin the previous day.[25]

Buford, not content to let them go, took personal charge of Gamble's dismounted pursuers. Hustling alongside troopers half his age, he tried to lead the way up the Hagerstown Road. Major Abner Hard of the Eighth Illinois, the division's chief surgeon and Buford's close friend, recorded that "the men had run so fast that they were completely tired out, but were pleased to see General Buford shake his fat sides, as he attempted to keep up with them." Doctor Hard quoted the winded but happy general as claiming that "these boys beat anything in the world in a foot skirmish!" Gamble's skirmishers were just as exultant; a member of the Twelfth Illinois wrote home that "Gen. Buford says ... the only fault he finds with us is that he can't stop us when we once get the Rebbs [sic] to running."[26]

But Buford was not all merriment. That night he sent Pleasonton's headquarters at Middletown a report of the day's action, claiming ultimate success but adding, "I have had a very rough day of it."[27]

Beaver Creek

Things eased a bit on the ninth. Only Devin's brigade was

engaged, and not until late in the day. One reason for the light schedule was that toward evening the head of Meade's column, the VI Corps of Major General John Sedgwick and the cavalry of David Gregg, emerged from the mountain gaps and closed up on Boonsboro. Still held immobile along the Potomac, continuing to strengthen the works that ran from Williamsport through Hagerstown and back to the river, Lee's army was not about to contest an advance by its heftier opponent.[28]

Buford, however, would not lay idle. By four P.M., no Rebels having drawn near Boonsboro, he sent Tom Devin to probe their lines; if Lee had shifted position, Meade would want to know. The result was a sharp but brief skirmish along Beaver Creek, an Antietam tributary. Feinting toward the left with a squadron of skirmishers, holding the center of his position with two guns of the recently attached Battery B/L (Albert Vincent's), Second United States Artillery, Devin launched a dismounted attack on the right, spearheaded by a larger skirmish force.[29]

Under Buford's watchful eye, the dismounted men crossed the creek against a rattling fire, then scrambled to the top of a ridge beyond in "a most gallant manner...and in a space of time remarkably short...." Cowed by the sight of screaming Yankees coming at them on the dead run, Stuart's men raced to their led horses, saddled, and took off down the road to Funkstown. Not content with a forced retreat, Devin's skirmishers kept right on going, driving the enemy, as one trooper put it, "about 2 miles like fun." Fun it might have been, but Buford, remembering his exertions of the previous day, chose not to join in this footrace.[30]

Funkstown

Next morning, while Meade's army closed in on Lee's

bridgehead, Buford's dismounted skirmishers, along with Kilpatrick's, started for Funkstown and the upper reaches of the Rebel line. Well to the rear marched Sedgwick's infantry—too far back to constitute a ready reserve. Buford, who was in high spirits this day, did not care. Between Beaver Creek and the main branch of Antietam Creek, his confident troopers encountered Stuart's advance guard and, as on previous occasions, drove it rapidly. The Rebels retreated toward Funkstown, above which sat a line of entrenchments crammed with Confederate infantry.

Buford mounted his troopers and pushed north. From about eight A.M. until noon he followed his adversary at what one New Yorker called "a rappid walk," skirmishing all the way to the Antietam. Below that stream, Stuart abruptly faced about and made a stand. The reason for his sudden tenacity was quickly apparent: unlike Buford, he had infantry friends close at hand. At a signal, a brigade of foot soldiers under Colonel W. W. White clambered out of the trenches, waded the Antietam, and came down on Buford's ranks, rifles spitting.[31]

Surprised but not confounded, Buford again dismounted his squadrons and placed them behind what little cover he could find in that area. He himself stood for a time in plain view of the enemy until a Rebel bullet tugged at his hunting blouse, "cutting five holes" in it. For a time his men held the line nicely against the foot soldiers, keeping them back with their rapid-fire capability—Gettysburg all over again. This day, however, their own infantry was not coming to their aid. Turning about, Buford was astonished to see the VI Corps so far back, and advancing so slowly, as to appear stationary.[32]

Riding to the head of the infantry line, he sought out its commander, Brigadier General Albion P. Howe (who as an artillery captain had served with Buford against the Sioux), to learn what was going on. "I have used a great deal of my ammunition," Buford said, trying to keep anger out of his voice, "...suppose you move up there, or send up a brigade, or even a part of one, and [help] hold that position." To his amazement, Howe plead that his hands were tied: General Sedgwick had ordered him to avoid becoming involved in "a general engagement."

For several minutes, as the Confederates pressed his men, Buford stood there in his bullet-torn blouse, trying to persuade the infantry to come into line on his flanks. During this period Howe sent several messages to the rear requesting the necessary permission from Sedgwick but each time was refused. The scene grew even more farcical when Howe finally agreed to challenge White's brigade but only if the cavalry evacuated its position. Apparently, the infantry did not wish to share with its mounted brethren any success to be won this day.

Shaking his head ruefully, Buford headed north to withdraw his troopers. After some further delay Howe's division moved up and retook the abandoned position. It was a strange ending to a strange day, but it confirmed Buford's long-held belief that the command arrangements in this army, and the willingness of its components to ease one another's burdens, left much to be desired.[33]

Falling Waters

After his relief by the infantry, Buford moved his tired men into a sheltered position behind Beaver Creek. There the division unsaddled for the first time in more than a week. Next day it remounted and moved upriver to Bakersville, close to the southern edge of Lee's defenses. The First Division remained in that area for the next three days, guarding the left flank of Meade's army, which had finally moved into close proximity to Lee's lines and had begun to maneuver into a position to attack the bridgehead.

To provide Meade with information on the defenses confronting him, by the thirteenth Buford had pushed patrols to within 800 yards of the trenches at Downsville. He sent back word that the Potomac was falling to the point at which Lee would be able to cross in safety. The Confederates had cobbled together a pontoon bridge at Falling Waters and the river was low enough at Williamsport that a fording would soon be possible. Buford realized that Lee would not linger indefinitely on Northern soil, awaiting an attack. Meade knew this as well, but when he finally nerved himself to strike on 14 July his action came one day too late.[34]

As Buford had anticipated, crossing operations began at Williamsport and Falling Waters after dark on the thirteenth. Within hours, Buford at Downsville and Kilpatrick, guarding Meade's right near Hagerstown, noticed that the works nearest them were empty. By seven A.M., after alerting the infantry, both generals started their men toward the river, Buford from the east, Kilpatrick from the north.

Buford hastened westward with a driving sense of purpose. Meade's "hot pursuit" of his enemy had been lukewarm at best, but there was still time to cut off a part of Lee's army from its home state, still time to strike a blow that would end on the proper note a campaign that had taken such a toll of Buford's command. A division of foot soldiers under General Pettigrew, protected by artillery, continued to man a line of entrenchments at Falling Waters. The infantry was waiting for stragglers to cross before it trod the pontoons and cut the bridge loose from the Virginia side. If these troops could be overtaken and destroyed, Meade's hesitant maneuvering would gain a measure of redemption.[35]

En route to Falling Waters, Buford heard the sounds of

battle from upriver, indicating that Kilpatrick's advance had tangled with the Rebels at Williamsport. Buford sent a messenger to his comrade, informing him that he would "put my whole force in on the enemy's rear and flank, and get possession of the road and bridge in their rear." Buford's implied intent was that Kilpatrick should distract Pettigrew, holding him immobile long enough for Buford's men to slice between the bridgehead and the river.

It was not to be. Like the VI Corps outside Funkstown, Kilpatrick had no intention of sharing the day's glory with anyone, even a senior colleague. Rushing south from Williamsport, he launched an ill-considered mounted assault against Pettigrew before Buford could reach the position from the other side. One hundred members of Custer's brigade charged the well-entrenched Confederates, who shredded the attackers, making casualties of more than thirty of them. Coming up to the river, Colonel Gamble, leading Buford's column, sized up Custer's charge as one of the sorriest tactical performances he had ever seen.[36]

Upon reaching the field of slaughter, Buford was distressed to find that instead of holding Pettigrew's troops in place Kilpatrick had alerted them to imminent danger. The troopers of Gamble and Devin, the latter coming up presently on the left, managed to nab a few hundred members of the rear guard as well as numerous stragglers. Thousands of potential prisoners, however, had slipped the trap with minutes to spare, scrambling across the pontoons to safety. The Gettysburg campaign had ended on a sour note after all, and no one's ears were more offended than John Buford's.[37]

While disgusted by the denouement, the general had nothing but admiration for his troopers' behavior; they had fought stubbornly and well, exchanging shots with the Rebel rear up to the moment it disappeared over the bridge that was now floating free in the choppy Potomac. Gaining control of himself, Buford wandered among his men at the bridgehead, many of them guarding prisoners, others milling about as though dazed and directionless. Buford lent them whatever words of encouragement he could summon up.

As ever, he was concerned with the condition of the wounded, Union and Confederate alike, and he took pains to see to their care. As he passed behind one severely injured trooper propped against a tree where Surgeon Hard was ministering to him, he heard the man say that painful though his wound was he was glad that he, and not General Buford, had been hit. Suddenly alert to Buford's presence, the surgeon looked up to see tears glistening in the general's eyes.[38]

CHAPTER XI

The Battles of Autumn

To Buford's acute regret, the war went on. Not even the recently received news of Ulysses S. Grant's capture of the Mississippi River citadel of Vicksburg relieved the gloom that beset him for several days after the fumbled opportunity at Falling Waters.

At least the army did not seem disposed to brood over its misfortune. Meade—as bitterly disappointed as anyone over Lee's escape—determined to renew the pursuit in Virginia. Based on early scouting reports, it appeared likely that the Confederates would return to the Rappahannock line by the same route they had taken north, the Shenandoah Valley; the swollen waters of the Shenandoah River would probably keep them beyond the mountains until able to swing east through the lower gaps of the Blue Ridge. If Meade could beat his enemy to the gaps, and push through before Lee could do so from the other side, he might take the long Confederate column in flank, slicing up the Army of Northern Virginia and defeating each of its segments in turn.[1]

On 15 July, one day before the infantry left the river,

Buford's division marched east from Falling Waters, past Sandy Hook (opposite Harpers Ferry) and through South Mountain, to Berlin, where Meade's engineers had bridged the Potomac with pontoons. Leading their horses across the swaying span, the troopers under Gamble, Devin, and Merritt bivouacked for the night near the bridgehead. Next day they started south, holding close to the eastern rim of the Blue Ridge until on the twentieth they neared Manassas and Chester Gaps. Lee's army was not yet in sight, and scouts reported both defiles lightly guarded.

As per his orders, Buford sent his advance component, Gamble's brigade, south to Chester Gap while leading the next brigade in column, Merritt's, toward the upper gorge. Although Gamble would be on his own, Merritt would have infantry support: coming up in his rear, in accord with Meade's strategy, was General French's command out of Frederick. The stage was thus set for a dramatic thrust at Lee's columns and the halting of his retreat.[2]

Manassas and Chester Gaps

To Buford's chagrin, the same lack of cooperation he had witnessed at Funkstown prevented the army from exploiting this new, gleaming opportunity. On the twenty-first Merritt seized his objective, pushing through along the line of the Manassas Gap Railroad. With the First United States Cavalry in the van, supported closely by the Second and Fifth Cavalry, Merritt shoved the Rebels into the valley in the direction of Front Royal, capturing twenty-six defenders. Rather than pursuing the fugitives, Merritt's troopers and Captain Graham's artillerymen fulfilled their instructions by securing the gorge and the surrounding hills. They held the position throughout the twenty-second against an intermittent skirmish fire, foiling several attempts to turn their flanks.[3]

French's command, the nearest supporting force to Merritt, had reached Union, sixteen miles northeast of the gap, on 20 July. But not until the morning of the twenty-third, with Meade's advance hard on their heels, did French's soldiers replace Merritt's on the summit, and not till that evening did they make progress toward Front Royal. The lost hours had the worst possible effect: the main body of Lee's army, the corps of Lieutenant General James Longstreet in advance, moved quickly enough along the other side of the mountains as to slip through French's hands.[4]

While Buford and Merritt watched their hard-won advantage go unexploited, Colonel Gamble was likewise shaking his head in dismay. By the time his brigade reached Chester Gap, late on the afternoon of the twenty-first, it found the area secured by a force Lee had sent south in advance of his main army: the remnants of George Pickett's shattered division, reinforced by cavalry and artillery. Gamble promptly attacked, driving his foe to the crest of the gorge. Thereafter, despite Pickett's weakness, the colonel could make no progress. "Not having a sufficient force to drive the enemy from the Gap, having no support nearer than 20 miles," Gamble fell back to Barbee's Cross Roads, where he was joined by Buford and the rest of the division. All Gamble had to show for his efforts was a herd of captured horses, mules, sheep, and cattle that had been en route to General Lee's commissary and whose value he somehow calculated at $46,000.[5]

Beef and mutton would not compensate the Army of the Potomac for another botched opportunity to bring Lee to heel. Buford was angered not only by the infantry's inability to reinforce Merritt in timely fashion and to reinforce Gamble at all, but by what Meade later called General

French's "very feeble effort" to defeat a defense force that Merritt had already demoralized. The upshot was that Lee's army was able to clear the lower gaps in the Blue Ridge; by the twenty-fourth Longstreet's corps had reoccupied the country between the Rappahannock and Rapidan. Meade followed dejectedly; by 25 July army headquarters was back at Warrenton and the relative positions of the opponents prior to Gettysburg had been restored.[6]

Buford's division had barely returned to the business of picketing the river that separated the armies when on the twenty-seventh it got new orders, and Buford a new dose of aggravation. To clear the far shore for the rebuilding of the flood-damaged bridge near Rappahannock Station, Pleasonton ordered most of Buford's troopers across the now-receding river. At the outset, confusion reigned. Buford had received the impression that a bridge was to be provided for his command, whereas the engineers of the army expected the cavalry to ford and clear the south shore before the pontoons were laid. Annoyed by the sight of engineers lounging by their bridging equipment, Buford sought cooperation but got none. In a fit of temper he complained to army headquarters that "if I am to advance, I would like to see some disposition shown to aid me. Everything seems to be awaiting orders." In time General Pleasonton intervened to smooth things over and Buford's men crossed the unbridged stream, some fording, others ferried across aboard the pontoons. The operation proved a success, but his run-in with the engineers left Buford in a foul mood.[7]

Culpeper Court House

Another unhappy encounter—with the enemy—did not improve his state of mind. Once on the far shore, his troopers squared off against a couple of Stuart's brigades, contesting the crossing. A nettled Buford thrust the Rebels steadily south until, about a mile and a half above Culpeper Court House, he found "the tables turned," as George Chapman put it: 5,000 infantry and three light batteries had come up from the south with uncharacteristic stealth to block his path. Aware that against such odds a pitched battle would be futile, Buford sought to disengage. With foot soldiers creeping up along both flanks and artillery pounding his front, the maneuver was a difficult and trying one. Only after suffering several casualties did Buford break free and retire to the familiar fields around Brandy Station. There, within range of infantry support north of the river, he could cover the bridge repair operation without further harm.[8]

By this point, however, the stress and strain of the past twelve hours had taken both a physical and an emotional toll. As he informed Pleasonton, it had been "a very severe day upon men and horses. I myself am worthless." The after-effects of 1 August were long-lived; as if to confirm Buford's worst opinion of journalism, two days later the New York newspapers claimed that the infantry had saved him from devastation outside Culpeper. "The reconnaissance ...was a success," he insisted to Pleasonton on the third, "yet the First Corps gets the credit of saving me from disaster." That same day he closed another dispatch with a burst of indignation: "How the newspapers lie!"[9]

By the time he wrote, Buford's temper had been fueled by yet another run-in with uncooperative, obstructive infantry commanders. On the afternoon of the third, General Slocum, whose XII Corps lay in camp along the Rappahannock, summarily countermanded Buford's orders to Colonel Devin. Not only did Slocum halt a reconnaissance mission that he considered "altogether unnecessary," for a time he appropriated Devin's men for his own use. This flagrant example of meddling in the mounted operations of the army—something a corps organization for cavalry had been designed to prevent—caused Buford to lose his equanimity in a most dramatic way. To Pleasonton he complained that "I am disgusted and worn out with the system that seems to prevail. There is so much apathy and so little disposition to fight and co-operate that I wish to be relieved from the Army of the Potomac. I do not wish to put myself and [my] soldiers in front where I cannot get a support.... I am willing to serve my country, but I do not wish to sacrifice the brave men under my command...."[10]

Such outbursts, so uncharacteristic of the man, suggested that his problems ranged beyond issues of cooperation and support. The merciless, inexorable machinery of war was beginning to wear John Buford down.

* * *

He needed a respite from the war, and he got one in early August, but it was no vacation. Buford's wife had gone to Kentucky weeks before to be with her ailing father; not only had he died during her visit to Georgetown, so had five-year-old Pattie Buford, the victim of a sudden disease perhaps contracted on the trip to Kentucky. The news had been late in reaching the general and in the midst of the hectic campaigning following Lee's retreat from Pennsylvania he had not taken the time to mourn. Now, the recent flurry of activity along the Rappahannock having died down, he had enough time to confront his grief.

Realizing that his wife's bereavement was greater than his own, he determined to go to her. After securing the necessary permission, on 10 August he turned the division over to General Merritt and took a train to Washington and then westward. He reached Georgetown on the evening of the eleventh to find his wife "broken-hearted" over "our darling daughter and ...her dear father."[11]

He remained with her for more than a week, not only comforting her but trying to put in order some affairs relating to her father's estate. He also took the time to write Ambrose Burnside, now commander of the Army and the Department of the Ohio, whose jurisdiction included Kentucky east of the Tennessee River. Buford's primary intent in contacting old "Burn" was to seek permission for his mother-in-law to visit her "erring nephew," Colonel Basil Duke of the Confederate army, then languishing in the Ohio State Penitentiary after his capture during John Hunt Morgan's recent raid across the Ohio River.

In his letter Buford could not refrain from alluding to his recent problems in command relations—the same sort of problems that had complicated Burnside's tenure. The army, he told his former superior, was in "about the same state as when you left it. The same faults exist among Corps Commanders as has [sic] always existed. Too much apathy, too much cold water...."[12]

Apathy and pessimism might surround him in Virginia, but he could not stay away. Leaving his wife to mourn amid her family, he returned east by himself, rejoining his command at Warrenton Junction on the twenty-first.[13]

He found that force smaller than when he left it. In his absence, corps headquarters had decreed a wholesale refurbishment of the casualty-depleted Reserve Brigade. As a body, Merritt's Regulars and their Pennsylvania comrades had gone to the District of Columbia to resupply and remount. The brigade would remain at "Camp Buford," adjacent to the new cavalry depot at Giesboro Point, across the Eastern Branch of the Potomac from the capital, until mid-October.[14]

For a brief time, Buford's division grew smaller still. The continuing quietude along the Rappahannock enabled him to grant an army headquarters request that a brigade be sent via the Loudoun Valley to Leesburg, there to break up bands of Confederate guerrillas—including partisan rangers under the "Gray Ghost," Major John Singleton Mosby—reputed to be terrorizing Unionist citizens and attacking wagon trains passing between Washington and the front. If Buford thought the assignment a wild-goose chase, as he may well have, his belief was borne out by the experience of Tom Devin, whose troopers performed the frustrating and unproductive task at hand. In summarizing the mission, which he completed in the first days of September, Devin reported that "the country [between Bristoe Station and Leesburg] has been completely scoured on both sides of Bull Run Mountain ...and that no force of any importance is on this side of the Blue Ridge or Valley...."[15]

* * *

Early in September intense activity returned to the Rappahannock basin, spawned by military operations hundreds of miles westward. In mid-August Major General William S. Rosecrans, leader of the largest Union army in the western theater, the Army of the Cumberland, had begun a march against Chattanooga, stronghold of General Braxton Bragg's Army of Tennessee. Within three weeks Rosecrans had maneuvered his weaker opponent out of the city and into northern Georgia, to which point the Army of the Cumberland pursued Bragg, setting up a momentous confrontation.

To assist Bragg in a theater that had become increasingly important to the Confederate war effort, on 9 September Robert E. Lee began to dispatch the majority of Longstreet's corps by rail to Georgia. Two days later Meade's scouts learned of the detaching and the army leader decided to take the offensive against his weakened opponent. His decision touched off a month's worth of advances and retreats between the Rappahannock and Rapidan that brought John Buford his share, and more, of both glory and grief.[16]

To the Rapidan

The opening gambit took place on 12 September when, at Meade's order, Buford crossed the upper river at Rappahannock Station while his associate, Kilpatrick, passed over at Kelly's Ford. Once the horsemen were on the south shore, Meade's main army crossed at various points in their rear. Meeting Stuart's skirmishers on the far shore, Buford steadily drove them with Devin's and Gamble's brigades, the latter now under the command of Colonel Chapman. Even when Stuart's main body intervened Buford continued to move south "as fast as possible." The nonplussed cavaliers went whirling through Culpeper Court House and points south toward Raccoon Ford. Behind Stuart, Robert E. Lee's abbreviated army fled the path of the blue onslaught, withdrawing below the line of the Rapidan.[17]

When his advance reached Raccoon Ford, Buford took a counterpunch. Stuart's horse artillery—which quickly increased to a total of eleven guns—got his range, dropping shells into the road the general occupied. One hit a nearby tree, "not a rod from him," according to Surgeon Hard, "and, glancing, struck the ground in our midst, the fuse burning and hissing. As if by instinct, the General and staff spurred their horses, and barely escaped as the next moment the shell exploded, the fragments passing over our heads...."[18]

To evade the deadly rain, which only increased in rapidity and accuracy, Buford moved his column into patches of timber along the stream. Later he led the men north to Stevensburg, where they remained, resting and refitting, until the twentieth. On that morning they returned to the offensive, accompanying Meade's vanguard to the line of the Rapidan. Early on the twenty-first, at Pleasonton's order, both Buford and Kilpatrick looped westward, crossing Robertson's River to Madison Court House. At that locale, scene of his maiden experience in field command back in August of 1862, Buford led both divisions southeastward to study the Rebel left near Liberty Mills.

Liberty Mills

En route to their common destination, the generals split up, Buford moving toward Gordonsville, Kilpatrick farther west along the direct route to the mills. Some miles from the river, Stuart crossed Buford's path and challenged him to battle; the troopers of Devin and Chapman readily obliged. When their struggle was at its height, however, Stuart abruptly turned his back on the First Division to lash out at Kilpatrick, who by reaching Liberty Mills had gotten into the Rebel rear. It was Brandy Station all over again, and this time the Union pincers closed on the Confederate commander, for as soon as Stuart faced about Buford treated him to carbine-fire and shot and shell, inflicting heavy casualties.[19]

Under heavy but not irresistible pressure, Kilpatrick's leading brigade, commanded by Brigadier General Henry E. Davies, gave way and retreated before George Custer's more steadfast command could relieve him. Extricating himself from trouble, Stuart slipped away from his antagonists and hastened across the Rapidan to safety.

Buford was not displeased by the outcome; Stuart's narrow escape put an exclamation point to Buford's most successful outing against the Beau Sabreur. After studying Confederate dispositions across the river, he sent a dispatch to Meade's headquarters pronouncing the mission "completely successful." Leaving Stuart's men huddling along the south bank, he led his divisions back over Robertson's River and north to Stevensburg, where they went into camp.[20]

All the way home Buford was in high spirits, for he had

throttled more than one nemesis on this expedition. The same day that he chased a worried Stuart across the Rapidan he arrested and sent to Pleasonton's headquarters a couple of New York reporters who had fallen in with the command, "after being notified that they could not be allowed to do so. Can they not be sent out of the army?" A general like Kilpatrick, who welcomed reporters for the publicity they provided him, would have been appalled that Buford would treat as common criminals correspondents of the august *Herald* and *Tribune*, but Buford felt he was going easy on the gentlemen of the press; given the power, he probably would have shot them.[21]

* * *

While Buford had been meeting with success south of Robertson's River, General Rosecrans had been meeting disaster in northern Georgia. On 19-20 September, Bragg's reinforced army surprised and routed the Army of the Cumberland near Rossville along the banks of Chickamauga Creek. A stunned Rosecrans fled north to Chattanooga, Bragg following and laying siege to the city.

To revive Union fortunes in that quarter, the War Department got up a multi-part relief force. Ulysses S. Grant and William T. Sherman were sent from Vicksburg to lift the siege and defeat Bragg. To augment their forces, it was decided to send the XI and XII Corps from Virginia to Tennessee.[22]

Between 25 September and 2 October trains containing Howard's and Slocum's soldiers rolled westward. The War Office hoped to keep the transfer, massive as it was, a secret for as long as possible, but those same irresponsible journalists that John Buford loathed ran stories about the operation only a day after it began. Within ten days, increased activity below the Rapidan suggested that General Lee had gotten the word; to prevent further detaching against Bragg, the Confederate commander prepared to assume the offensive for the first time in four months.[23]

On 9 October, one day after Buford and Pleasonton reviewed the First Division in its camps at Stevensburg, both of Lee's remaining corps began to forge across the Rapidan along a route pointing toward Meade's right flank. For the first couple of days of the movement Lee's opponent remained in the dark as to its meaning. Believing the increased activity along the Rapidan signalled a Confederate withdrawal rather than an advance, Meade dispatched his foot soldiers to investigate, Buford's and Kilpatrick's troopers riding in advance to clear the way.[24]

Morton's Ford and Third Brandy Station

Buford's orders were to force a crossing of the Rapidan, despite opposition from Stuart, at Germanna Ford; once on the lower bank he would move west to Morton's Ford. There he would link with Major General John Newton's First Army Corps, which would accompany him in studying Lee's dispositions. The assignment sounded relatively straightforward, but it broke down in execution. Leaving Stevensburg at eight-thirty in the morning of the tenth, Buford reached Germanna Ford at about noon with the troopers of Devin and Chapman, Vincent's Battery B/L, Second Artillery, and the newly attached Battery D of the same regiment under Lieutenant Edward B. Williston. About one P. M. Chapman's skirmishers "most handsomely" fought their way across the ford, shoving back a large force of Stuart's cavalry under Fitzhugh Lee.[25]

Once Buford's column moved upriver to Morton's Ford, trouble began. Arriving at that crossing-site after dark, the cavalry failed to find Newton's foot soldiers—rumor said they had pulled north to Culpeper—but Buford did encounter Confederate pickets and the occupants of a line of riverside entrenchments. Promptly attacking, he cleared the exterior works, then bivouacked on the ground, awaiting further orders. These reached him next morning, by which time they were twenty-four hours out of date: Meade's headquarters, finally aware that the enemy was coming on rather than falling back, warned the cavalry not to cross the Rapidan for fear of being cut off.

An angry Buford quickly moved to clear the area. After flinging the remaining Rebels out of their trenches and across the river, Buford began to follow them over the ford. The fleeing enemy retreated west toward Raccoon Ford, where they were joined by a portion of Fitz Lee's command. Thus fortified, the force rushed back to a position from which to retard Buford's crossing. Colonel Chapman, however, foiled Lee's attempt to take the Federals in flank, then covered the crossing of the artillery, followed by Devin's brigade.

The division got over in tolerable order but only after taking losses heavier than Buford would have preferred—for which he held army headquarters responsible. During the operation Devin was "sorely pressed," Buford reported, "as his force on the enemy's side decreased, but he, by frequent dashing and telling charges, and the two batteries by their fire from the north side, kept the enemy from closing on his rear." The general added pointedly that "Colonel Devin's command on this occasion was beautifully handled, though too bravely, and consequently suffered quite severely."[26]

Once the Second Brigade was on firm ground, Colonel Chapman—a bespectacled schoolmaster-type who was also a hard-driving cavalryman much admired by his men—turned about to meet the main force under Lee, marching up from Raccoon Ford, sabers and pistols at the ready. A devoted disciple of Buford's brand of warfare, Chapman dismounted his brigade and placed it behind cover along the riverbank, from which it met Lee's charge with a powerful blow that left the Confederates "dismayed, in confusion, and terribly punished." Only when a considerable force of infantry came up in Lee's rear did Chapman follow Devin, Vincent, and Williston on their northward jaunt to Stevensburg, trailed at a distance by the bruised but still pugnacious Lee.

En route to his old camp, Buford received word that at least a portion of Meade's army was withdrawing north of the Rappahannock. Halting near Stevensburg only long enough to escort a small train of supply wagons to Kelly's Ford, he marched crosscountry to old, familiar Brandy Station, "without a [great] deal of molestation from the enemy, although closely followed by him." Reaching the Orange & Alexandria depot, Buford made contact with his friends in the infantry, a segment of Meade's rear guard trudging through Brandy Station toward the river. Learning that Kilpatrick was marching in rear of this column, Buford decided to remain in the area till able to join him in fording the river, each commander covering the other's rear.[27]

When, toward evening, Kilpatrick finally came in on Buford's right flank, the Rebels who had been trailing the First Division suddenly turned against the newcomers, some of them interposing between Kilpatrick's column and the river it must cross. At the same time, the Third Division took blows to the rear from another large body of cavalry, Stuart in command, which had been following it for some distance.

To lend assistance, Buford charged two of Devin's regiments against Fitz Lee's vanguard, overpowering it with sabers and pistols. Though Devin suffered some loss, the attack relieved much of the pressure Kilpatrick had been under, enabling him to concentrate against Stuart and precipitating what one regimental leader called a "wild and exciting" fight. That fight lasted until after dark, when Stuart and Lee drew off, permitting the First and Third Divisions to reach the river; by eight o'clock the Federals were safely over.[28]

Culpeper to Centreville

Buford must have wondered why he had bothered to cross; on the morning of the twelfth he was ordered back to Brandy Station, this time in company with much of the V and VI Corps under overall command of General Sedgwick. Lee's advance appeared to have slowed, as though the Confederates had relinquished their hope of outflanking Meade; the Union commander wished to know why.

Back across the river went the weary Buford and his troopers, forging ahead of the foot troops. Encountering a much reduced force of Rebel cavalry, the First Division drove it to within two miles of Culpeper, at which point Sedgwick recalled Buford to Brandy Station. Returning to the scene of the previous day's combat, his men were able to collect their more severely wounded, whom they had been forced to leave behind, and to recover several unburied dead, now minus items of clothing and equipment. Ever the soldier's general, Buford stressed that "it was truly gratifying to be able to recover these wounded men, and to bury the men that had been stripped and abandoned by the enemy." After a few hours on the fields around Brandy, both cavalry and infantry recrossed the Rappahannock, Buford getting over by daylight on 13 October.[29]

After resting on the north bank through much of that day—a respite Buford desperately needed, his young troopers perhaps less so—the division received a new and especially taxing assignment: to escort the long line of supply wagons rumbling north in rear of the main army. Meade had decided to pull back across Bull Run to Centreville, thirty miles from the Rappahannock; he had already begun to entrench near the Bull Run battlefields. That was a long way to conduct slow-moving wagons pulled by balky teams and driven by teamsters who were sometimes as hard to move as the mules. But there was no help for it; suddenly tired all over again, early on the fourteenth Buford started his people north, overtook the wagons at Catlett's Station, and prepared for the slow trek to Centreville. Already Buford did not like the looks of things. His quartermaster's eye could see that the train was not only too long to guard properly but "badly conducted." He informed Pleasonton that he would "do the best I can, but ...I apprehend trouble."[30]

His pessimism was warranted; from the first, the journey was a study in delay, disorder, and aggravation. After a late start, the train made slow progress, Buford's men nervously scanning the country in rear for pursuers. Upon reaching Brentsville, several miles shy of their destination, the column ground to a halt. While Buford seethed over the delay—probably caused by broken-down wagons blocking the road—he was also furious to find that "little disposition to move was displayed by the few quartermasters I could find." As the halt continued, his men deployed to meet some of Stuart's cavalry, seen creeping up on the south. After dark the column finally resumed its progress—prodded into life by the sounds of heavy firing down along the railroad, where Meade's rear guard, the II Corps of Major General G. K. Warren and the cavalry of David Gregg, was blocking Lee's advance at Bristoe Station. Toward evening—by which time the firing had ceased, Lee having been severely checked by his well-entrenched enemy—the train slowly approached Bull Run, the last obstacle to a safe haven at Centreville.[31]

As the wagons struggled to cross the stream at Wood Yard Ford, Buford's pursuers came close enough to fire into the column. In gathering darkness Buford made the best dispositions he could, while cautioning Pleasonton that "I cannot do much in the night...." Detecting the anxiety in Buford's words, the cavalry commander directed Gregg's division to move from Bristoe Station to his assistance. Pleasonton also persuaded Meade to order an infantry brigade to Wood Yard Ford.[32]

Thanks to blocked roads, neither reinforcement came up quickly. The train was still under fire when Gregg's advance reached Bull Run near daylight on the fifteenth. A bystander heard Buford greet its commander with more than a hint of impatience: "Where have you been, sir? You have had time to come from Washington!"[33]

By the time Gregg appeared, most of the train was across the ford. Believing himself home free, Buford crossed to the north side only to find that the head of the column had taken a wrong road that led it back across Bull Run toward their pursuers. Hustling his troopers and Gregg's to the danger point, Buford arrived just in time to repulse an enemy attack, which, as he observed, "fortunately struck me, instead of the flank of the trains." Cursing the errant teamsters, Buford's men quickly turned their ire on the enemy: "Every man of the command had made up his mind that there should be no child's play on his part, so when he [the enemy] did appear, with a determined will we went at him and before long drove him back." Finally able to devote full attention to the train, Buford corrected its heading and escorted it back across the water.

In the early hours of 16 October the tag end of the column—the army's pontoon train—crossed the creek. Then, as the wagons rumbled on to Centreville, Buford detailed his men to picket duty along both sides of Bull Run. That done, he sat down to inform General Pleasonton of his safe passage. Danger past, he wrote with his customary confidence, boasting that not only had the lengthy column gotten across the stream intact but "the rebels have made nothing off of me yet. My loss is trifling."[34]

* * *

For several days Meade's army remained on the north side of the run, skirmishing with Rebel troops who had ventured close to the opposite side. Finding his enemy too strongly positioned to attack with any hope of success, on the seventeenth General Lee withdrew south. Within hours of his leave-taking, Buford's cavalry was well into a brisk pursuit. Merritt's brigade, recently returned to the army from Washington, wrestled with Lee's rear guard near Bristoe Station—an encounter that constituted the extent of the First Division's combat experience during the brief campaign, which closed with a Confederate recrossing of the Rappahannock on 20 October.[35]

It was well that Buford did not see more extensive participation in the move south. Merritt's brigade might be fresh, but the rest of the division had been reduced to 2,000 able-bodied men and perhaps 1,000 serviceable horses. These figures did not tell the full story of the command's weakened condition. Weeks of almost constant campaigning, much of it in inclement weather, too much stress and strain and too little sleep, had drained John Buford to an alarming degree, a truth he tried to hide beneath a stoic demeanor. On 19 October, Lieutenant Colonel Theodore Lyman of Meade's staff found Buford "cold and tired and wet," but noted that "the General takes his hardships good-naturedly." A few weeks later, however, the aide found Buford prostrated at his field headquarters with "rheumatism," which, Lyman added, "he bore with his usual philosophy."[36]

Although Buford could feel himself winding down like an old clock, he refused to give in to his infirmities. As early as

3 November he was in such poor condition, racked by body aches and fever, that Secretary of War Stanton granted him sick leave in Washington. He refused to go, however, and by sheer effort of will he made a partial recovery. He went from sickbed to saddle in time to take part in Meade's 7-8 November recrossing of the Rappahannock. As the defensive-minded Lee fell back, once again, across the Rapidan, Buford's division charged along the army's right flank to Culpeper, from which point the general threw a picket line along the river opposite the enemy's new position.[37]

At Culpeper he tended to the daily routine as best he could, supervising the placement of pickets, studying scouting reports, interrogating prisoners. Increasingly, despite his every attempt to prevent it, his deteriorating health distracted and disrupted him. On 15 November he took urgent leave in the capital, ostensibly to oversee "family matters" but more likely to consult Surgeon Major R. O. Abbott, Medical Director of the Department of Washington, and his staff. He did not remain in the city but returned quickly to his field quarters. Five days later, however, he suffered a relapse, stricken with fever and debility, and had to be invalided to Washington. By then he was deathly ill.[38]

EPILOGUE

"I Wish I Could Have Lived Now"

Surgeon Hard of the Eighth Illinois, Buford's medical director, believed the general to be suffering from a rheumatic condition, "on account of which he is unable to perform military duty," and which might prove fatal under continued exposure to the rigors of field service. In all likelihood, however, Buford had been prostrated by typhoid fever, an insidious bacterial infection possibly contracted from a contaminated water supply.

It is not surprising that his condition confounded medical personnel of his day; because a typhoid bacillus had not been cultured by 1863, medical science lacked a means of confirming a clinical diagnosis. Typhoid—characterized by high fever, body pains, malaise and, at its height, stupor and delirium—had been described as early as 1643, but more than two centuries later it remained an amorphous part of a wide spectrum of febrile diseases known as "continued fevers."[1]

When transferred from his field headquarters to Washington, Buford at first had no place to go; his wife and son were hundreds of miles away—then visiting his family in Illinois. The only person on whom he could have counted for round-the-clock care was his long-time servant, a freed black named Edward. Fortunately, a home opened up to Buford: the Pennsylvania Avenue residence of his old superior, George Stoneman, who since late July had headed the Cavalry Bureau, a War Department office charged with overseeing the equipping, mounting, and inspecting of Buford's arm.

Under Stoneman's care and the medical attention of Surgeon Abbott, by early December Buford appeared to make a slight recovery, although his prognosis remained guarded. The strain of overwork, stress-fatigue, and prolonged exposure had so lowered his resistance that his condition worsened as the month wore on. Buford's temperature soared to 104 degrees and remained there for several days; complications including dysentery further weakened his system; and he began to slip in and out of delirium.[2]

In his lucid moments, he conversed with members of his staff, who clustered about his sickbed, and he happily if weakly received visitors including the officers and non-coms of his command. George Sanford of the First Cavalry happened to be visiting in the city when he learned that the general wished to see him. The young lieutenant—who only recently had recovered from a less virulent strain of the disease—felt "very anxious" about Buford's condition. Still, when he called at Stoneman's house he found the patient "bright and cheerful—said that he had been anxious to see an officer of the Reserve Brigade as he had a message to send to the command."

A week after Chickamauga, General Rosecrans, seeking an "able" replacement for his wounded chief of cavalry, had asked the War Department to send him Buford. Rosecrans had been relieved shortly after he made the request and nothing came of it. Now, however, Buford had learned that a similar application had been made by William T. Sherman, commander of the Army of the Tennessee. When Sanford expressed pleased surprise, the sick man replied: "Well it is true. I have been offered the command of all the cavalry in the West ...and I have replied that I will accept it on one condition ...that I may be allowed to take with me my own brigade"—meaning the Reserves. The idea of a new command and increased authority appeared to buoy him somewhat, but then he grew fatigued and before Sanford could say anything more "Gen. Stoneman motioned to me that I must say good-bye. I did so, and for the last time."[3]

Just before mid-December Buford took a turn for the worse; the news drew his closest companions, including Myles Keogh, to his side. On the fourteenth, Pattie Buford, already borne down by the death of a father and a daughter, left Rock Island, Illinois, for Washington, dreading what she would find at the end of her journey.[4]

Early on 16 December, with the general sinking rapidly, an appointment as major general of volunteers reached the Stoneman home from another Pennsylvania Avenue address. Told that Buford's death was imminent, President Lincoln had persuaded Secretary Stanton—long an opponent of deathbed promotions, especially in the case of Southern-born officers—to make the gesture. Reportedly Stanton had agreed to the appointment only after being assured that Buford would not live to fill it. Upon learning of the honor, Buford is supposed to have whispered, "I wish I could have lived now." One of his aides signed Buford's name to the acceptance form and another served as witness.[5]

For the rest of that day, the sixteenth, Buford was intermittently delirious. At one point he began to berate Edward for some supposed dereliction but recovered to apologize to the teary-eyed servant. A bit later he was heard giving orders to his officers, warning them to patrol the roads and halt fugitives from the front. These were his last intelligible words; as the shadows of late afternoon filled the room, he lapsed into a deep sleep from which he never awoke.[6]

* * *

A well-arranged and well-attended funeral was held for John Buford on 20 December at the Presbyterian church at Thirteenth and "H" Streets. General Stoneman was in charge of the military escort that bore Buford's remains to the church; a regiment of infantry, a battery of Regular artillery, and a squadron of cavalry constituted the honor guard; as part of the cortege, a riderless Grey Eagle was led in rear of the casket.

The church was filled with prominent soldiers and civilians although the general's widow, prostrated by grief, was unable to attend. Mourners included President Lincoln, General-in-Chief Halleck, numerous other stalwarts of field and War Department, lesser-ranking officers from Buford's division including every member of the staff, and cabinet members including the war secretary who had so grudgingly paid Buford the final honor of his career.[7]

In his eulogy, the Reverend Ralph Randolph Gurley characterized the deceased as a model soldier, "modest, yet brave; retiring, yet efficient; quiet, but vigilant; careful of the lives of his men with an almost parental solicitude, yet never shirking from action, however fraught with peril, when the time and place for such action had come. His skill and courage were put to stern and decisive tests on many hardfought fields, and they were always equal to every emergency...."[8]

Such sentiments were echoed, albeit less eloquently, by the

rank-and-file. When news of Buford's passing swept the camps along the Rapidan, mourning was widespread but nowhere was it more in evidence than in the regiments of the First Cavalry Division, which a *New York Tribune* correspondent found "enshrouded in gloom." Every member of Buford's division, the reporter observed, "loved him as a father, and placed the utmost confidence in him as a commander and a soldier. He was confessedly the finest cavalry officer in the service...." Many of Buford's units held memorial services in their camps; others voted resolutions of bereavement and regret, which they delivered to the general's widow.[9]

At eight-thirty on the morning after the funeral, Buford's flag-draped coffin was escorted through the capital to the train station. Transported to New York City, it continued its northward journey on the Hudson River Railroad, reaching West Point late that day. Though supposedly the general had requested to be buried in the Buford family plot in Rock Island, his officers had strongly urged interment in the Military Academy cemetery; Academy officials readily agreed, considering it fitting that his hillside resting place should "look down upon the scenes of his cadet life."[10]

Over his grave at West Point a monument, fully twenty-five feet high, was later erected through subscription among veterans of his division. A second, more modest memorial, a life-size bronze statue of the general, field-glasses in hand, scanning the hostile terrain, was unveiled at Gettysburg on 1 July 1893. Standing beside the Chambersburg Pike near the point at which the First Cavalry Division met Heth's advance on the first day of the battle, the monument is surrounded by four 3-inch ordnance rifles. Three of these wrought-iron guns saw action with Battery A, Second United States Artillery during the battle in which Buford reached the height of his fame; one rifle is supposed to have fired the opening round of the engagement.[11]

Another, more enduring monument to Buford's memory is the legacy he bequeathed to the soldiers who fought through the remaining year and a half of the war, as well as to soldiers of later generations. In the realm of tactical theory, he has come down through history as the embodiment of dismounted, dragoon-style fighting, as illustrated by the splendid, against-all-odds delaying action at Gettysburg. On the other hand, his inspired use of the mounted attack—which he employed effectively at Second Bull Run, Brandy Station, at the foot of Cemetery Ridge on 1 July 1863, and in numerous skirmishes and engagements throughout his sixteen months in field command—is an equally prominent aspect of the Buford heritage.

In fact, his approach to cavalry theory was an eclectic one. "A true dragoon, as well as a true cavalier," he opted for operational flexibility and versatility over slavish devotion to a particular tactical model. Above all, he strove to enhance and promote the basic qualities of the mounted soldier, speed and mobility. Those qualities have carried over from the horse cavalry of Buford's era; salient characteristics of the mechanized warfare of today, they have significantly influenced the conduct of every major conflict since World War II. In this sense, Buford's deathbed wish—that he might live on in his profession—has been granted.

Notes

Abbreviations Used in Notes:

AGO	Adjutant General's Office
B&L	*Battles and Leaders of the Civil War*
CWTI	*Civil War Times Illustrated*
HSP	Historical Society of Pennsylvania
JUSCA	*Journal of the United States Cavalry Association* (also known as *Cavalry Journal*)
LC	Library of Congress
M-, r-	Microcopy, reel
MR	Monthly Return
NA	National Archives
OR	*War of the Rebellion: A Compilation of the Official Records of the Union and Confederate Armies*
RG-, E-	Record Group, Entry
USMA	United States Military Academy

CHAPTER I:

1. James Harrison Wilson, "Major-General John Buford," *JUSCA* 8 (1895): 173; Marcus Bainbridge Buford, *A Genealogy of the Buford Family in America, with Records of a Number of Allied Families* (San Francisco, 1903), 5-7.
2. Marcus Bainbridge Buford, George Washington Buford, and Mildred Buford Minter, *History and Genealogy of the Buford Family in America, with Records of a Number of Allied Families* (La Belle, Mo., 1924), 29-32, 169, 306; Wilson, "Major-General John Buford," 174; Theodore F. Rodenbough, *From Everglade to Canon with the Second Dragoons . . .* (New York, 1875), 457; William E. Railey, *History of Woodford County* (Versailles, Ky., 1968), 90-91; Mary E. Wharton and Ellen F. Williams, eds., *Peach Leather and Rebel Gray: Bluegrass Life and the War, 1860-1865* (Lexington, Ky., 1986), i-iii.
3. Buford, Buford, and Minter, *History and Genealogy of the Buford Family*, 306-07, 311-12, 318, 321; Wilson, "Major-General John Buford," 174; *Rock Island* (Ill.) *Argus*, 30 Dec. 1863; 22 Jan. 1942; 15 Jan. 1945; 19 Nov. 1954; Railey, *History of Woodford County*, 91.
4. *Woodford* (County, Ky.) *Sun*, 19 May 1932; *Rock Island Argus*, 22 Jan. 1942, 19 Nov. 1954; *Pisgah [Presbyterian Church], 1784-1984, Woodford County, Kentucky* (n.p., 1984), 145; Railey, *History of Woodford County*, 91; George W. Wickstrom, *The Town Crier* (Rock Island, Ill., 1948), 69; Ermina Jett Darnell, *Forks of Elkhorn Church* (Baltimore, 1980), 97; Records of the 1830 Census, Versailles District, Woodford County, Kentucky, Woodford County Historical Society, Versailles, Ky; Rowena Lawson, *Woodford County, Kentucky, 1810-1840 Censuses* (Bowie, Md., 1987), 40; Ruth M. Coyle, Curator, Woodford County Historical Society, Versailles, Ky., to author, 15 Feb. 1994; author's interviews of Mrs. Coyle, 3, 24 Feb. 1994.
5. Railey, *History of Woodford County*, 91; *Rock Island Argus*, 29 June 1916; Thomas Marshall Green, *Historic Families of Kentucky . . .* (Baltimore, 1982), 100-02; Wharton and

Williams, *Peach Leather and Rebel Gray,* iii; "Revolutionary Army Orders for the Main Army Under Washington, 1777-1779," *Virginia Magazine of History and Biography* 15 (1907-08): 170n.; "Virginia's Soldiers in the Revolution," *Ibid.*, 20 (1912): 185, 189, 275, 277.

6. Buford, Buford, and Minter, *History and Genealogy of the Buford Family,* 311; Wilson, "Major-General John Buford," 174; Ezra J. Warner, *Generals in Blue: Lives of the Union Commanders* (Baton Rouge, La., 1964), 53-54; *Rock Island Argus,* 28 Mar. 1883.

7. "John Buford, Major General, U. S. Army," [p. 3], TS. in Rock Island Arsenal Museum, Rock Island, Ill.

8. *Rock Island Argus,* 22 Jan. 1942; 15 Jan. 1945; 19 Nov. 1954; B. J. Elsner, ed., *Rock Island: Yesterday, Today & Tomorrow* (Rock Island, Ill., 1988), 66.

9. Author's interview of Mrs. N. Lucille Sampson, Archivist, Rock Island County Historical Society, Rock Island, Ill., 28 Jan. 1994; *Rock Island Argus,* 29 June 1916; Thomas Ford to J. C. Spencer, 16 Feb. 1843, Cadet Records, USMA Library.

10. Eric J. Wittenberg, "John Buford and the Gettysburg Campaign," *Gettysburg Magazine* 11 (July 1994): 22-23; Napoleon B. Buford to Salmon P. Chase, 7 Nov. 1842, Chase Papers, HSP; John Buford to William Wilkins, 20 Apr. 1844, Commission Branch Files, M-1064, r-9, NA.

11. James L. Morrison, Jr., ed., "Getting Through West Point: The Cadet Memoirs of John C. Tidball, Class of 1848," *Civil War History* 26 (1980): 306; Charles Dickens, *American Notes* (Gloucester, Mass., 1968), 249.

12. Morrison, ed., "Getting Through West Point," 306-07.

13. Wilson, "Major-General John Buford," 175.

14. Morrison, ed., "Getting Through West Point," 312.

15. Morris Schaff, *The Spirit of Old West Point, 1858-1862* (Boston, 1907), 38.

16. "Class of 1848," *Army and Navy Journal* 39 (1902): 1028; Morrison, ed., "Getting Through West Point," 313.

17. George W. Cullum, comp., *Biographical Register of Officers and Graduates of the United States Military Academy . . .* (2 vols. New York, 1891), 2: 349-61; "Class of 1848," 1028.

18. Schaff, *Spirit of Old West Point*, 67-68; James L. Morrison, Jr., *"The Best School in the World": West Point, the Pre-Civil War Years, 1833-1866* (Kent, Ohio, 1986), 56, 60.

19. *Ibid.*, 25, 49-51; James L. McDonough, *Schofield: Union General in the Civil War and Reconstruction* (Tallahassee, Fla., 1972), 10.

20. "Class of 1848," 1028; *Official Register of the Officers and Cadets of the U. S. Military Academy, West Point, N. Y.* (West Point, N. Y., 1845), 21; "John Buford, Jr.'s Academic Record at the United States Military Academy, 1 July 1844-1 July 1848," 1, USMA Archives.

21. "Register of Delinquencies," 54: 141, USMA Archives.

22. Morrison, *"Best School in the World"*, 73-74; Morrison, ed., "Getting Through West Point," 318-19.

23. "Register of Delinquencies," 54: 141.

24. Wilson, "Major-General John Buford," 175.

25. *Official Register of the Officers and Cadets of the U. S. Military Academy, West Point, N. Y.* (West Point, N. Y., 1846), 21; "John Buford, Jr.'s Academic Record," 1; Michael Phipps and John S. Peterson, *"The Devil's to Pay": Gen. John Buford, USA* (Gettysburg, Pa., 1995), 10.

26. K. Jack Bauer, *The Mexican War, 1846-1848* (New York, 1974), 7-10, 16-29, 32-43, 46-63, 66-68; James I. Robertson, Jr., *General A. P. Hill: The Story of a Confederate Warrior* (New York, 1987), 13-14.

27. George S. Pappas, *To the Point: The United States Military Academy, 1802-1902* (Westport, Conn., 1993), 219; *Official Register of the Officers and Cadets of the U. S. Military Academy, West Point, N. Y.* (West Point, N. Y., 1847), 23; "John Buford, Jr.'s Academic Record," 1.

28. Morrison, *"Best School in the World"*, 98-100.

29. "Class of 1848," 1028; Morrison, ed., "Getting Through West Point," 321.

30. "Register of Delinquencies," 54: 141; "John Buford, Jr.'s Academic Record," 1-2.

31. *Ibid.*, 1; *Official Register of the Officers and Cadets of the U. S. Military Academy, West Point, N. Y.* (West Point, N. Y., 1848), 22.

32. *Rock Island Argus*, 22 Jan. 1942; Buford, Buford, and Minter, *History and Genealogy of the Buford Family*, 307; "John Buford, Jr.'s Academic Record," 1-2.

33. Wilson, "Major-General John Buford," 174; Cullum, comp., *Biographical Register of Officers and Graduates*, 2: 353; Theodore F. Rodenbough and William L. Haskin, eds., *The Army of the United States: Historical Sketches of Staff and Line* . . . (New York, 1896), 173-75.

CHAPTER II:

1. Theophilus F. Rodenbough and William L. Haskin, eds., *The Army of the United States: Historical Sketches of Staff and Line*. . . . (New York, 1896), 153-58, 174, 193; Harold B. Simpson, *Cry Comanche: The 2nd U. S. Cavalry in Texas, 1855-1861* (Hillsboro, Tex., 1979), 7-11.

2. MRs, First U. S. Dragoons, July, Oct. 1848, M-744, r-3, NA.

3. *Ibid.*, July, Aug., Oct. 1848.

4. *Ibid.*, Nov., Dec. 1848; George W. Cullum, comp., *Biographical Register of the Officers and Graduates of the U. S. Military Academy* . . . (2 vols. New York, 1891), 2: 353; Robert W. Frazer, *Forts of the West: Military Forts . . . West of the Mississippi River to 1898* (Norman, Okla., 1965), 57-58; Francis B. Heitman, comp., *Historical Register and Dictionary of the United States Army* . . . (2 vols. Washington, D. C., 1903), 1: 856.

5. Randy Steffen, *The Horse Soldier, 1776-1943: The United States Cavalryman—His Uniforms, Arms, Accoutrements, and Equipments* (4 vols. Norman, Okla., 1977-80), 1: 128-36; R. T. Huntington, *Hall's Breechloaders: John H. Hall's*

Invention and Development of a Breechloading Rifle . . . (York, Pa., 1972), 89-90, 207, 217; Author's interview of Mr. Arnold Schofield, Historian, Fort Scott, Kan., 13 Aug. 1994.

6. Steffen, *Horse Soldier,* 1: 177; D. H. Mahan, *An Elementary Treatise on Advanced-Guard, Out-Post, and Detachment Service of Troops* . . . (New York, 1853), 56-59; Dabney H. Maury, *Recollections of a Virginian in the Mexican, Indian, and Civil Wars* (New York, 1894), 95-96, 104-05; Grady McWhiney and Perry D. Jamieson, *Attack and Die: Civil War Military Tactics and the Southern Heritage* (University, Ala., 1982), 126-32.

7. James Harrison Wilson, "Major-General John Buford," *JUSCA* 8 (1895): 176.

8. Cullum, comp., *Biographical Register of Officers and Graduates,* 2: 353; Heitman, comp., *Historical Register and Dictionary,* 1: 260; MR, Second U. S. Dragoons, Apr. 1849, M-744, r-16, NA.

9. Simpson, *Cry Comanche,* 8-11; Theophilus F. Rodenbough, *From Everglade to Canon with the Second Dragoons* . . . (New York, 1875), 1-161, 432-33; J. Henry Carleton, *The Prairie Logbooks: Dragoon Campaigns to the Pawnee Villages in 1844, and to the Rocky Mountains in 1845,* ed. Louis Pelzer (Lincoln, Neb., 1983), 155.

10. Robert M. Utley, *Frontiersmen in Blue: The United States Army and the Indian, 1848-1865* (New York, 1967), 23; Edward S. Wallace, *General William Jenkins Worth, Monterey's Forgotten Hero* (Dallas, 1953), 68.

11. *Ibid.*; Utley, *Frontiersmen in Blue,* 128.

12. *Ibid.*, 115, 119-20; P. T. Turnley, *Reminiscences of Parmenas Taylor Turnley* . . . (Chicago, 1892), 130, 171-72.

13. John Buford, Quartermaster Receipt, 25 Dec. 1849, Ferdinand Dreer Collection, HSP; MRs, Second U. S. Dragoons, Jan.-Feb. 1851, M-744, r-16, NA; "John Buford, Major General, U. S. Army," [p. 2], TS. in Rock Island Arsenal Museum, Rock Island, Ill.

14. MRs, Second U. S. Dragoons, Jan.-Feb. 1851, July-Aug. 1852, M-744, r-16, NA.

15. *Ibid.*, Sept. 1851, Mar. 1852; Marcus Bainbridge Buford, George Washington Buford, and Mildred Buford Minter, *History and Genealogy of the Buford Family in America, with Records of a Number of Allied Families* (La Belle, Mo., 1924), 169, 312.

16. Rodenbough, *From Everglade to Canon*, 167; Frazer, *Forts of the West*, 155; MR, Second U. S. Dragoons, July 1852, M-744, r-16, NA.

17. *Ibid.*, Aug. 1852; Cullum, comp., *Biographical Register of Officers and Graduates*, 2: 353; Maury, *Recollections of a Virginian*, 105.

18. Rodenbough, *From Everglade to Canon*, 433, 525-26; MRs, Second U. S. Dragoons, Aug. 1852, Mar., May, Aug. 1853, M-744, r-16, NA.

19. *Ibid.*, July-Aug. 1853, July-Aug. 1854; Heitman, comp., *Historical Register and Dictionary*, 1: 260; 2: 400-01; Rodenbough, *From Everglade to Canon*, 176-80, 433.

20. Buford, Buford, and Minter, *History and Genealogy of the Buford Family*, 169; "John Buford Biography," [p. 1], TS. in United States Cavalry Museum, Fort Riley, Kan.; Frank B. Borries, Jr., "General John Buford, Civil War Union Cavalryman," 3, M. A. thesis, University of Kentucky, 1960.

21. W. S. Harney to AGO, 5 Apr. 1855, Letterbook, Sioux Expedition, RG-393, E-5504A, NA; Rodenbough, *From Everglade to Canon*, 526-27; Utley, *Frontiersmen in Blue*, 113-15.

22. W. S. Harney to AGO, 2 June 1855, Letterbook, Sioux Expedition, RG-393, E-5504A, NA.

23. *Ibid.*; Almira Russell Hancock, *Reminiscences of Winfield Scott Hancock, by His Wife* (New York, 1887), 21; Ray H. Mattison, ed., "The Harney Expedition Against the Sioux: The Journal of Capt. John B. S. Todd," *Nebraska History* 43 (1962): 91-92.

24. "John Buford, Major General, U. S. Army," [pp. 1-2]; MR,

Second U. S. Dragoons, May 1855, M-744, r-16; W. S. Harney to AGO, 25 Apr. 1855, Letterbook, Sioux Expedition, RG-393, E-5504A; both, NA; Wilson, "Major-General John Buford," 175.

25. AGO to Jefferson Davis, 6 Oct. 1855, Office of the Secretary of War, Orders and Endorsements Sent, M-444, r-3; MR, Second U. S. Dragoons, May 1855, M-744, r-16; both, NA; Mattison, ed., "Harney Expedition," 92.

26. *Ibid.*, 100, 103, 107.

27. *Ibid.*, 92, 108-11; W. S. Harney to AGO, 5 Sept. 1855, Letterbook, Sioux Expedition, RG-393, E-5504A, NA; Henry Heth, *The Memoirs of Henry Heth*, ed. James L. Morrison, Jr. (Westport, Conn., 1974), xxviii-xxix; Richard C. Drum, "Reminiscences of the Indian Fight at Ash Hollow, 1855," *Collections of the Nebraska State Historical Society* 16 (1911): 144-45; Robert Harvey, "The Battle Ground of Ash Hollow," *Ibid.*, 152-53; R. Eli Paul, ed., "Battle of Ash Hollow: The 1909-1910 Recollections of General N. A. M. Dudley," *Nebraska History* 62 (1981): 380.

28. W. S. Harney to AGO, 5 Sept. 1855, Letterbook, Sioux Expedition, RG-393, E-5504A, NA; Rodenbough, *From Everglade to Canon*, 181; Utley, *Frontiersmen in Blue*, 116; Mattison, ed., "Harney Expedition," 111-12; Drum, "Reminiscences of the Indian Fight," 145-46; Paul, ed., "Battle of Ash Hollow," 381; Heth, *Memoirs*, 127-28; *Daily Missouri Republican* (St. Louis), 27 Sept. 1855; Emerson Gifford Taylor, *Gouverneur Kemble Warren: The Life and Letters of an American Soldier, 1830-1882* (Boston, 1932), 24-25.

29. W. S. Harney to AGO, 5 Sept. 1855, Letterbook, Sioux Expedition, RG-393, E-5504A, NA; Rodenbough, *From Everglade to Canon*, 182-84, 433; Utley, *Frontiersmen in Blue*, 117; Mattison, ed., "Harney Expedition," 113-14; Paul, ed., "Battle of Ash Hollow," 382; Heth, *Memoirs*, 128; *Daily Missouri Republican* (St. Louis), 27 Sept. 1855; Taylor, *Gouverneur Kemble Warren*, 25-27.

30. Drum, "Reminiscences of the Indian Fight," 149-50; Taylor,

Gouverneur Kemble Warren, 27-29; Utley, *Frontiersmen in Blue*, 118-20.

CHAPTER III:

1. W. S. Harney to AGO, 26 Sept. 1855, Letterbook, Sioux Expedition, RG-393, E-5504A; MR, Second U. S. Dragoons, Oct. 1855, M-744, r-16; both, NA; Ray H. Mattison, ed., "The Harney Expedition Against the Sioux: The Journal of Capt. John B. S. Todd," *Nebraska History* 43 (1962): 115-17; Theophilus F. Rodenbough, *From Everglade to Canon with the Second Dragoons . . .* (New York, 1875), 171-72.
2. Mattison, ed., "Harney Expedition," 130; Robert M. Utley, *Frontiersmen in Blue: The United States Army and the Indian, 1848-1865* (New York, 1967), 119; Rodenbough, *From Everglade to Canon*, 170, 529.
3. MRs, Second U. S. Dragoons, Dec. 1855, M-744, r-16; Feb., June, Oct. 1856, M-744, r-17; all, NA.
4. Rodenbough, *From Everglade to Canon*, 184; *Report of the Secretary of War: Senate Executive Document 5* (34th Cong., 3rd Sess., 1 Dec. 1856), 48; Jay Monaghan, *Civil War on the Western Border, 1854-1865* (Boston, 1955), 56-59; Thomas A. McMullin and David Walker, *Biographical Directory of American Territorial Governors* (Westport, Ct., 1984), 163-64.
5. *Report of the Secretary of War* (1 Dec. 1856), 48-49, 88.
6. *Ibid.*, 49, 80-81.
7. *Ibid.*, 81-83; Percival G. Lowe, *Five Years a Dragoon ('49 to '54) and Other Adventures on the Great Plains* (Kansas City, Mo., 1906), 229-30, 238-39.
8. *Report of the Secretary of War* (1 Dec. 1856), 81-82, 101-03, 120-23, 131-40; Monaghan, *Civil War on the Western Border*, 82-87; McMullin and Walker, *American Territorial Governors*, 164-66; G. Murlin Welch, *Border Warfare in Southeastern Kansas, 1856-1859* (Pleasonton, Kan., 1977), 7.
9. *Report of the Secretary of War* (1 Dec. 1856), 137, 144-45;

MR, Second U. S. Dragoons, Oct. 1856, M-744, r-17, NA; Lowe, *Five Years a Dragoon*, 229.

10. *Ibid.*, 146; MR, Second U. S. Dragoons, Dec. 1856, M-744, r-17, NA.

11. *Report of the Secretary of War: Senate Executive Document 11* (35th Cong., 1st Sess., 5 Dec. 1857), 6-7.

12. *Ibid.*, 7-9, 32-33; Norman F. Furniss, *The Mormon Conflict, 1850-1859* (New Haven, Conn., 1960), 11-61; Donald R. Moorman and Gene A. Sessions, *Camp Floyd and the Mormons: The Utah War* (Salt Lake City, 1992), 3-24; Harold D. Langley, ed., *To Utah with the Dragoons . . .* (Salt Lake City, 1974), 2-6.

13. Furniss, *Mormon Conflict*, 101, 104; Rodenbough, *From Everglade to Canon*, 205, 207; MR, Second U. S. Dragoons, May 1857, M-744, r-17, NA.

14. *Ibid.*, July 1857; Rodenbough, *From Everglade to Canon*, 185, 207; McMullin and Walker, *American Territorial Governors*, 166-68; Welch, *Border Warfare in Southeastern Kansas*, 33-36.

15. Furniss, *Mormon Conflict*, 96-98, 116-17; Rodenbough, *From Everglade to Canon*, 185; McMullin and Walker, *American Territorial Governors*, 292-94.

16. Furniss, *Mormon Conflict*, 69, 95, 98-99, 112; Charles P. Roland, *Albert Sidney Johnston, Soldier of Three Republics* (Austin, Tex., 1964), 185-89.

17. *Report of the Secretary of War* (5 Dec. 1857), 24; Yearly Return, Second U. S. Dragoons, 1857, M-744, r-17, NA; Furniss, *Mormon Conflict*, 117; Rodenbough, *From Everglade to Canon*, 185-87, 208-10; Wesley Merritt, "Life and Services of General Philip St. George Cooke, U. S. Army," *JUSCA* 8 (1895): 83.

18. Allen Johnson, et al., eds., *Dictionary of American Biography* (27 vols. to date. New York, 1927-), 3: 243; Rodenbough, *From Everglade to Canon*, 187.

19. Lowe, *Five Years a Dragoon*, 295-96.

20. Rodenbough, *From Everglade to Canon*, 187-88.

21. Philip St. George Cooke, et al., to John B. Floyd, 24 Oct. 1857, AGO Letters Received (Main Series), 1822-60, M-567, r-596, NA.

22. Rodenbough, *From Everglade to Canon*, 188; Roland, *Albert Sidney Johnston*, 193; *Report of the Secretary of War: Senate Executive Document 1* (35th Cong., 2nd Sess., 6 Dec. 1858), 6.

23. Rodenbough, *From Everglade to Canon*, 188-89; Moorman and Sessions, *Camp Floyd and the Mormons*, 29.

24. Rodenbough, *From Everglade to Canon*, 189-91; Yearly Return, Second U. S. Dragoons, 1857, M-744, r-17, NA; Merritt, "General Philip St. George Cooke," 83; Furniss, *Mormon Conflict*, 117-18; Roland, *Albert Sidney Johnston*, 195-96; Jerry Thompson, *Henry Hopkins Sibley: Confederate General of the West* (Natchitoches, La., 1987), 146-48.

25. Rodenbough, *From Everglade to Canon*, 192, 218; Moorman and Sessions, *Camp Floyd and the Mormons*, 30; Furniss, *Mormon Conflict*, 116.

26. *Report of the Secretary of War* (6 Dec. 1858), 37; Rodenbough, *From Everglade to Canon*, 218-28.

27. Furniss, *Mormon Conflict*, 192-200; Moorman and Sessions, *Camp Floyd and the Mormons*, 41-42; Roland, *Albert Sidney Johnston*, 206-11; Langley, ed., *To Utah with the Dragoons*, 13-16; *Utah: A Guide to the State* (New York, 1945), 71-72.

28. *Report of the Secretary of War* (6 Dec. 1858), 122-25; Rodenbough, *From Everglade to Canon*, 229-30; Moorman and Sessions, *Camp Floyd and the Mormons*, 44-58; Furniss, *Mormon Conflict*, 198-203; John Gibbon, *Personal Recollections of the Civil War* (New York, 1928), 3-4.

29. MR, Second U. S. Dragoons, Aug. 1858, M-744, r-17, NA; Cullum, George W., comp., *Biographical Register of Officers and Graduates*, 2: 353; Rodenbough, *From Everglade to Canon*, 192; Lowe, *Five Years a Dragoon*, 317.

30. John Buford to AGO, 26 Jan., 5 Mar. 1859, AGO Letters Received (Main Series), 1822-60, M-567, r-596, NA.

31. John Buford to AGO, 1 Apr. 1859, *ibid.*; John Buford to

AGO, 10 June 1859, *ibid.*, r-597; AGO to John Buford, 19 Sept. 1859, *ibid.*; MR, Second U. S. Dragoons, Aug. 1859, M-744, r-17; all, NA; Cullum, comp., *Biographical Register of Officers and Graduates*, 2: 353; Heitman, *Historical Register and Dictionary*, 1: 260.

32. MRs, Second U. S. Dragoons, Oct. 1859, Mar. 1860, M-744, r-17; AGO to John Buford, 19 Sept. 1859, AGO Letters Received (Main Series), 1822-60, M-567, r-597; all, NA; Langley, ed., *To Utah with the Dragoons*, 11; *Report of the Secretary of War: Senate Executive Document 1* (36th Cong., 2nd Sess., 3 Dec. 1860), 191.

33. Rodenbough, *From Everglade to Canon*, 173, 192; Special Order #112, 11 Sept. 1860; #131, 14 Nov. 1860; #138, 18 Dec. 1860; #139, 21 Dec. 1860; #1, 8 Jan. 1861; #2, 18 Jan. 1861; #8, 9 Mar. 1861; #10, 14 Mar. 1861; #14, 19 Mar. 1861; #19, 4 Apr. 1861; #21, 1 May 1861; #30, 27 May 1861; all, HQ Dept. of Utah Order Books, 1857-61, RG-393, E-5035, vol. 7, NA.

34. MRs, Second U. S. Dragoons, June, Aug. 1861, M-744, r-17, NA; Eben Swift, "General Wesley Merritt," *JUSCA* 21 (1911): 829.

35. Rodenbough, *From Everglade to Canon*, 192; Moorman and Sessions, *Camp Floyd and the Mormons*, 274-75; Gibbon, *Personal Recollections*, 5; Thompson, *Henry Hopkins Sibley*, 208-09.

36. Richard W. Etulain, ed., "A Virginian in Utah Chooses the Union . . .," *Utah Historical Quarterly* 42 (1974): 381-85; Frank Moore, *The Civil War in Song and Story, 1860-1865* (New York, 1889), 254; Michael Phipps and John S. Peterson, *"The Devil's to Pay": Gen. John Buford, USA* (Gettysburg, Pa., 1995), 19.

37. Merritt, "General Philip St. George Cooke," 85; Swift, "General Wesley Merritt," 829-30; F.E. Hunt, R.E. Clary, and J.B. Porter to Simon Cameron, 15 June 1861, AGO Letters Received, 1848-63, M-619, R-80, NA.

38. Rodenbough, *From Everglade to Canon*, 192-93; MRs,

Second U.S. Dragoons, Aug.-Sept. 1861, M-744, r-17, NA; Gibbon, *Personal Recollections*, 5-6.

CHAPTER IV:

1. MRs, Second U. S. Dragoons (Second U. S. Cavalry), Aug.-Sept. 1861, M-744, r-17, NA; Wesley Merritt, "Life and Services of General Philip St. George Cooke, U. S. Army," *JUSCA* 8 (1895): 85; Eben Swift, "General Wesley Merritt," *ibid.*, 21 (1911): 831; John Gibbon, *Personal Recollections of the Civil War* (New York, 1928), 6.
2. *Ibid.*, 6-9.
3. *Ibid.*, 8-10; MR, Second U. S. Dragoons (Second U. S. Cavalry), Oct. 1861, M-744, r-17, NA; Merritt, "General Philip St. George Cooke," 86.
4. Theophilus F. Rodenbough and William L. Haskin, eds., *The Army of the United States: Historical Sketches of Staff and Line . . .* (New York, 1896), 153, 193; Stephen Z. Starr, *The Union Cavalry in the Civil War* (3 vols. Baton Rouge, La., 1979-85), 1: 58-59.
5. *Ibid.*, 72, 84, 85n.-86n.; John Pope, "The Second Battle of Bull Run," *B&L*, 2: 491; Allan G. Bogue, *The Earnest Men: Republicans of the Civil War Senate* (Ithaca, N. Y., 1981), 47-48.
6. Francis B. Heitman, comp., *Historical Register and Dictionary of the United States Army . . .* (2 vols. Washington, D. C., 1903), 1: 856; Ezra J. Warner, *Generals in Blue: Lives of the Union Commanders* (Baton Rouge, La., 1964), 310-11; *Report of the Secretary of War: Senate Executive Document 1* (35th Cong., 2nd Sess., 6 Dec. 1858), 7-8; John Buford to AGO, 15 Nov. 1861, AGO Letters Received, 1848-63, M-619, r-7, NA; James Harrison Wilson, "Major-General John Buford," *JUSCA* 8 (1895): 175.
7. MR, Second U. S. Dragoons (Second U. S. Cavalry), Nov. 1861, M-744, r-17; John Buford to AGO, 8 Dec. 1861 [p. 1], AGO Letters Received, 1848-63, M-619, r-9; both, NA.
8. *Ibid.*, [pp. 1-2].

9. *Ibid.*, [p. 9]; John Buford to AGO, 1 Jan. 1862 [pp. 8, 11], *ibid.*, r-74.

10. John Buford to AGO, 8 Dec. 1861 [pp. 1-2, 5-6], *ibid.*, r-9; John Buford to AGO, 1 Jan. 1862 [pp. 1, 5, 9, 12-13], *ibid.*, r-74.

11. John Buford to AGO, 8 Dec. 1861 [pp. 2, 6], *ibid.*, r-9; John Buford to AGO, 1 Jan. 1862 [pp. 6-7, 11], *ibid.*, r-74; John Buford to AGO, 27 June 1862 [p. 1], *ibid.*, r-77.

12. John Gibbon to his wife, 15 Aug. 1862, Gibbon Papers, HSP.

13. John Buford to "Col. Gregory," 4 June 1862, Office of the Secretary of War, Telegrams Received, 1860-70, M-504, r-32, NA; Stephen W. Sears, *To the Gates of Richmond: The Peninsula Campaign* (New York, 1992), 9-39.

14. Warner, *Generals in Blue*, 53-54; Benton McAdams, "Napoleon Bonaparte: The Other Buford," *CWTI* 33 (Nov.-Dec. 1994): 82-85.

15. John Buford to AGO, 27 June 1862, AGO Letters Received, 1848-63, M-619, r-77, NA; Frank B. Borries, Jr., "General John Buford, Civil War Union Cavalryman," 6, M. A. thesis, University of Kentucky, 1960; Warner, *Generals in Blue*, 376-77.

16. Russell F. Weigley, "John Buford," *CWTI* 5 (June 1966): 16; John Buford, Personnel Return, June 1862, Union Staff Officers' Files, RG-94, NA; Pope, "Second Battle of Bull Run," 491.

17. Sears, *To the Gates of Richmond*, 335-56; *OR*, I, 12, pt. 2: 20-23; John Codman Ropes, *The Army Under Pope* (New York, 1882), 15-16.

18. Wallace J. Schutz and Walter N. Trenerry, *Abandoned by Lincoln: A Military Biography of General John Pope* (Urbana, Ill., 1990), 87-88; John J. Hennessy, *Return to Bull Run: The Campaign and Battle of Second Manassas* (New York, 1993), 24-25, 40; *OR*, I, 12, pt. 2: 23-24; pt. 3: 475-76, 481-82, 484-86, 512; *New York Times*, 6 Aug. 1862;

Philadelphia Inquirer, 26 July 1862; Starr, *Union Cavalry*, 1: 291-92.

19. Delevan Arnold to his mother, 25 July 1862; to his father, 29 July 1862, Arnold Correspondence, Kalamazoo Public Museum, Kalamazoo, Mich.; *OR*, I, 12, pt. 2: 24; pt. 3: 514; 30, pt. 3: 395; Starr, *Union Cavalry in the Civil War*, 1: 292-93; Edwin M. Stanton to anon., 27 July 1862, AGO Letters Received, 1848-62, M-619, r-78, NA; John Buford to AGO, 27 July 1862, *ibid.*

20. *OR*, I, 12, pt. 3: 583; Starr, *Union Cavalry*, 1: 59.

21. Delevan Arnold to his mother, 13 Aug. 1862, Arnold Correspondence; Willard Glazier, *Three Years in the Federal Cavalry* (New York, 1870), 79; *New York Herald*, 2 Sept. 1862.

22. *OR*, I, 27, pt. 3: 835; 29, pt. 1: 140; Borries, "General John Buford," 56-57.

CHAPTER V:

1. *OR*, I, 12, pt. 3: 525-26; *New York Times*, 8 Aug. 1862; Theodore Lyman, *Meade's Headquarters, 1863-1865: Letters of Colonel Theodore Lyman from the Wilderness to Appomattox*, ed. George R. Agassiz (Boston, 1922), 21.

2. Theophilus F. Rodenbough, *From Everglade to Canon with the Second Dragoons . . .* (New York, 1875), 271; James A. Bell to Augusta Hallock, 11 July 1863, Bell Correspondence, Henry E. Huntington Library, San Marino, Calif.; Daniel Oakey, *History of the Second Massachusetts Regiment of Infantry: Beverly Ford . . .* (Boston, 1884), 10.

3. *OR*, I, 12, pt. 1: 200; pt. 2: 24, 326; Edward J. Stackpole, *From Cedar Mountain to Antietam, August-September 1862 . . .* (Harrisburg, Pa., 1959), 32; Ezra J. Warner, *Generals in Blue: Lives of the Union Commanders* (Baton Rouge, La., 1964), 26.

4. *OR*, I, 12, pt. 2: 88-89; pt. 3: 544; *Proceedings of the Buford Memorial Association . . .* (New York, 1895), 20.

5. *OR*, I, 12, pt. 3: 548.

6. *Ibid.*, pt. 1: 158, 201; pt. 2: 25-26, 55, 145, 180-81; Robert K. Krick, *Stonewall Jackson at Cedar Mountain* (Chapel Hill, N. C., 1990), 31, 49; Stackpole, *From Cedar Mountain to Antietam*, 45.
7. Delevan Arnold to his mother, 13 Aug. 1862, Arnold Correspondence, Kalamazoo Public Museum, Kalamazoo, Mich.; *New York Times*, 13 Aug. 1862.
8. *OR*, I, 12, pt. 2: 88-91, 133-35, 140-42, 145-53, 157-61, 178-79, 181-85, 188-91, 214-33, 235-36; Samuel J. Bayard, *The Life of George Dashiell Bayard . . .* (New York, 1874), 228-29; John Pope, "The Second Battle of Bull Run," *B&L*, 2: 459.
9. *OR*, I, 12, pt. 2: 27-28, 134, 240; 51, pt. 1: 121; Bayard, *Life of Bayard*, 229; Myles Keogh, "Etat de Service of Major Genl Jno. Buford from his promotion to Brig Genl to his death" [p. 1], MS. in Special Collections, USMA Library, West Point, N. Y.; Delevan Arnold to his mother, 13 Aug. 1862, Arnold Correspondence.
10. *OR*, I, 12, pt. 2: 28.
11. *Ibid.*, 5, 8-11, 28; Stephen W. Sears, *To the Gates of Richmond: The Peninsula Campaign* (New York, 1992), 353-56; John J. Hennessy, *Return to Bull Run: The Campaign and Battle of Second Manassas* (New York, 1993), 8-10, 30.
12. *OR*, I, 12, pt. 2: 551-52, 563, 641; Hennessy, *Return to Bull Run*, 22-24, 31-37.
13. *OR*, I, 12, pt. 2: 28, 726; pt. 3: 589; 51, pt. 1: 740; *Buford Memorial Association*, 20; Willard Glazier, *Three Years in the Federal Cavalry* (New York, 1870), 84-85; Louis N. Boudrye, *Historic Records of the Fifth New York Cavalry . . .* (Albany, 1868), 39-40; Ford H. Rogers, *"Jeb" Stuart's Hat: War Papers Read Before the Commandery of the State of Michigan, Military Order of the Loyal Legion of the United States* (Detroit, 1893), 3-6; Emory M. Thomas, *Bold Dragoon: The Life of J. E. B. Stuart* (New York, 1986), 142-44; *Detroit Advertiser & Tribune*, 6 Sept. 1862.

14. *OR*, I, 12, pt. 2: 28-29; pt. 3: 592, 601; 51, pt. 1: 745-46; Glazier, *Three Years in the Federal Cavalry*, 85; Rogers, *"Jeb" Stuart's Hat*, 6-7; Kenneth P. Williams, *Lincoln Finds a General: A Military Study of the Civil War* (5 vols. New York, 1949-59), 1: 277-79.

15. *OR*, I, 12, pt. 2: 89-90, 726-27; pt. 3: 601, 604; Boudrye, *Fifth New York Cavalry*, 40.

16. *OR*, I, 12, pt. 2: 30; pt. 3: 609-10, 623; John Gibbon to his wife, 22 Aug. 1862, Gibbon Papers, HSP.

17. *OR*, I, 12, pt. 1: 202, 211; pt. 2: 30, 32, 34-35, 60-61, 64, 332.

18. *Ibid.*, 34, 334, 552-54, 564, 642-43, 730-32; Thomas, *Bold Dragoon*, 145-50; Hennessy, *Return to Bull Run*, 74-79, 92-101, 107-22.

19. *OR*, I, 12, pt. 1: 263; pt. 2: 68, 271, 277, 333-34, 352; pt. 3: 657-58, 669, 685.

20. *Ibid.*, pt. 1: 263; pt. 2: 271, 277, 350.

21. *Ibid.*, 271, 277; pt. 3: 658.

22. *Ibid.*, pt. 1: 144; pt. 2: 277, 335, 564; *New York Herald*, 4 Sept. 1862; Williams, *Lincoln Finds a General*, 1: 316; John Codman Ropes, *The Army Under Pope* (New York, 1882), 66-67; A. L. Long, *Memoirs of Robert E. Lee: His Military and Personal History . . .* (New York, 1886), 192.

23. *OR*, I, 12, pt. 2: 335-36; Hennessy, *Return to Bull Run*, 141-42.

24. *OR*, I, 12, pt. 2: 91, 383-84; *Buford Memorial Association*, 21; Stackpole, *From Cedar Mountain to Antietam*, 200.

25. *OR*, I, 12, pt. 2: 271-72, 277; *Buford Memorial Association*, 21; Fletcher Pratt, *Eleven Generals: Studies in American Command* (New York, 1949), 106.

26. *OR*, I, 12, pt. 2: 272, 277.

27. *Ibid.*, 338, 908, 1010-11; pt. 3: 729-30; Hennessy, *Return to Bull Run*, 233; Wallace J. Schutz and Walter N. Trenerry, *Abandoned by Lincoln: A Military Biography of General John Pope* (Urbana, Ill., 1990), 202.

28. *OR*, I, 12, pt. 1: 263; pt. 2: 851, 853, 903-04, 1010; Hennessy, *Return to Bull Run*, 234; Pratt, *Eleven Generals*, 106; Williams, *Lincoln Finds a General*, 1: 326.

29. Austin C. Stearns, *Three Years with Company K . . . 13th Massachusetts Infantry*, ed. Arthur A. Kent (Rutherford, N. J., 1976), 101-02.

30. Hennessy, *Return to Bull Run*, 329, 430; *Proceedings of Buford Memorial Association*, 21; *New York Times*, 2 Sept. 1862; *Philadelphia Inquirer*, 2 Sept. 1862.

31. Hennessy, *Return to Bull Run*, 231-361.

32. *Ibid.*, 430; Boudrye, *Fifth New York Cavalry*, 40; *Buford Memorial Association*, 21.

33. *OR*, I, 12, pt. 2: 272, 274, 737, 746; *New York Times*, 2 Sept. 1862; *Philadelphia Inquirer*, 2 Sept. 1862.

34. *OR*, I, 12, pt. 2: 274; Hennessy, *Return to Bull Run*, 431.

35. *OR*, I, 12, pt. 2: 746, 748.

36. *New York Times*, 2 Sept. 1862; *New York Tribune*, 4 Sept. 1862; Keogh, "Etat de Service" [pp. 1-2]; John Robertson, comp., *Michigan in the War* (Lansing, 1882), 565.

37. *OR*, I, 12, pt. 2: 746, 748.

38. *Ibid.*, 748; *Philadelphia Inquirer*, 2 Sept. 1862; *Detroit Advertiser & Tribune*, 2, 5, 6 Sept. 1862.

39. *OR*, I, 12, pt. 2: 746, 748, 752; Hennessy, *Return to Bull Run*, 432-33; Stackpole, *From Cedar Mountain to Antietam*, 234.

40. Hennessy, *Return to Bull Run*, 433; Abner Doubleday, *Chancellorsville and Gettysburg* (New York, 1882), 83; Eric J. Wittenberg, "John Buford and the Gettysburg Campaign," *Gettysburg Magazine* 11 (July 1994): 23.

41. *New York Tribune*, 4 Sept. 1862; Keogh, "Etat de Service" [p. 1]; Alfred G. Ryder, Diary, 30 Aug. 1862, University of Michigan Library, Ann Arbor, Mich.; John Buford to AGO, 5 Oct. 1862, AGO Letters Received, 1848-63, M-619, r-80, NA.

42. *OR*, I, 12, pt. 2: 737; Hennessy, *Return to Bull Run*, 434.

CHAPTER VI:

1. *New York Herald*, 2 Sept. 1862; Fletcher Pratt, *Eleven Generals: Studies in American Command* (New York, 1949), 106; Ezra J. Warner, *Generals in Blue: Lives of the Union Commanders* (Baton Rouge, La., 1964), 53.
2. Author's interview of Colonel Adrian Wheat, USA, Chief of Surgery, McDonald Army Community Hospital, Fort Eustis, Virginia, 4 Apr. 1995; *OR*, I, 12, pt. 2: 46, 86, 275; pt. 3: 786, 963.
3. *Ibid.*, pt. 2: 49.
4. John Hennessy, *Return to Bull Run: The Campaign and Battle of Second Manassas* (New York, 1993), 451-55; Stephen W. Sears, *Landscape Turned Red: The Battle of Antietam* (New York, 1983), 74-80.
5. Hennessy, *Return to Bull Run*, 466-72; Thornton F. Brodhead to his wife, 31 Aug. 1862, Brodhead Correspondence, Detroit Public Library, Detroit, Mich.; E. S. Williams, ed., "Col. Thornton Broadhead's [Brodhead's] Last Letter," *Michigan Historical Collections* 9 (1886): 208-09; "Letters of a Civil War Surgeon," *Indiana Magazine of History* 27 (1931): 140-41; George D. Bayard to his father, 31 Aug. 1862, Bayard Correspondence, USMA Library, West Point, N. Y.; Samuel J. Bayard, *The Life of George Dashiell Bayard . . .* (New York, 1874), 240-41.
6. *OR*, I, 19, pt. 1: 208; pt. 2: 185; 51, pt. 1: 787, 799-800; Alfred Pleasonton, Generals' Reports of Service, War of the Rebellion, 1: 111-12, RG-94, E-160, NA.
7. *OR*, I, 12, pt. 2: 45; 51, pt. 1: 789; Bayard to his father, 31 Aug. 1862, Bayard Correspondence.
8. Warner, *Generals in Blue*, 373-74; Edward G. Longacre, "Alfred Pleasonton, 'The Knight of Romance'," *CWTI* 13 (Dec. 1974): 11-14; Stephen Z. Starr, *The Union Cavalry in the Civil War* (3 vols. Baton Rouge, La., 1979-85), 1: 313-14; *OR*, I, 19, pt. 1: 97, 180.
9. *Ibid.*, pt. 2: 242; 51, pt. 1: 797.
10. Starr, *Union Cavalry*, 1: 313; *OR*, I, 19, pt. 1: 187, 209-10;

pt. 2: 334; James V. Murfin, *The Gleam of Bayonets: The Battle of Antietam and the Maryland Campaign of 1862* (South Brunswick, N. J., 1965), 173-74; W. N. Pickerill, *History of the Third Indiana Cavalry* (Indianapolis, 1906), 29-30; "Letters of a Civil War Surgeon," 144; Myles Keogh, "Etat de Service of Major Genl Jno. Buford from his promotion to Brig Genl to his death" [p. 2], MS. in Special Collections, USMA Library.

11. *OR*, I, 19, pt. 1: 199-200, 202, 211-13; Sears, *Landscape Turned Red*, 103, 172, 270-71; Pleasonton, Generals' Reports of Service, 1: 114-15, RG-94, E-160, NA; Pickerill, *Third Indiana Cavalry*, 30; "Letters of a Civil War Surgeon," 144, 149; Robert Milligan to "Dear Levi," 7 Oct. 1862, Milligan Correspondence, State Historical Society of Wisconsin, Madison, Wis.; Silas D. Wesson diary, 17 Sept. 1862, United States Army Military History Institute, Carlisle Barracks, Pa.; S. L. Gracey, *Annals of the Sixth Pennsylvania Cavalry* (Philadelphia, 1868), 100; Benjamin W. Crowninshield and D. H. L. Gleason, *A History of the First Regiment of Massachusetts Cavalry Volunteers* (Boston, 1891), 14-15; Starr, *Union Cavalry*, 1: 316-17.

12. *OR*, I, 19, pt. 2: 485, 490-91, 496; Sears, *Landscape Turned Red*, 323-32; "Letters of a Civil War Surgeon," 149.

13. *OR*, I, 19, pt. 1: 74, 77-81; Crowninshield and Gleason, *First Massachusetts Cavalry*, 34.

14. *OR*, I, 19, pt. 1: 72-74; pt. 2: 38-45; 51, pt. 1: 878; Gracey, *Sixth Pennsylvania Cavalry*, 105-06; Silas D. Wesson diary, 7 Oct. 1862; Edward G. Longacre, *Mounted Raids of the Civil War* (South Brunswick, N. J., 1975), 40-44.

15. *OR*, I, 19, pt. 1: 82-87; pt. 2: 103; Sears, *Landscape Turned Red*, 335-38.

16. *OR*, I, 21: 83, 99-101; William Marvel, *Burnside* (Chapel Hill, N. C., 1991), 163.

17. *OR*, I, 21: 84-85, 103-04, 550-51; Starr, *Union Cavalry*, 1: 324; Charles D. Rhodes, *History of the Cavalry of the Army of the Potomac . . .* (Kansas City, Mo., 1900), 28.

18. *OR*, I, 19, pt. 2: 526, 541; 21: 6-7, 13-14, 21, 23-25; Crowninshield and Gleason, *First Massachusetts Cavalry*, 16; Edward P. Tobie, *History of the First Maine Cavalry, 1861-1865* (Boston, 1887), 102-03; Starr, *Union Cavalry*, 1: 309-10; John Buford to "Comdg ofr 8th NY Cavly," ca. 1 Nov. 1862, Office of the Secretary of War, Telegrams Received, 1860-70, M-504, r-32, NA.

19. *Joint Committee on the Conduct of the War* (3 vols. in 8. Washington, D. C., 1863-68), 1863, pt. 1: 747.

20. *OR*, I, 21: 71, 89-91, 219, 355-56, 449-50.

21. *Ibid.*, 92-95, 219-20, 480-81, 510-12; James Longstreet, "The Battle of Fredericksburg," *B&L*, 3: 78-82.

22. *OR*, I, 21: 220-21; Pickerill, *Third Indiana Cavalry*, 38; Edward J. Stackpole, *Drama on the Rappahannock: The Fredericksburg Campaign* (Harrisburg, Pa., 1957), 198, 235-38; Pleasonton, Generals' Reports of Service, 1: 120, RG-94, R-160, NA; Starr, *Union Cavalry*, 1: 325-26; *New York Times*, 15, 16 Dec. 1862; Bayard, *Life of Bayard*, 273-75; Charles F. Adams, Jr., et. al., *A Cycle of Adams Letters, 1861-1865* . . ., ed. Chauncey Worthington Ford (2 vols. Boston, 1920), 1: 211.

23. *Joint Committee*, 1863, pt. 1: 747-48; Rhodes, *Cavalry of the Army of the Potomac*, 30; Stackpole, *Drama on the Rappahannock*, 240-42.

24. *OR*, I, 12, pt. 2: 1010-11; Wallace J. Schutz and Walter N. Trenerry, *Abandoned by Lincoln: A Military Biography of General John Pope* (Urbana, Ill., 1990), 200-04; Benton McAdams, "Napoleon Bonaparte: The Other Buford," *CWTI* 33 (Nov.-Dec. 1994): 88.

25. John Buford to "Maj R. Williams," 21 Jan. 1863, AGO Letters Received, 1848-63, M-619, r-160; John Buford to "Lt Spangler," 21 Jan. 1863, Office of the Secretary of War, Telegrams Received, 1860-70, M-504, r-32; both, NA; Starr, *Union Cavalry*, 1: 336-37.

26. *OR*, I, 12, pt. 1: 262-63; John Buford, Personnel Returns, Jan., Mar. 1863, Union Staff Officers' Files, RG-94, NA.

27. *OR*, I, 25, pt. 2: 3-5; 51, pt. 1: 977.

28. Michael Phipps and John S. Peterson, *"The Devil's to Pay": Gen. John Buford, USA* (Gettysburg, Pa., 1995), 28.

29. *OR*, I, 25, pt. 2: 59; 51, pt. 1: 983.

30. *Ibid.*, 25, pt. 2: 93; John Buford, Personnel Return, Mar. 1863, Union Staff Officers' Files, RG-94, NA.

CHAPTER VII:

1. *OR*, I, 25, pt. 1: 170; pt. 2: 72; Stephen Z. Starr, *The Union Cavalry in the Civil War* (3 vols. Baton Rouge, La., 1979-85), 1: 339; Edward G. Longacre, *The Cavalry at Gettysburg: A Tactical Study of Mounted Operations During the Civil War's Pivotal Campaign, 9 June-14 July 1863* (Rutherford, N. J., 1986), 73.

2. Ezra J. Warner, *Generals in Blue: Lives of the Union Commanders* (Baton Rouge, La., 1964), 90; Starr, *Union Cavalry*, 1: 275-78.

3. Francis B. Heitman, comp., *Historical Register and Dictionary of the United States Army . . .* (2 vols. Washington, D. C., 1903), 1: 260; Marcus Bainbridge Buford, George Washington Buford, and Mildred Buford Minter, *History and Genealogy of the Buford Family in America, with Records of a Number of Allied Families* (La Belle, Mo., 1924), 311.

4. George F. Price, comp., *Across the Continent with the Fifth Cavalry* (New York, 1883), 331-34; Longacre, *Cavalry at Gettysburg*, 52.

5. Starr, *Union Cavalry*, 1: 337-39; Daniel Butterfield, "Reminiscences of the Cavalry in the Army of [the] Potomac" [p. 1], RG-94, NA.

6. Willard Glazier, *Three Years in the Federal Cavalry* (New York, 1870), 124-26; William H. Medill to "Dear Sister Kate," 15 Mar. 1863, Hanna-McCormick Papers, Library of Congress, Washington, D. C.

7. *OR*, I, 25, pt. 2: 51, 71-72; Starr, *Union Cavalry*, 1: 339-40; Glazier, *Three Years in the Federal Cavalry*, 125-26.

8. George B. Sanford, *Fighting Rebels and Redskins: Experiences*

in Army Life of Colonel George B. Sanford, 1861-1892, ed. E. R. Hagemann (Norman, Okla., 1969), 194.

9. Longacre, *Cavalry at Gettysburg*, 46; Walter S. Newhall to "My Dear Bob," 14 Feb. 1863, Newhall Correspondence, HSP.
10. Edward G. Longacre, "Alfred Pleasonton, 'The Knight of Romance'," *CWTI* 13 (Dec. 1974): 11, 13; Charles F. Adams, Jr., et. al., *A Cycle of Adams Letters, 1861-1865 . . .*, ed. Chauncey Worthington Ford (2 vols. Boston, 1920), 2: 8.
11. Warner, *Generals in Blue*, 12-13; Robert B. Boehm, "The Unfortunate Averell," *CWTI* 5 (Aug. 1966): 30.
12. Longacre, *Cavalry at Gettysburg*, 50; William H. Medill to "Dear Sister Kate," 15 Mar. 1863, Hanna-McCormick Papers; Alphonso D. Rockwell, *Rambling Recollections: An Autobiography* (New York, 1920), 164.
13. *OR*, I, 25, pt. 1: 169-70; Joseph Hooker to Samuel P. Bates, 12 July 1878, Bates Papers, Pennsylvania State Archives, Harrisburg, Pa.
14. Starr, *Union Cavalry*, 1: 342-43, 345-46.
15. *OR*, I, 25, pt. 1: 47-64; Sanford, *Fighting Rebels and Redskins*, 195-96; Price, comp., *Fifth Cavalry*, 114-15; Wiley Sword, "Cavalry on Trial at Kelly's Ford," *CWTI* 13 (Apr. 1974): 33-40.
16. Walter S. Newhall to his father, 18 Mar. 1863, Newhall Correspondence.
17. S. L. Gracey, *Annals of the Sixth Pennsylvania Cavalry* (Philadelphia, 1868), 130-31; Newel Cheney, comp., *History of the Ninth Regiment, New York Volunteer Cavalry, War of 1861 to 1865* (Poland Center and Jamestown, N. Y., 1901), 81-83; Sanford, *Fighting Rebels and Redskins*, 196; Daniel W. Pulis to his parents, 8 Apr. 1863, Pulis Correspondence, Rochester Public Library, Rochester, N. Y.
18. OR, I, 25, pt. 1: 1066; Edward G. Longacre, "The Raid That Failed," *CWTI* 26 (Jan. 1988): 15.
19. *Ibid.*, 16; *OR*, I, 25, pt. 1: 1087-88.

20. *Ibid.*, 83-84, 1088; pt. 2: 204-05, 212, 215; Sanford, *Fighting Rebels and Redskins*, 197.

21. *Ibid.*, 197-98; *OR*, I, 25, pt. 1: 1088; Edward P. Tobie, *History of the First Maine Cavalry, 1861-1865* (Boston, 1887), 129-30; Daniel W. Pulis to his parents, 1 May 1863, Pulis Correspondence.

22. *OR*, I, 25, pt. 2: 213-14; Longacre, "Raid That Failed," 16, 18; Edward G. Longacre, *Mounted Raids of the Civil War* (South Brunswick, N. J., 1975), 154-55.

23. *OR*, I, 25, pt. 1: 1088; pt. 2: 232, 242; Benjamin W. Crowninshield and D. H. L. Gleason, *A History of the First Regiment of Massachusetts Cavalry Volunteers* (Boston, 1891), 120; Gracey, *Sixth Pennsylvania Cavalry*, 136.

24. *OR*, I, 25, pt. 2: 244-45.

25. *Ibid.*, pt. 1: 1058, 1096; Gracey, *Sixth Pennsylvania Cavalry*, 136-37; Sanford, *Fighting Rebels and Redskins*, 198.

26. *OR*, I, 25, pt. 1: 1058, 1088; Price, comp., *Fifth Cavalry*, 115.

27. *OR*, I, 25, pt. 1: 1059-60, 1088; Gracey, *Sixth Pennsylvania Cavalry*, 138; *New York Times*, 10 May 1863; Albert G. Brackett, *History of the United States Cavalry . . . to the 1st of June 1863 . . .* (New York, 1865), 306.

28. *OR*, I, 25, pt. 1: 1060, 1081, 1089-92, 1094-95; Gracey, *Sixth Pennsylvania Cavalry*, 139-42, 145-46; Price, comp., *Fifth Cavalry*, 116; Sanford, *Fighting Rebels and Redskins*, 200; Brackett, *History of the United States Cavalry*, 306-08.

29. *OR*, I, 25, pt. 1: 1089, 1093-94, 1097-98; Gracey, *Sixth Pennsylvania Cavalry*, 146-47; Sanford, *Fighting Rebels and Redskins*, 200; Price, comp., *Fifth Cavalry*, 116-17; *New York Times*, 10 May 1863; Heitman, comp., *Historical Register and Dictionary*, 1: 260.

30. *OR*, I, 25, pt. 1: 1060, 1089, 1094; Gracey, *Sixth Pennsylvania Cavalry*, 148-50; Sanford, *Fighting Rebels and Redskins*, 201-03; Longacre, *Mounted Raids of the Civil War*, 164-71.

31. *OR*, I, 25, pt. 1: 1062-63, 1089-90, 1094, 1096-97; pt. 2:

560-61; Sanford, *Fighting Rebels and Redskins*, 203-04; Price, comp., *Fifth Cavalry*, 117; Gracey, *Sixth Pennsylvania Cavalry*, 151-52; *New York Times*, 10 May 1863; W. N. Pickerill, *History of the Third Indiana Cavalry* (Indianapolis, 1906), 72.

32. *OR*, I, 25, pt. 1: 1090.

CHAPTER VIII:

1. *OR*, I, 25, pt. 1: 1090; George B. Sanford, *Fighting Rebels and Redskins: Experiences in Army Life of Colonel George B. Sanford, 1861-1892*, ed. E. R. Hagemann (Norman, Okla., 1969), 204; Stephen Z. Starr, *The Union Cavalry in the Civil War* (3 vols. Baton Rouge, La., 1979-85), 1: 358-60.

2. *Ibid.*, 361-62; *OR*, I, 25, pt. 1: 1072-80; William E. Doster, *Lincoln and Episodes of the Civil War* (New York, 1915), 200-01; William G. H. Carter, *From Yorktown to Santiago with the Sixth U. S. Cavalry* (Baltimore, 1900), 78; Emory M. Thomas, *Bold Dragoon: The Life of J. E. B. Stuart* (New York, 1986), 208-10.

3. *OR*, I, 25, pt. 2: 468-69, 474-75, 533; 27, pt. 3: 11 and n.

4. Charles F. Adams, Jr., et. al., *A Cycle of Adams Letters, 1861-1865*, ed. Worthington Chauncey Ford (2 vols. Boston, 1920), 2: 8; Walter S. Newhall to his father, 14 May 1863, Newhall Correspondence, HSP.

5. *OR*, I, 25, pt. 2: 474, 498, 533.

6. *Ibid.*, 536-38, 542-43; Wilbur S. Nye, *Here Come the Rebels!* (Baton Rouge, La., 1965), 31; Edwin B. Coddington, *The Gettysburg Campaign: A Study in Command* (New York, 1968), 49-50.

7. *OR*, I, 25, pt. 1: 1119; pt. 2: 593, 595; 27, pt. 1: 29.

8. Nye, *Here Come the Rebels!*, 33; Coddington, *Gettysburg Campaign*, 51.

9. *OR*, I, 27, pt. 1: 29, 32, 902; pt. 3: 8, 12; Coddington, *Gettysburg Campaign*, 53-54; Starr, *Union Cavalry*, 1: 373.

10. *OR*, I, 27, pt. 3: 14, 25-26, 37; Coddington, *Gettysburg Campaign*, 54; Edward G. Longacre, *The Cavalry at*

Gettysburg: A Tactical Study of Mounted Operations During the Civil War's Pivotal Campaign, 9 June-14 July 1863 (Rutherford, N. J., 1986), 62.

11. *OR*, I, 27, pt. 1: 168-70; pt. 3: 15-17, 27-30; Coddington, *Gettysburg Campaign*, 55-56; Longacre, *Cavalry at Gettysburg*, 62-63.

12. *OR*, I, 27, pt. 1: 1047, 1053; *Annals of the War, Written by Leading Participants North and South* (Philadelphia, 1879), 448-49; S. L. Gracey, *Annals of the Sixth Pennsylvania Cavalry* (Philadelphia, 1868), 157-58, 170; Newel Cheney, comp., *History of the Ninth Regiment, New York Volunteer Cavalry, War of 1861 to 1865* (Poland Center and Jamestown, N. Y., 1901), 95; James A. Bell to Augusta Hallock, 10 June 1863, Bell Correspondence, Henry E. Huntington Library, San Marino, Calif.; Fairfax Downey, *Clash of Cavalry: The Battle of Brandy Station, June 9, 1863* (New York, 1959), 93-94. The definitive source on John Buford's role in the battle is Clark B. Hall, "Buford at Brandy Station," *Civil War* 8 (July-Aug. 1990): 12-17, 66-67.

13. *Annals of the War*, 138-39.

14. Starr, *Union Cavalry*, 1: 378-79; Longacre, *Cavalry at Gettysburg*, 65-67; Downey, *Clash of Cavalry*, 95-96.

15. *New York Times*, 7 Apr. 1878; Ezra J. Warner, *Generals in Blue: Lives of the Union Commanders* (Baton Rouge, La., 1964), 123-24; Samuel H. Bradley, *Recollections of Army Life* . . . (Olean, N. Y., 1912), 14.

16. Longacre, *Cavalry at Gettysburg*, 72; *OR*, I, 27, pt. 1: 1043-44.

17. *Ibid.*, 1045, 1047; *Annals of the War*, 139, 449; Downey, *Clash of Cavalry*, 95; Gracey, *Sixth Pennsylvania Cavalry*, 158; Abner Hard, *History of the Eighth Cavalry Regiment, Illinois Volunteers, During the Great Rebellion* (Aurora, Ill., 1868), 65; James A. Bell to Augusta Hallock, 10 June 1863, Bell Correspondence.

18. Daniel W. Pulis to his parents, 11 June 1863, Pulis

Correspondence, Rochester Public Library, Rochester, N. Y.; *Annals of the War*, 449.

19. W. N. Pickerill, *History of the Third Indiana Cavalry* (Indianapolis, 1906), 73; *OR*, I, 27, pt. 1: 1047.

20. *Ibid.*, 1045, 1047; Coddington, *Gettysburg Campaign*, 65; John Buford, report of Brandy Station, 13 June 1863, Joseph Hooker Papers, Henry E. Huntington Library, San Marino, Calif.; H. P. Moyer, comp., *History of the Seventeenth Regiment Pennsylvania Volunteer Cavalry . . .* (Lebanon, Pa., 1911), 45; Cheney, comp., *Ninth New York Cavalry*, 96.

21. Longacre, *Cavalry at Gettysburg*, 71-72; Starr, *Union Cavalry*, 1: 379.

22. *Annals of the War*, 140; Gracey, *Sixth Pennsylvania Cavalry*, 159-61; Eric J. Wittenberg, "John Buford and the Gettysburg Campaign," *Gettysburg Magazine* 11 (July 1994): 31; Henry C. Whelan to his sister, 11 June 1863, Cadwalader Family Papers, HSP.

23. *OR*, I, 27, pt. 1: 1045; *Annals of the War*, 449; Longacre, *Cavalry at Gettysburg*, 73-77; Starr, *Union Cavalry*, 1: 380-85.

24. Longacre, *Cavalry at Gettysburg*, 83-85; *Annals of the War*, 141-43; *OR*, I, 27, pt. 1: 822; Daniel Oakey, *History of the Second Massachusetts Regiment of Infantry: Beverly Ford . . .* (Boston, 1884), 10-13; Starr, *Union Cavalry*, 1: 387; Gracey, *Sixth Pennsylvania Cavalry*, 163-64; Wittenberg, "Buford and the Gettysburg Campaign," 32; Henry C. Whelan to his sister, 11 June 1863, Cadwalader Family Papers; Theophilus F. Rodenbough, *From Everglade to Canon with the Second Dragoons . . .* (New York, 1875), 288-89.

25. *OR*, I, 27, pt. 1: 951, 1045, 1048; pt. 3: 49; *Annals of the War*, 141-42, 449-50; Nye, *Here Come the Rebels!*, 57; Longacre, *Cavalry at Gettysburg*, 85-86.

26. *OR*, I, 27, pt. 1: 951, 961-62, 1045, 1048; *Annals of the War*, 143-45, 450; James A. Bell to Augusta Hallock, 10

June 1863, Bell Correspondence; Gracey, *Sixth Pennsylvania Cavalry*, 164; Downey, *Clash of Cavalry*, 142.

27. Buford report, 13 June 1863, Hooker Papers; Coddington, *Gettysburg Campaign*, 66; *OR*, I, 27, pt. 1: 168-70, 905; pt. 2: 719.

28. *Ibid.*, pt. 1: 903-04, 1045; James A. Bell to Augusta Hallock, 8, 10 June 1863, Bell Correspondence.

29. *OR*, I, 27, pt. 1: 141, 1029; pt. 3: 30, 33, 93; Hard, *Eighth Illinois Cavalry*, 35, 247; Warner, *Generals in Blue*, 165; "Colonel Samuel H. Starr" [pp. 1-2], Starr Papers, Missouri Historical Society, St. Louis, Mo.

30. *OR*, I, 27, pt. 2: 295, 305-06, 440; pt. 3: 45-47, 55-59.

31. *Ibid.*, pt. 1: 141; pt. 2: 306, 357; pt. 3: 80-84, 87-89, 99-107; Coddington, *Gettysburg Campaign*, 80-85.

32. *OR*, I, 27, pt. 1: 142; pt. 3: 64, 116-17; Moyer, comp., *Seventeenth Pennsylvania Cavalry*, 46-47, 386; Hillman A. Hall, W. B. Besley, and Gilbert G. Wood, comps., *History of the Sixth New York Cavalry . . . 1861-1865* (Worcester, Mass., 1908), 129; *Annals of the War*, 450.

33. *OR*, I, 27, pt. 1: 142, 906-07, 952-53, 962-64.

34. *Ibid.*, 907-10, 1029; *Annals of the War*, 377, 450-51; Hall, Besley, and Wood, comps., *Sixth New York Cavalry*, 129; Cheney, comp., *Ninth New York Cavalry*, 98; Charles Brown to his sister, 18 June 1863, Brown Correspondence, New York State Library, Albany, N. Y.; Hard, *Eighth Illinois Cavalry*, 250.

35. *OR*, I, 27, pt. 1: 910-11, 953-54, 975-76; pt. 2: 759; pt. 3: 210; *Annals of the War*, 377; Nye, *Here Come the Rebels!*, 195-96.

36. *OR*, I, 27, pt. 1: 911, 920; pt. 3: 229-30.

37. Cheney, comp., *Ninth New York Cavalry*, 98; *OR*, I, 27, pt. 1: 920-21; Nye, *Here Come the Rebels!*, 197.

38. *Ibid.*, 201-02; *OR*, I, 27, pt. 1: 921, 946.

39. *Ibid.*, 921, 932-33, 946-47, 1029; Benjamin Engel to

Samuel H. Starr, 7 Aug. 1891, Starr Papers; Nye, *Here Come the Rebels!*, 199, 202-03.

40. *Ibid.*, 203-05; *OR*, I, 27, pt. 1: 921, 933; Hard, *Eighth Illinois Cavalry*, 251-53; Hall, Besley, and Wood, comps., *Sixth New York Cavalry*, 130; Wittenberg, "Buford and the Gettysburg Campaign," 35; William H. Redman to his mother, 24 June 1863, Redman Correspondence, University of Virginia Library, Charlottesville, Va.

41. *OR*, I, 27, pt. 1: 946-47; Nye, *Here Come the Rebels!*, 207-08.

42. *OR*, I, 27, pt. 1: 913; Daniel W. Pulis to his parents, 23 June 1863, Pulis Correspondence.

43. *OR*, I, 27, pt. 1: 946-47; Nye, *Here Come the Rebels!*. 207-8.

44. *Ibid.*, pt. 1: 143; pt. 3: 305-06, 337, 349, 353, 370, 377; Longacre, *Cavalry at Gettysburg*, 162-64.

45. OR, I, 27, pt. 1: 143, 913, 938, 1030; pt. 3: 333, 336-37, 349, 353, 369, 374; Coddington, *Gettysburg Campaign*, 126; Hard, *Eight Illinois Cavalry*, 254; George H. Chapman diary, 26-27 June 1863, Indiana Historical Society, Indianapolis, Ind.; James A. Bell to Augusta Hallock, 28 June 1863, Bell Correspondence; George Gordon Meade to his wife, 29 June 1863, Meade Papers, HSP.

46. Longacre, *Cavalry at Gettysburg*, 168; Isaac R. Pennypacker, *General Meade* (New York, 1901), 141.

47. OR, I, 27, pt. 3: 373; Coddington, *Gettysburg Campaign*, 220-21.

48. Moyer, comp., *Seventeenth Pennsylvania Cavalry*, 58; Hard, *Eighth Illinois Cavalry*, 260.

CHAPTER IX:

1. *OR*, I, 27, pt. 3: 400; Coddington, *Gettysburg Campaign*, 232; *Annals of the War, Written by Leading Participants North and South* (Philadelphia, 1879), 453; Joseph Hooker to E. D. Townsend, 28 Sept. 1875; to "Counsilor McConaughy," 17 Oct. 1875; both, Hooker Papers, Gettysburg College Library, Gettysburg, Pa.

2. *OR*, I, 27, pt. 1: 144; Edwin B. Coddington, *The Gettysburg Campaign: A Study in Command* (New York, 1968), 229.

3. *OR*, I, 27, pt. 1: 938, 1030; Hillman A. Hall, W. B. Besley, and Gilbert G. Wood, comps., *History of the Sixth New York Cavalry . . . 1861-1865* (Worcester, Mass., 1908), 132-33; Newel Cheney, comp., *History of the Ninth Regiment, New York Volunteer Cavalry, War of 1861 to 1865* (Poland Center and Jamestown, N. Y., 1901), 100-02; George H. Chapman diary, 29-30 June 1863, Indiana Historical Society, Indianapolis, Ind.

4. *Ibid.*, 30 June 1863; *OR*, I, 27, pt. 1: 923, 926, 938; Coddington, *Gettysburg Campaign*, 232.

5. *OR*, I, 27, pt. 1: 923; H. P. Moyer, comp., *History of the Seventeenth Regiment Pennsylvania Volunteer Cavalry . . .* (Lebanon, Pa., 1911), 49, 329; Cheney, comp., *Ninth New York Cavalry*, 100-01; George H. Chapman diary, 29 June 1863; Daniel W. Pulis to his parents, 6 July 1863, Pulis Correspondence, Rochester Public Library, Rochester, N. Y.

6. *OR*, I, 27, pt. 1: 923; pt. 2: 213, 443, 464-65; pt. 3: 344, 349, 353, 363, 370, 377; Hall, Besley, and Wood, comps., *Sixth New York Cavalry*, 133.

7. *Ibid.*, 133-34; *OR*, I, 27, pt. 1: 923; Cheney, comp., *Ninth New York Cavalry*, 102-03; Moyer, comp., *Seventeenth Pennsylvania Cavalry*, 49-50; Michael Jacobs, *Notes on the Rebel Invasion and the Battle of Gettysburg* (Philadelphia, 1864), 22.

8. Moyer, comp., *Seventeenth Pennsylvania Cavalry*, 379-80; Coddington, *Gettysburg Campaign*, 233; Edward G. Longacre, *The Cavalry at Gettysburg: A Tactical Study of Mounted Operations During the Civil War's Pivotal Campaign, 9 June-14 July 1863* (Rutherford, N. J., 1986), 181-82.

9. Warren W. Hassler, Jr., "The First Day's Battle at Gettysburg," *Civil War History* 6 (1960): 261; Gary Kross, "'Fight Like the Devil to Hold Your Own': General John Buford's Cavalry at Gettysburg on July 1, 1863," *Blue and*

Gray 12 (Feb. 1995): 1014; Coddington, *Gettysburg Campaign*, 237-240, 283-84; Daniel A. Skelly, *A Boy's Experiences During the Battles of Gettysburg* (Gettysburg, Pa., 1932), 10.

10. David G. Martin, *Gettysburg, July 1* (Conshohocken, Pa., 1995), 583-86; Coddington, *Gettysburg Campaign*, 302-03.

11. *OR*, I, 27, pt. 1: 922-24; Kross, "'Fight Like the Devil to Hold Your Own'," 10-11.

12. David L. Ladd and Audrey J. Ladd, eds., *The Bachelder Papers: Gettysburg in Their Own Words . . .* (Dayton, 1994), 201; *Proceedings of the Buford Memorial Association . . .* (New York, 1895), 24-25.

13. *OR*, I, 27, pt. 1: 927, 934, 938-39; Hall, Besley, and Wood, comps., *Sixth New York Cavalry*, 137-38; Kross, "'Fight Like the Devil to Hold Your Own'," 12-13; William Gamble to William L. Church, 10 Mar. 1864, Chicago Historical Society, Chicago, Ill.

14. *OR*, I, 27, pt. 1: 922-24; *Buford Memorial Association*, 25; Stephen Z. Starr, *The Union Cavalry in the Civil War* (3 vols. Baton Rouge, La., 1979-85), 1: 423.

15. *OR*, I, 27, pt. 1: 923-24, 927.

16. Hall, Besley, and Wood, comps., *Sixth New York Cavalry*, 136; *Buford Memorial Association*, 17-18; Martin, *Gettysburg July 1*, 47.

17. Abner Hard, *History of the Eighth Cavalry Regiment, Illinois Volunteers, During the Great Rebellion* (Aurora, Ill., 1868), 256; Hall, Besley, and Wood, comps., *Sixth New York Cavalry*, 137; Coddington, *Gettysburg Campaign*, 266-67; William Gamble to William L. Church, 10 Mar. 1864; Longacre, *Cavalry at Gettysburg*, 186.

18. Coddington, *Gettysburg Campaign*, 263-64; Longacre, *Cavalry at Gettysburg*, 148-60, 193-202; Emory M. Thomas, *Bold Dragoon: The Life of J. E. B. Stuart* (New York, 1986), 239-46.

19. Ladd and Ladd, eds., *Bachelder Papers*, 201; James Harrison

Wilson, "Major-General John Buford," JUSCA 8 (1895): 178.

20. Abner Doubleday, *Chancellorsville and Gettysburg* (New York, 1882), 126n.

21. *OR*, I, 27, pt. 1: 927, 934, 1030-31; W. N. Pickerill, *History of the Third Indiana Cavalry* (Indianapolis, 1906), 82; Coddington, *Gettysburg Campaign*, 266-67; George H. Chapman diary, 1 July 1863; Warren W. Hassler, Jr., *Crisis at the Crossroads: The First Day at Gettysburg* (University, Ala., 1970), 30; John H. Calef, "Gettysburg Notes: The Opening Gun," *Journal of the Military Service Institution of the United States* 40 (1907): 47-48; Moyer, comp., *Seventeenth Pennsylvania Cavalry*, 62.

22. William Gamble to William L. Church, 10 Mar. 1864; Martin, *Gettysburg July 1*, 73-74; George H. Chapman diary, 1 July 1863.

23. Coddington, *Gettysburg Campaign*, 266, 272-73; Martin, *Gettysburg July 1*, 69-72.

24. *OR*, I, 27, pt. 1: 924, 934; Cheney, comp., *Ninth New York Cavalry*, 108-09; Flavius J. Bellamy to his parents, 3 July 1863, Bellamy Correspondence, Indiana State Library, Indianapolis, Ind.; Hassler, "First Day's Battle," 264; Kross, "'Fight Like the Devil to Hold Your Own'," 15; Martin, *Gettysburg July 1*, 86, 590; Michael Phipps and John S. Peterson, *"The Devil's To Pay": Gen. John Buford*, USA (Gettysburg, Pa., 1995), 47.

25. Charles H. Veil to "D. McConaughy Esq.," 7 Apr. 1864, Veil Papers, Gettysburg College Library, Gettysburg, Pa.; Coddington, *Gettysburg Campaign*, 262.

26. *Ibid.*, 262-63, 267; Ladd and Ladd, eds., *Bachelder Papers*, 201; Moyer, comp., *Seventeenth Pennsylvania Cavalry*, 62; Hall, Besley, and Wood, comps., *Sixth New York Cavalry*, 138-39; Samuel P. Bates, *The Battle of Gettysburg* (Philadelphia, 1875), 59-60; *Buford Memorial Association*, 18.

27. *Philadelphia North American*, 29 June 1913; Eric J.

Wittenberg, "John Buford and the Gettysburg Campaign," *Gettysburg Magazine* 11 (July 1994): 42n.

28. Charles H. Veil to "D. McConaughy Esq.," 7 Apr. 1864, Veil Papers; Calef, "Gettysburg Notes," 47; *OR*, I, 27, pt. 1: 927, 934; Flavius J. Bellamy to his parents, 3 July 1863, Bellamy Correspondence; Longacre, *Cavalry at Gettysburg*, 188.

29. *OR*, I, 27, pt. 1: 244-46, 265-67, 281-82, 927, 934; Coddington, *Gettysburg Campaign*, 267-69; Cheney, comp., *Ninth New York Cavalry*, 109.

30. *OR*, I, 27, pt. 1: 244-45, 696-702; pt. 2: 607, 637-39.

31. Calef, "Gettysburg Notes," 48.

32. *Ibid.*, 48-52; *OR*, I, 27, pt. 1: 927, 1031; Pickerill, *Third Indiana Cavalry*, 82; Almira Russell Hancock, *Reminiscences of Winfield Scott Hancock, by His Wife* (New York, 1887), 189.

33. *OR*, I, 27, pt. 1: 934; Martin, *Gettysburg July 1*, 82, 88, 102-65, 170, 186-87; George H. Chapman diary, 1 July 1863.

34. Martin, *Gettysburg July 1*, 170, 205; *OR*, I, 27, pt. 2: 552.

35. *Ibid.*, I, 27, pt. 1: 701-02, 939; Cheney, comp., *Ninth New York Cavalry*, 109; Coddington, *Gettysburg Campaign*, 280-82; Kross, "'Fight Like the Devil to Hold Your Own'," 17, 19; Martin, *Gettysburg July 1*, 278; Moyer, comp., *Seventeenth Pennsylvania Cavalry*, 63.

36. *Ibid.*, 63-64; Martin, *Gettysburg July 1*, 280-81; Kross, "'Fight Like the Devil to Hold Your Own'," 19; *OR*, I, 27, pt. 1: 702-03, 728, 939.

37. *Ibid.*, pt. 2: 468-69, 554, 639; Martin, *Gettysburg July 1*, 342-89, 394-400.

38. *Ibid.*, 28, 73, 76; Phipps and Peterson, *"The Devil's to Pay"*, 52; Harry W. Pfanz, *Gettysburg: Culp's Hill and Cemetery Hill* (Chapel Hill, N. C., 1993), 44; Daniel W. Pulis to his parents, 6 July 1863, Pulis Correspondence.

39. Martin, *Gettysburg July 1*, 422; Flavius J. Bellamy to his parents, 3 July 1863, Bellamy Correspondence; Hard, *Eighth Illinois Cavalry*, 258; *OR*, I, 27, pt. 2: 661-62.

40. Ken Bandy and Florence Freeland, comps., *The Gettysburg Papers* (2 vols. Dayton, 1978), 1: 177; James A. Bell to Augusta Hallock, 2 July 1863, Bell Correspondence, Henry E. Huntington Library, San Marino, Calif.; *OR*, I, 27, pt. 2: 665.

41. *Ibid.*, pt. 1: 702-04, 729-30; Oliver O. Howard, *Autobiography of Oliver Otis Howard* (2 vols. New York, 1907), 1: 417.

42. Coddington, *Gettysburg Campaign*, 284-85; OR, I, 27, pt. 1: 366-67.

43. *Ibid.*, 367-68, 925; Cheney, comp., *Ninth New York Cavalry*, 113; John A. Carpenter, "General O.O. Howard at Gettysburg," *Civil War History* 9 (1963): 265.

44. Bandy and Freeland, comps., *Gettysburg Papers*, 1: 155-57; E. P. Halstead, "Incidents of the First Day at Gettysburg," *B&L* 3: 285.

45. Hancock, *Winfield Scott Hancock*, 189; *OR*, I, 27, pt. 1: 366; pt. 2: 665; Flavius J. Bellamy to his parents, 3 July 1863, Bellamy Correspondence; William Gamble to William L. Church, 10 Mar. 1864; Francis A. Walker, *History of the Second Army Corps in the Army of the Potomac* (New York, 1886), 266 and n.

46. *OR*, I, 27, pt. 1: 482, 531, 758-59, 777; Coddington, *Gettysburg Campaign*, 317-21; Martin, *Gettysburg July 1*, 523-51.

47. Cheney, comp., *Ninth New York Cavalry*, 114; Moyer, comp., *Seventeenth Pennsylvania Cavalry*, 398; Wilson, "Major-General John Buford," 181; Calef, "Gettysburg Notes," 51; Martin, *Gettysburg July 1*, 493.

48. *New York Tribune*, 17 Dec. 1863; *OR*, I, 27, pt. 1: 927, 939.

CHAPTER X:

1. Hillman A. Hall, W. B. Besley, and Gilbert G. Wood, comps., *History of the Sixth New York Cavalry . . . 1861-1865* (Worcester, Mass., 1908), 142; Newel Cheney, comp., *History of the Ninth Regiment, New York Volunteer*

Cavalry, War of 1861 to 1865 (Poland Center and Jamestown, N. Y., 1901), 114; Harry W. Pfanz, *Gettysburg: The Second Day* (Chapel Hill, N. C., 1987), 88-89; *OR*, I, 27, pt. 1: 927-28, 939, 1032.

2. Cheney, comp., *Ninth New York Cavalry*, 115.
3. *OR*, I, 27, pt. 1: 185, 930, 1032.
4. *Ibid.*, pt. 3: 1086; Edwin B. Coddington, *The Gettysburg Campaign: A Study in Command* (New York, 1968), 351.
5. George H. Chapman diary, 2 July 1863, Indiana Historical Society, Indianapolis, Ind.; *OR*, I, 27, pt. 1: 145, 914, 927-28, 939, 1032; Hall, Besley, and Wood, comps., *Sixth New York Cavalry*, 143; Cheney, comp., *Ninth New York Cavalry*, 115.
6. *OR*, I, 27, pt. 1: 131, 515, 939; Coddington, *Gettysburg Campaign*, 343-56, 385-410.
7. Coddington, *Gettysburg Campaign*, 351-52; Edward G. Longacre, *The Cavalry at Gettysburg: A Tactical Study of Mounted Operations During the Civil War's Pivotal Campaign, 9 June-14 July 1863* (Rutherford, N. J., 1986), 205-06.
8. *OR*, I, 27, pt. 1: 1032; Cheney, comp., *Ninth New York Cavalry*, 115; George H. Chapman diary, 3 July 1863.
9. *Ibid.*, 3-4 July 1863; *OR*, I, 27, pt. 1: 145, 928, 939.
10. George H. Chapman diary, 4 July 1863; *OR*, I, 27, pt. 3: 517-18, 538, 544-45; Hall, Besley, and Wood, comps., *Sixth New York Cavalry*, 144; H. P. Moyer, comp., *History of the Seventeenth Regiment Pennsylvania Volunteer Cavalry . . .* (Lebanon, Pa., 1911), 51; Ezra J. Warner, *Generals in Blue: Lives of the Union Commanders* (Baton Rouge, La., 1964), 162.
11. *OR*, I, 27, pt. 1: 185, 943, 948-49; Longacre, *Cavalry at Gettysburg*, 235-37, 240-41.
12. *OR*, I, 27, pt. 1: 489, 928, 1032; pt. 3: 524, 538; S. L. Gracey, *Annals of the Sixth Pennsylvania Cavalry* (Philadelphia, 1868), 182-83; George H. Chapman diary, 5 July 1863; Stephen Z. Starr, *The Union Cavalry in the Civil War* (3 vols. Baton Rouge, La., 1979-85), 1: 451; Willard

Glazier, *Three Years in the Federal Cavalry* (New York, 1870), 283; Coddington, *Gettysburg Campaign*, 552.

13. John D. Imboden, "The Confederate Retreat from Gettysburg," *B&L*, 3: 421-25; *OR*, I, 27, pt. 1: 928.

14. *Ibid.*, 145, 928, 995; Longacre, *Cavalry at Gettysburg*, 248; Starr, *Union Cavalry*, 1: 453.

15. *OR*, I, 27, pt. 1: 995.

16. *Ibid.*, 81, 925; Abner Hard, *History of the Eighth Cavalry Regiment, Illinois Volunteers, During the Great Rebellion* (Aurora, Ill., 1868), 261; Imboden, "Confederate Retreat from Gettysburg," 426-27.

17. *OR*, I, 27, pt. 1: 916, 928, 935, 939-40, 943, 1032; Imboden, "Confederate Retreat from Gettysburg," 427; Coddington, *Gettysburg Campaign*, 552-54; Hard, *Eighth Illinois Cavalry*, 261-62; James A. Bell to Augusta Hallock, 8 July 1863, Bell Correspondence, Henry E. Huntington Library, San Marino, Calif.; Hall, Besley, and Wood, comps., *Sixth New York Cavalry*, 145.

18. *OR*, I, 27, pt. 1: 916, 928, 935; Gracey, *Sixth Pennsylvania Cavalry*, 183; George H. Chapman diary, 6 July 1863; William H. Redman to his mother, 10 July 1863, Redman Correspondence, University of Virginia Library, Charlottesville, Va.

19. *OR*, I, 27, pt. 1: 928, 935, 943, 995; Coddington, *Gettysburg Campaign*, 552-53; Starr, *Union Cavalry*, 1: 453-54; Hard, *Eighth Illinois Cavalry*, 262; *New York Times*, 21 July 1863; Gracey, *Sixth Pennsylvania Cavalry*, 184; Louis N. Boudrye, *Historic Records of the Fifth New York Cavalry* . . . (Albany, 1868), 69.

20. *OR*, I, 27, pt. 1: 928, 935, 940, 995, 1032; Imboden, "Confederate Retreat from Gettysburg," 427-28; George H. Chapman diary, 6 July 1863; *New York Times*, 21 July 1863.

21. *OR*, I, 27, pt. 1: 146, 928, 940, 1032-33; Gracey, *Sixth Pennsylvania Cavalry*, 185.

22. *OR*, I, 27, pt. 1: 940, 948-49; pt. 2: 703, 754, 760-61; Hall, Besley, and Wood, comps., *Sixth New York Cavalry*, 146-47;

Cheney, comp., *Ninth New York Cavalry*, 118-19; Moyer, comp., *Seventeenth Pennsylvania Cavalry*, 52-53; Starr, *Union Cavalry*, 1: 456; George H. Chapman diary, 7 July 1863.

23. *OR*, I, 27, pt. 1: 929, 935, 940; pt. 2: 703.

24. *Ibid.*, pt. 1: 935, 940-41, 944, 1033; Hall, Besley, and Wood, comps., *Sixth New York Cavalry*, 147-48; Moyer, comp., *Seventeenth Pennsylvania Cavalry*, 53.

25. *OR*, I, 27, pt. 1: 935-36; pt. 3: 602, 604; Glazier, *Three Years in the Federal Cavalry*, 281; Boudrye, *Fifth New York Cavalry*, 69-70.

26. *OR*, I, 27, pt. 1: 936; Hard, *Eighth Illinois Cavalry*, 263; William H. Redman to his mother, 10 July 1863, Redman Correspondence.

27. *OR*, I, 27, pt. 1: 925.

28. *Ibid.*, 146; Longacre, *Cavalry at Gettysburg*, 262.

29. *OR*, I, 27, pt. 1: 941, 1022; Hall, Besley, and Wood, comps., *Sixth New York Cavalry*, 148; George H. Chapman diary, 9 July 1863.

30. *OR*, I, 27, pt. 1: 929, 941; Gracey, *Sixth Pennsylvania Cavalry*, 187; Hard, *Eighth Illinois Cavalry*, 263; Hall, Besley, and Wood, comps., *Sixth New York Cavalry*, 149; Flavius J. Bellamy to his brother, 11 July 1863, Bellamy Correspondence, Indiana State Library, Indianapolis, Ind.; Daniel W. Pulis to his parents, 11 July 1863, Pulis Correspondence, Rochester Public Library, Rochester, N. Y.

31. *OR*, I, 27, pt. 1: 929, 936, 941-42, 1033; Gracey, *Sixth Pennsylvania Cavalry*, 188; Hall, Besley, and Wood, comps., *Sixth New York Cavalry*, 149.

32. *OR*, I, 27, pt. 1: 936, 942, 1033; Hard, *Eighth Illinois Cavalry*, 264.

33. *OR*, I, 27, pt. 1: 686-87, 692, 694, 929, 936, 942, 1033; Glazier, *Three Years in the Federal Cavalry*, 284-87.

34. Cheney, comp., *Ninth New York Cavalry*, 120-22; *OR*, I, 27, pt. 1: 929, 942; pt. 3: 647, 656-58; Myles Keogh, "Etat de Service of Major Genl Jno. Buford from his promotion to Brig Genl to his death" [pp. 2-3], MS. in Special

Collections, USMA Library, West Point, N. Y.; Starr, *Union Cavalry*, 1: 458-59; Coddington, *Gettysburg Campaign*, 565-69.

35. *Ibid.*, 570; *OR*, I, 27, pt. 1: 210, 929, 936, 942; Hall, Besley, and Wood, comps., *Sixth New York Cavalry*, 150; Daniel W. Pulis to his parents, 17 July 1863, Pulis Correspondence; George H. Chapman diary, 14 July 1863.

36. *OR*, I, 27, pt. 1: 929, 936, 990, 998, 1000; *New York Times*, 21 July 1863.

37. *OR*, I, 29, pt. 1: 929, 937, 942, 990-91; George H. Chapman diary, 14 July 1863.

38. Hard, *Eighth Illinois Cavalry*, 265.

CHAPTER XI:

1. *OR*, I, 27, pt. 1: 83; Edwin B. Coddington, *The Gettysburg Campaign: A Study in Command* (New York, 1968), 564; E. B. Long, "The Battle That Almost Was—Manassas Gap," *CWTI* 11 (Dec. 1972): 21-22.

2. *OR*, I, 27, pt. 1: 148-49, 929, 945; pt. 3: 721, 729; H. P. Moyer, comp., *History of the Seventeenth Regiment Pennsylvania Volunteer Cavalry . . .* (Lebanon, Pa., 1911), 330-31; S. L. Gracey, *Annals of the Sixth Pennsylvania Cavalry* (Philadelphia, 1868), 192-93; Charles Munroe diary, 15-18 July 1863, American Antiquarian Society, Worcester, Mass.

3. *OR*, I, 27, pt. 1: 495-96, 945; pt. 3: 734-36, 740, 742, 756.

4. Long, "Battle That Almost Was," 24-26; *OR*, I, 27, pt. 1: 489-490, 495-96, 945; Willard Glazier, *Three Years in the Federal Cavalry* (New York, 1870), 301-02; Gracey, *Sixth Pennsylvania Cavalry*, 193.

5. *OR*, I, 27, pt. 1: 932-33, 937; pt. 3: 729, 735, 741-42; Abner Hard, *History of the Eighth Cavalry Regiment, Illinois Volunteers, During the Great Rebellion* (Aurora, Ill., 1868), 267; George H. Chapman diary, 21-22 July 1863, Indiana Historical Society, Indianapolis, Ind.; William Gamble to anon., ca. 1 Oct. 1864, Commission Branch Files, M-1064, r-9, NA.

6. *OR*, I, 27, pt. 1: 149, 929-30, 937; Moyer, comp., *Seventeenth Pennsylvania Cavalry*, 331; Hard, *Eighth Illinois Cavalry*, 267.
7. *OR*, I, 27, pt. 3: 772, 787-88, 819-21; Hillman A. Hall, W. B. Besley, and Gilbert G. Wood, comps., *History of the Sixth New York Cavalry . . . 1861-1865* (Worcester, Mass., 1908), 153; George H. Chapman diary, 27-31 July 1863.
8. *Ibid.*, 1-2 Aug. 1863; *OR*, I, 27, pt. 1: 111, 932; pt. 3: 822, 825, 827; Charles Munroe diary, 1 Aug. 1863.
9. *OR*, I, 27, pt. 3: 827, 835.
10. *Ibid.*, 835, 839-40; Stephen Z. Starr, *The Union Cavalry in the Civil War* (3 vols. Baton Rouge, La., 1979-85), 2: 20.
11. Hard, *Eighth Illinois Cavalry*, 269; John Buford to Ambrose E. Burnside, 12 Aug. 1863, George Hay Stuart Papers, LC.
12. *Ibid.*
13. John Buford to Alfred Pleasonton, 21 Aug. 1863, General's Papers, RG-94, E-159, NA; George H. Chapman diary, 21-22 Aug. 1863.
14. *OR*, I, 29, pt. 1: 224 and n., 353; pt. 2: 51-52; George B. Sanford, *Fighting Rebels and Redskins: Experiences in Army Life of Colonel George B. Sanford, 1861-1892*, ed. E. R. Hagemann (Norman, Okla., 1969), 207n., 208-12; George F. Price, comp., *Across the Continent with the Fifth Cavalry* (New York, 1883), 119.
15. *OR*, I, 29, pt. 1: 94-95; pt. 2: 103, 108; Newel Cheney, comp., *History of the Ninth Regiment, New York Volunteer Cavalry, War of 1861 to 1865* (Poland Center and Jamestown, N. Y., 1901), 131-32.
16. *OR*, I, 29, pt. 2: 167, 169, 172, 706, 720-21.
17. *Ibid.*, pt. 1: 111; Starr, *Union Cavalry*, 2: 21; Charles Munroe diary, 12-13 Sept. 1863; Hall, Besley, and Wood, comps., *Sixth New York Cavalry*, 156; Louis N. Boudrye, *Historic Records of the Fifth New York Cavalry . . .* (Albany, 1868), 74, 77; George H. Chapman diary, 12 Sept. 1863; Walter S. Newhall to his father, 15 Sept. 1863, Newhall Correspondence, HSP; *New York Times*, 15 Sept. 1863.

18. *OR*, I, 29, pt. 1: 111-12, 118-21, 134-35; pt. 2: 720; *New York Times*, 16-17 Sept. 1863; Charles Munroe diary, 14 Sept. 1863; Glazier, *Three Years in the Federal Cavalry*, 314-15; Hard, *Eighth Illinois Cavalry*, 271-72.

19. *OR*, I, 29, pt. 1: 140; pt. 2: 742; Starr, *Union Cavalry*, 2: 22-23; Glazier, *Three Years in the Federal Cavalry*, 317-18; Hard, *Eighth Illinois Cavalry*, 274-75; W. N. Pickerill, *History of the Third Indiana Cavalry* (Indianapolis, 1906), 95-96; Charles Munroe diary, 21-22 Sept. 1863; Alfred Pleasonton to John Buford, 5 Nov. 1863, Headquarters, Cavalry Corps, Army of the Potomac, Letters Sent, 1863-65, RG-393, E-1439, NA.

20. *OR*, I, 29, pt. 1: 141-43; pt. 2: 224; Starr, *Union Cavalry*, 2: 23; Glazier, *Three Years in the Federal Cavalry*, 319-20; Emory M. Thomas, *Bold Dragoon: The Life of J. E. B. Stuart* (New York, 1986), 263-64; Andrew A. Humphreys to George Gordon Meade, 23 Sept. 1863, General's Papers, RG-94, E-159, NA.

21. *OR*, I, 29, pt. 1: 140; *New York Times*, 17 Sept. 1863.

22. *OR*, I, 29, pt. 1: 146-48; pt. 2: 220, 227.

23. *Ibid.*, pt. 1: 148-95; Starr, *Union Cavalry*, 2: 23.

24. Hall, Besley, and Wood, comps., *Sixth New York Cavalry*, 159; Cheney, comp., *Ninth New York Cavalry*, 136; *OR*, I, 29, pt. 1: 9-10; pt. 2: 268, 279-80.

25. *Ibid.*, pt. 1: 347-48; pt. 2: 268, 272-74; Hard, *Eighth Illinois Cavalry*, 277; Hall, Besley, and Wood, comps., *Sixth New York Cavalry*, 159.

26. *Ibid.*, 160; *OR*, I, 29, pt. 1: 342, 348; Cheney, comp., *Ninth New York Cavalry*, 136; Pickerill, *Third Indiana Cavalry*, 96-97.

27. George H. Chapman diary, 11 Oct. 1863; *OR*, I, 29, pt. 1: 348-49; Pickerill, *Third Indiana Cavalry*, 97.

28. *OR*, I, 29, pt. 1: 349, 381, 394-95; Starr, *Union Cavalry*, 2: 24-27; Glazier, *Three Years in the Federal Cavalry*, 326-27; Thomas, *Bold Dragoon*, 264-65; Hall, Besley, and Wood, comps., *Sixth New York Cavalry*, 160-61; Cheney, comp.,

Ninth New York Cavalry, 137-38; Boudrye, *Fifth New York Cavalry*, 79-80; Myles Keogh, "Etat de Service of Major Genl Jno. Buford from his promotion to Brig Genl to his death" [p. 3], MS. in Special Collections, USMA Library, West Point, N. Y.; S. A. Clark, "Brandy Station, October, 1863," *Maine Bugle* n.s. 3 (1896): 226-28; *New York Times*, 14 Oct. 1863; *Philadelphia Inquirer*, 14 Oct. 1863.

29. *OR*, I, 29, pt. 1: 9-10, 236, 349, 999; pt. 2: 293, 295-99; 51, pt. 1: 1102; Hall, Besley, and Wood, comps., *Sixth New York Cavalry*, 162; Hard, *Eighth Illinois Cavalry*, 279; Cheney, comp., *Ninth New York Cavalry*, 138; George H. Chapman diary, 12 Oct. 1863; Pickerill, *Third Indiana Cavalry*, 98-99; Keogh, "Etat de Service" [p. 3].

30. *OR*, I, 29, pt. 1: 346, 349-50; pt. 2: 305-07; Hard, *Eighth Illinois Cavalry*, 279-80.

31. *OR*, I, 29, pt. 1: 346, 350, 1000; pt. 2: 314; *History of the Third Pennsylvania Cavalry, Sixtieth Regiment Pennsylvania Volunteers, in the American Civil War, 1861-1865* (Philadelphia, 1905), 346; Keogh, "Etat de Service" [pp. 3-4]; William Rawle Brooke to his mother, 22 Oct. 1863, Brooke Correspondence, War Library, National Commandery, Military Order of the Loyal Legion of the United States, Philadelphia, Pa..

32. *Ibid.*, 21 Oct. 1863; *OR*, I, 29, pt. 1: 333, 346 and n., 362; pt. 2: 328-29; *Third Pennsylvania Cavalry*, 346-50.

33. *Ibid.*, 350.

34. *OR*, I, 29, pt. 1: 334, 337, 347, 350; pt. 2: 325; John Buford to Alfred Pleasonton, 16 Oct. 1863, Office of the Secretary of War, Telegrams Received, 1860-70, M-504, r-32, NA.

35. Starr, *Union Cavalry*, 2: 28-29; *OR*, I, 29, pt. 1: 351-54, 997-98; Gracey, *Sixth Pennsylvania Cavalry*, 199-200.

36. *OR*, I, 29, pt. 2: 400; Theodore Lyman, *Meade's Headquarters, 1863-1865: Letters of Colonel Theodore Lyman from the Wilderness to Appomattox*, ed. George R. Agassiz (Boston, 1922), 35, 50.

37. Edwin M. Stanton to anon., 3 Nov. 1863, General's Papers,

RG-94, E-159, NA; *OR*, I, 29, pt. 2: 426, 428, 430, 432, 438-39, 441; 51, pt. 1: 1121; George H. Chapman diary, 8-9 Nov. 1863; Charles Munroe diary, 7-10 Nov. 1863; Sarah Butler Wister, *Walter S. Newhall: A Memoir* (Philadelphia, 1864), 127; Gracey, *Sixth Pennsylvania Cavalry*, 204-05; Hard, *Eighth Illinois Cavalry*, 282; Hall, Besley, and Wood, comps., *Sixth New York Cavalry*, 165.

38. *OR*, I, 29, pt. 2: 459-61; John Buford to C. Ross Smith, 13 Nov. 1863; to Alfred Pleasonton, ca. 14 Nov. 1863; both, Office of the Secretary of War, Telegrams Received, 1860-70, M-504, r-32; to J. H. Taylor, 15 Mar. 1863 [two MSS.], General's Papers, RG-94, E-159; to C. Ross Smith, 20 Nov. 1863, *ibid.*; John Buford, Personnel Return, Nov. 1863, Union Staff Officers' Files, RG-94; all, NA.

EPILOGUE:

1. Endorsement to John Buford to C. Ross Smith, 20 Nov. 1863, General's Papers, RG-94, E-159, NA; author's interview of Colonel Adrian Wheat, USA, Chief of Surgery, McDonald Army Community Hospital, Fort Eustis, Virginia, 4 Apr. 1995.
2. Frank Moore, *The Civil War in Song and Story, 1860-1865* (New York, 1889), 254; Frank B. Borries, Jr., "General John Buford, Civil War Union Cavalryman," 61, M. A. thesis, University of Kentucky, 1960; Stephen Z. Starr, *The Union Cavalry in the Civil War* (3 vols. Baton Rouge, La., 1979-85), 2: 4-6.
3. George B. Sanford, *Fighting Rebels and Redskins: Experiences in Army Life of Colonel George B. Sanford, 1861-1892*, ed. E. R. Hagemann (Norman, Okla., 1969), 214-15; *OR*, I, 30, pt. 4: 9; *New York Tribune*, 17 Dec. 1863.
4. A. J. Alexander to C. Ross Smith, 13 Dec. 1863, General's Papers, RG-94, E-159, NA; *Rock Island* (Ill.) *Argus*, 18 Dec. 1863.
5. Sanford, *Fighting Rebels and Redskins*, 215; Abraham Lincoln to Edwin M. Stanton, 16 Dec. 1863, Special Collections, USMA Library, West Point, N. Y.; Borries, "General John

Buford," 62; Moore, *Civil War in Song and Story*, 254; A. J. Alexander to anon., 16 Dec. 1863, Commission Branch Files, M-1064, r-9, NA.

6. Moore, *Civil War in Song and Story*, 254; "Anecdotes of General Buford," *National Tribune*, 18 Feb. 1882; *New York Times*, 17 Dec. 1863; *New York Tribune*, 17 Dec. 1863; *Philadelphia Daily Evening Bulletin*, 17 Dec. 1863.
7. J. P. Taylor to John P. Slough, 19 Dec. 1863, General's Papers, RG-94, E-159, NA; George W. Wickstrom, *The Town Crier* (Rock Island, Ill., 1948), 67; *Rock Island Argus*, 28 Dec. 1863.
8. S. L. Gracey, *Annals of the Sixth Pennsylvania Cavalry* (Philadelphia, 1868), 213.
9. *New York Tribune*, 17 Dec. 1863; Gracey, *Sixth Pennsylvania Cavalry*, 211-13; Abner Hard, *History of the Eighth Cavalry Regiment, Illinois Volunteers, During the Great Rebellion* (Aurora, Ill., 1868), 285-87; Hillman A. Hall, W. B. Besley, and Gilbert G. Wood, comps., *History of the Sixth New York Cavalry . . . 1861-1865* (Worcester, Mass., 1908), 168.
10. George Stoneman to John A. Dix, 21 Dec. 1863, General's Papers, RG-94, E-159, NA; Wickstrom, *Town Crier*, 67-68; *Rock Island Argus*, 29 June 1916.
11. Fisher & Bird Co. to AGO, 20 June 1870, Commission Branch Files, M-1064, r-9, NA; Borries, "General John Buford," 62; *Proceedings of the Buford Memorial Association. . .* (New York, 1895), 31-44; John H. Calef, "Gettysburg Notes: The Opening Gun," *Journal of the Military Service Institution of the United States* 40 (1907): 40, 53-57.

Bibliography

I. UNPUBLISHED MATERIALS:

Arnold, Delevan. Correspondence. Kalamazoo Public Museum, Kalamazoo, Mich.

Bayard, George D. Correspondence. United States Military Academy Library, West Point, N. Y.

Bell, James A. Correspondence. Henry E. Huntington Library, San Marino, Calif.

Bellamy, Flavius J. Diary, 1863, and Correspondence. Indiana State Library, Indianapolis, Ind.

Bloss, Josiah. Diary, 1863, and Correspondence. Pennsylvania Historical and Museum Commission, Harrisburg, Pa.

Borries, Frank B., Jr. "General John Buford, Civil War Union Cavalryman." M. A. thesis, University of Kentucky, 1960.

Brodhead, Thornton F. Correspondence. Detroit Public Library, Detroit, Mich.

Brooke, William Rawle. Diary, 1863, and Correspondence. War Library, National Commandery, Military Order of the Loyal Legion of the United States, Philadelphia, Pa.

Brown, Charles. Correspondence. New York State Library, Albany, N. Y.

Buford John. Academic Record. United States Military Academy Archives.

_____. Cadet Records. United States Military Academy Library.

_____. Correspondence. Adjutant General's Office, Letters Received, 1848-63. Microcopy 619, reels 3, 7, 9, 74, 77, 78, 80, 160, National Archives, Washington, D. C.

_____. Correspondence. Adjutant General's Office, Letters Received (Main Series), 1822-1860. Microcopy 567, reels 596-97, National Archives.

_____. Correspondence. Commission Branch Files. Microcopy 1064, reel 9, National Archives.

_____. Correspondence. General's Papers. Record Group 94, National Archives.

_____. Correspondence, Office of the Secretary of War, Telegrams Received, 1860-70. Microcopy 504, reel 32, National Archives.

_____. Delinquency Register. United States Military Academy Archives.

_____. Letter of 26 April 1863. Simon Gratz Collection. Historical Society of Pennsylvania, Philadelphia, Pa.

_____. Letter of 12 August 1863. George Hay Stuart Papers. Library of Congress, Washington, D. C.

_____. Personnel Returns. Union Staff Officers' Files. Record Group 94, National Archives.

_____. Quartermaster's Receipts. Ferdinand Dreer Collection, Historical Society of Pennsylvania.

Butterfield, Daniel. "Reminiscences of the Cavalry in the Army of [the] Potomac." Record Group 94, National Archives.

Census of 1830, Versailles District, Woodford County, Kentucky. Woodford County Historical Society, Versailles, Ky.

Chapman, George H. Diaries, 1862-63. Indiana Historical Society, Indianapolis, Ind.

Chase, Salmon P. Papers. Historical Society of Pennsylvania.

Gamble, William. Letter of 10 March 1864. Chicago Historical Society, Chicago, Ill.

Gibbon, John. Papers. Historical Society of Pennsylvania.

Headquarters, Cavalry Corps, Army of the Potomac. Letters Sent, 1863-65. Record Group 393, Entry 1439, National Archives.

Headquarters, Department of Utah. Order Books, 1857-61. Record Group 393, Entry 5035, vol. 7, National Archives.

Headquarters, First Cavalry Division, Army of the Potomac. Letters and Telegrams Received, 1861-64. Record Group 393, Entry 1508, National Archives.

Headquarters, First Cavalry Division, Army of the Potomac. Letters Sent, 1863-65. Record Group 393, Entry 1439, National Archives.

Headquarters, First United States Dragoons. Regimental Returns, 1848-49. Microcopy 744, reel 3, National Archives.

Headquarters, Second United States Dragoons. Regimental Returns, 1849-61. Microcopy 744, reels 16-17, National Archives.

Hooker, Joseph. Correspondence. Samuel P. Bates Papers. Pennsylvania State Archives, Harrisburg, Pa.

_____. Papers. Gettysburg College Library, Gettysburg, Pa.

_____. Papers. Henry E. Huntington Library.

"John Buford Biography." Typescript in United States Cavalry Museum, Fort Riley, Kan.

"John Buford, Major General." Typescript in Rock Island Arsenal Museum, Rock Island, Ill.

Keogh, Myles. "Etat de Service of Major Genl Jno. Buford from his promotion to Brig Genl to his death." Manuscript in Special Collections, United States Military Academy Library.

Meade, George Gordon. Papers. Historical Society of Pennsylvania.

Medill, William H. Correspondence. Hanna-McCormick Papers. Library of Congress.

Milligan, Robert. Correspondence. State Historical Society of Wisconsin, Madison, Wis.

Munroe, Charles. Diary, 1863. American Antiquarian Society, Worcester, Mass.

Newhall, Walter S. Correspondence. Historical Society of Pennsylvania.

Nolan, James D. "'A Bold and Fearless Rider': The Life of Major General John Buford." M.A. thesis, St. John's University, 1994.

Pleasonton, Alfred. Generals' Reports of Service, War of the Rebellion. Record Group 94, Entry 160, National Archives.

Pulis, Daniel W. Correspondence. Rochester Public Library, Rochester, N. Y.

Redman, William H. Correspondence. University of Virginia Library, Charlottesville, Va.

Ryder, Alfred G. Correspondence and Diary, 1862. University of Michigan Library, Ann Arbor, Mich.

Secretary of War, Office of the. Orders and Endorsements Sent, 1855. Microcopy 444, reel 3, National Archives.

Sioux Expedition, 1855-56. Letterbook. Record Group 393, Entry 5504A, National Archives.

Starr, Samuel H. Papers. Missouri Historical Society, Saint Louis, Mo.

Veil, Charles H. Papers. Gettysburg College Library.

Wesson, Silas D. Diary, 1862. United States Army Military History Institute, Carlisle Barracks, Pa.

Whelan, Henry C. Letter of 11 June 1863. Cadwalader Family Papers. Historical Society of Pennsylvania.

NEWSPAPERS:

Army and Navy Journal (New York, N. Y.)

Daily Missouri Republican (St. Louis)

Detroit Advertiser & Tribune

New York Herald

New York Times

New York Tribune

Philadelphia Daily Evening Bulletin

Philadelphia Inquirer

Philadelphia North American

Rock Island (Ill.) *Argus*

Woodford (County, Ky.) *Sun*

ARTICLES AND ESSAYS:

"Anecdotes of General Buford." *National Tribune*, 18 February 1882.

Boehm, Robert B. "The Unfortunate Averell." *Civil War Times Illustrated* 5 (August 1966): 30-36.

Calef, John H. "Gettysburg Notes: The Opening Gun." *Journal of the Military Service Institution of the United States* 40 (1907): 40-58.

Carpenter, John A. "General O. O. Howard at Gettysburg." *Civil War History* 9 (1963): 261-76.

Clark, S. A. "Brandy Station, October, 1863." *Maine Bugle* n.s. 3 (1896): 226-29.

Crowninshield, Benjamin W. "Cavalry in Virginia During the War of the Rebellion." *Papers of the Military Historical Society of Massachusetts* 13 (1913): 3-31.

Davis, George B. "The Bristoe and Mine Run Campaigns." *Papers of the Military Historical Society of Massachusetts* 3 (1903): 470-502.

Drum, Richard C. "Reminiscences of the Indian Fight at Ash Hollow, 1855." *Collections of the Nebraska State Historical Society* 16 (1911): 143-51.

Etulain, Richard W., ed. "A Virginian in Utah Chooses the Union ..." *Utah Historical Quarterly* 42 (1974): 381-85.

Hall, Clark B. "Buford at Brandy Station." *Civil War* 8 (July-August 1990): 12-17, 66-67.

Halstead, E.P. "Incidents of the First Day at Gettysburg." *Battles and Leaders of the Civil War* 3 (1887-88): 255-84.

Harvey, Robert. "The Battle Ground of Ash Hollow." *Collections of the Nebraska State Historical Society* 16 (1911): 152-64.

Hassler, Warren W., Jr. "The First Day's Battle of Gettysburg." *Civil War History* 6 (1960): 259-76.

Hunt, Henry J. "The First Day at Gettysburg." *Battles and Leaders of the Civil War ...* 3 (1887-88): 255-84.

_____. "The Second Day at Gettysburg." *Battles and Leaders of the Civil War ...* 3 (1887-88): 290-313.

Imboden, John D. "The Confederate Retreat from Gettysburg." *Battles and Leaders of the Civil War ...* 3 (1887-88): 420-29.

Kross, Gary. "'Fight Like the Devil to Hold Your Own': General John Buford's Cavalry at Gettysburg on July 1, 1863." *Blue and Gray* 12 (February 1995): 9-22.

"Letters of a Civil War Surgeon." *Indiana Magazine of History* 27 (1931): 132-63.

Long, E. B. "The Battle That Almost Was—Manassas Gap." *Civil War Times Illustrated* 11 (December 1972): 21-28.

Longacre, Edward G. "Alfred Pleasonton, 'The Knight of Romance'." *Civil War Times Illustrated* 13 (December 1974): 11-23.

_____. "The Raid That Failed." *Civil War Times Illustrated* 26 (January 1988): 15-21, 44-45, 49.

Longstreet, James. "The Battle of Fredericksburg." *Battles and Leaders of the Civil War ...* 3 (1887-88): 70-85.

Mattison, Ray H., ed. "The Harney Expedition Against the Sioux: The Journal of Capt. John B. S. Todd." *Nebraska History* 43 (1962): 89-130.

McAdams, Benton. "Napoleon Bonaparte: The Other Buford." *Civil War Times Illustrated* 33 (November-December 1994): 82-92.

Merritt, Wesley. "Life and Services of General Philip St. George Cooke, U. S. Army." *Journal of the United States Cavalry Association* 8 (1895): 79-92.

Morrison, James L., ed. "Getting Through West Point: The Cadet Memoirs of John C. Tidball, Class of 1848." *Civil War History* 26 (1980): 304-25.

Paul, R. Eli, ed. "Battle of Ash Hollow: The 1909-1910 Recollections of General N. A. M. Dudley." *Nebraska History* 62 (1981): 373-99.

Pope, John. "The Second Battle of Bull Run." *Battles and Leaders of the Civil War* ... 2 (1887-88): 449-94.

"Revolutionary Army Orders for the Main Army Under Washington, 1777-1779." *Virginia Magazine of History and Biography* 20 (1912): 181-94, 267-81.

Swift, Eben. "General Wesley Merritt." *U. S. Cavalry Journal* 21 (1911): 829-37.

Sword, Wiley. "Cavalry on Trial at Kelly's Ford." *Civil War Times Illustrated* 13 (April 1974): 33-40.

"Virginia's Soldiers in the Revolution." *Virginia Magazine of History and Biography* 20 (1912): 181-94, 267-81.

Weigley, Russell F. "John Buford." *Civil War Times Illustrated* 5 (June 1966): 15-23.

Williams, E. S., ed. "Col. Thornton Broadhead's [Brodhead's] Last Letter." *Michigan Historical Collections* 9 (1886): 208-09.

Wilson, James Harrison. "Major-General John Buford." *Journal of the United States Cavalry Association* 8 (1895): 171-83.

Wittenberg, Eric J. "John Buford and the Gettysburg Campaign." *Gettysburg Magazine* 11 (July 1994): 19-55.

BOOKS AND PAMPHLETS:

Adams, Charles F., Jr., et al. *A Cycle of Adams Letters, 1861-1865* ... Edited by Chauncey Worthington Ford. 2 vols. Boston: Houghton, Mifflin Co., 1920.

Annals of the War, Written by Leading Participants North and South. Philadelphia: Times Publishing Co., 1879.

Bandy, Ken, and Florence Freeland, comps. *The Gettysburg Papers.* 2 vols. Dayton: Press of Morningside Bookshop, 1978.

Bates, Samuel P. *The Battle of Gettysburg.* Philadelphia: T.H. Davis & Co., 1875.

Bauer, K. Jack. *The Mexican War, 1846-1848.* New York: Macmillan Co., 1974.

Bayard, Samuel J. *The Life of George Dashiell Bayard* ... New York: G. P. Putnam's Sons, 1874.

The Biographical Encyclopedia of Kentucky of ... the Nineteenth Century. Cincinnati: J. M. Armstrong & Co., 1878.

Bogue, Allan G. *The Earnest Men: Republicans of the Civil War Senate.* Ithaca, N. Y.: Cornell University Press, 1981.

Boudrye, Louis N. *Historic Records of the Fifth New York Cavalry* ... Albany, N. Y.: J. Munsell, 1868.

Boynton, Edward C. *History of West Point ... and the Origin and Progress of the United States Military Academy.* New York: D. Van Nostrand, 1863.

Brackett, Albert G. *History of the United States Cavalry ... to the 1st of June 1863* ... New York: Harper & Brothers, 1865.

Bradley, Samuel H. *Recollections of Army Life* ... Olean, N. Y.: privately issued, 1912.

Buford, Marcus Bainbridge. *A Genealogy of the Buford Family in America, with Records of a Number of Allied Families.* San Francisco: privately issued, 1903.

______, George Washington Buford, and Mildred Buford Minter. *History and Genealogy of the Buford Family in America, with Records of a Number of Allied Families.* Le Belle, Mo.: privately issued, 1924.

Carleton, J. Henry. *The Prairie Logbooks: Dragoon Campaigns to the Pawnee Villages in 1844, and to the Rocky Mountains in 1845.* Edited by Louis Pelzer. Lincoln: University of Nebraska Press, 1983.

Carter, William G. H. *From Yorktown to Santiago with the Sixth U. S. Cavalry.* Baltimore: Lord Baltimore Press, 1900.

Cheney, Newel, comp. *History of the Ninth Regiment, New York Volunteer Cavalry, War of 1861 to 1865.* Poland Center and Jamestown, N. Y.: Martin Merz & Son, 1901.

Cleaves, Freeman. *Meade of Gettysburg.* Norman: University of Oklahoma Press, 1960.

Coddington, Edwin B. *The Gettysburg Campaign: A Study in Command.* New York: Charles Scribner's Sons, 1968.

Crowninshield, Benjamin W., and D. H. L. Gleason. *A History of the First Regiment of Massachusetts Cavalry Volunteers.* Boston: Houghton, Mifflin & Co., 1891.

Cullum, George Washington, comp. *Biographical Register of the Officers and Graduates of the U. S. Military Academy* ... 2 vols. New York: D. Van Nostrand, 1891.

Darnell, Ermina Jett. *Forks of Elkhorn Church.* Baltimore: Genealogical Publishing Co., Inc., 1980.

Dickens, Charles. *American Notes.* Gloucester, Mass.: Peter Smith, 1968.

Doster, William E. *Lincoln and Episodes of the Civil War.* New York: G. P. Putnam's Sons, 1915.

Doubleday, Abner. *Chancellorsville and Gettysburg.* New York: Charles Scribner's Sons, 1882.

Downey, Fairfax. *Clash of Cavalry: The Battle of Brandy Station, June 9, 1863.* New York: David McKay Co., Inc., 1959.

Elsner, B. J., ed. *Rock Island Yesterday, Today & Tomorrow.* Rock Island, Ill.: Rock Island History Book Committee, 1988.

Frazer, Robert W. *Forts of the West: Military Forts ... West of the Mississippi River to 1898.* Norman: University of Oklahoma Press, 1965.

Furniss, Norman F. *The Mormon Conflict, 1850-1859.* New Haven, Conn.: Yale University Press, 1960.

Gibbon, John. *Personal Recollections of the Civil War.* New York: G. P. Putnam's Sons, 1928.

Glazier, Willard. *Three Years in the Federal Cavalry.* New York: R. H. Ferguson & Co., 1870.

Gracey, S. L. *Annals of the Sixth Pennsylvania Cavalry.* Philadelphia: E. H. Butler & Co., 1868.

Green, Thomas Marshall. *Historic Families of Kentucky* ... Baltimore: Regional Publishing Co., 1964.

Hall, Hillman A., W. B. Besley, and Gilbert G. Wood, comps. *History of the Sixth New York Cavalry ... 1861-1865.* Worcester, Mass.: Blanchard Press, 1908.

Hancock, Almira Russell. *Reminiscences of Winfield Scott Hancock, by His Wife.* New York: Charles L. Webster & Co., 1887.

Hard, Abner. *History of the Eighth Cavalry Regiment, Illinois Volunteers, During the Great Rebellion.* Aurora, Ill.: privately issued, 1868.

Hassler, Warren W., Jr. *Crisis at the Crossroads: The First Day at Gettysburg.* University, Ala: University of Alabama Press, 1970.

Heitman, Francis B., comp. *Historical Register and Dictionary of the United States Army* ... 2 vols. Washington, D. C.: Government Printing Office, 1903.

Hennessy, John J. *Return to Bull Run: The Campaign and Battle of Second Manassas.* New York: Simon & Schuster, 1993.

Heth, Henry. *The Memoirs of Henry Heth.* Edited by James L. Morrison, Jr. Westport, Conn.: Greenwood Press, 1974.

Hinkley, Julian W. *A Narrative of Service with the Third Wisconsin Infantry* ... Madison: Wisconsin History Commission, 1912.

History of the Third Pennsylvania Cavalry, Sixtieth Regiment Pennsylvania Volunteers, in the American Civil War, 1861-1865. Philadelphia: Franklin Printing Co., 1905.

Howard, Oliver O. *Autobiography of Oliver Otis Howard.* 2 vols. New York: Baker & Taylor Co., 1907.

Huntington, R. T. *Hall's Breechloaders: John H. Hall's Invention and Development of a Breechloading Rifle* ... York, Pa.: George Shumway, 1972.

Jacobs, Michael. *Notes on the Rebel Invasion and the Battle of Gettysburg.* Philadelphia: J.B. Lippincott Co., 1864.

Johnson, Allen, et al., eds. *Dictionary of American Biography.* 27 vols. to date. New York: Charles Scribner's Sons, 1927-.

Joint Committee on the Conduct of the War. 3 vols. in 8. Washington, D.C.: Government Printing Office, 1863-68.

Krick, Robert K. *Stonewall Jackson at Cedar Mountain.* Chapel Hill: University of North Carolina Press, 1990.

Ladd, David L., and Audrey J. Ladd, eds. *The Bachelder Papers: Gettysburg in Their Own Words* ... Dayton: Morningside, 1994.

Langley, Harold D., ed. *To Utah with the Dragoons* ... Salt Lake City: University of Utah Press, 1974.

Lawson, Rowena. *Woodford County, Kentucky, 1810-1840 Censuses.* Bowie, Md.: Heritage Books, 1987.

Long, A. L. *Memoirs of Robert E. Lee: His Military and Personal History* ... New York: J. M. Stoddart & Co., 1886.

Longacre, Edward G. *The Cavalry at Gettysburg: A Tactical Study of Mounted Operations During the Civil War's Pivotal Campaign, 9 June-14 July 1863.* Rutherford, N. J.: Fairleigh Dickinson University Press, 1986.

_____. *Mounted Raids of the Civil War.* South Brunswick, N. J.: A. S. Barnes & Co., Inc., 1975.

Lowe, Percival G. *Five Years a Dragoon ('49 to '54) and Other Adventures on the Great Plains.* Kansas City, Mo.: F. Hudson Publshing Co., 1906; Norman: University of Oklahoma Press, 1965.

Lyman, Theodore. *Meade's Headquarters, 1863-1865: Letters of Colonel Theodore Lyman from the Wilderness to Appomattox.* Edited by George R. Agassiz. Boston: Atlantic Monthly Press, 1922.

Mahan, D. H. *An Elementary Treatise on Advanced-Guard, Out-Post,and Detachment Service of Troops* ... New York: John Wiley, 1853.

Martin, David G. *Gettysburg July 1.* Conshohocken, Pa.: Combined Books, 1995.

Marvel, William. *Burnside.* Chapel Hill: University of North Carolina Press, 1991.

Maury, Dabney H. *Recollections of a Virginian in the Mexican, Indian, and Civil Wars.* New York: Charles Scribner's Sons, 1894.

McDonough, James L. *Schofield: Union General in the Civil War and Reconstruction.* Tallahassee: Florida State University Press, 1972.

McMullin, Thomas A., and David Walker. *Biographical Directory of American Territorial Governors.* Westport, Conn.: Meckler Publishing, 1984.

McWhiney, Grady, and Perry D. Jamieson. *Attack and Die: Civil*

War Military Tactics and the Southern Heritage. University, Ala.: University of Alabama Press, 1982.

Meade, George G. *The Life and Letters of George Gordon Meade, Major-General United States Army*. 2 vols. New York: Charles Scribner's Sons, 1913.

Monaghan, Jay. *Civil War on the Western Border, 1854-1865*. Boston: Little, Brown & Co., 1955.

Moore, Frank. *The Civil War in Song and Story, 1860-1865*. New York: P. F. Collier, 1889.

Moorman, Donald R., and Gene A. Sessions. *Camp Floyd and the Mormons: The Utah War*. Salt Lake City: University of Utah Press, 1992.

Morrison, James L. *"The Best School in the World": West Point, the Pre-Civil War Years, 1833-1866*. Kent, Ohio: Kent State University Press, 1986.

Moyer, H. P., comp. *History of the Seventeenth Regiment Pennsylvania Volunteer Cavalry* ... Lebanon, Pa.: Sowers Printing Co., 1911.

Murfin, James V. *The Gleam of Bayonets: The Battle of Antietam and the Maryland Campaign of 1862*. South Brunswick, N. J.: Thomas Yoseloff, 1965.

Norton, Henry. *Deeds of Daring; or, History of the Eighth N. Y. Volunteer Cavalry* ... Norwich, N. Y.: Chenango Telegraph Printing House, 1889.

Nye, Wilbur S. *Here Come the Rebels!* Baton Rouge: Louisiana State University Press, 1965.

Oakey, Daniel. *History of the Second Massachusetts Regiment of Infantry: Beverly Ford* ... Boston: Geo. H. Ellis, 1884.

Official Register of the Officers and Cadets of the U. S. Military Academy, West Point, N. Y. West Point: Published for the Academy, 1845-48.

O'Neill, Robert F., Jr. *The Cavalry Battles of Aldie, Middleburg and Upperville* . . . Lynchburg, Va.: H.E. Howard, Inc., 1993.

Pappas, George S. *To the Point: The United States Military Academy, 1802-1902*. Westport, Conn.: Praeger Publishers, 1993.

Paris, Comte de. *History of the Civil War in America* ... 4 vols. Philadelphia: Porter & Coates, 1876-88.

Patrick, Marsena R. *Inside Lincoln's Army: The Diary of Marsena Rudolph Patrick, Provost Marshal General, Army of the Potomac.* Edited by David S. Sparks. New York: Thomas Yoseloff, 1964.

Patten, George. *Patten's Cavalry Drill, and Sabre Exercise* ... New York: J. W. Fortune, 1861.

Pennypacker, Isaac R. *General Meade.* New York: D. Appleton & Co., 1901.

Pfanz, Harry W. *Gettysburg: Culp's Hill and Cemetery Hill.* Chapel Hill: University of North Carolina Press, 1993.

_____. *Gettysburg: The Second Day.* Chapel Hill: University of North Carolina Press, 1987.

Phipps, Michael, and John S. Peterson. *"The Devil's to Pay": Gen. John Buford, USA.* Gettysburg, Pa.: Farnsworth Military Impressions, 1995.

Pickerill, W. N. *History of the Third Indiana Cavalry.* Indianapolis: Aetna Printing Co., 1906.

Pisgah [Presbyterian Church], 1784-1984, Woodford County, Kentucky. n. p.: privately issued, 1984.

Pratt, Fletcher. *Eleven Generals: Studies in American Command.* New York: William Sloane Associates, 1949.

Price, George F., comp. *Across the Continent with the Fifth Cavalry.* New York: D. Van Nostrand, 1883.

Proceedings of the Buford Memorial Association ... New York: Buford Memorial Association, 1895.

Railey, William E. *History of Woodford County.* Versailles, Ky.: Woodford Improvement League, 1968.

Record [of the] First Michigan Cavalry: Civil War, 1861-1865. Kalamazoo: Ihling Bros. & Everhard, 1905.

Report of the Secretary of War: Senate Executive Document 1 (35th Congress, 2nd Session), 6 December 1858.

Report of the Secretary of War: Senate Executive Document 1 (36th Congress, 2nd Session), 3 December 1860.

Report of the Secretary of War: Senate Executive Document 2 (36th Congress, 1st Session), 1 December 1859.

Report of the Secretary of War: Senate Executive Document 5 (34th Congress, 3rd Session), 1 December 1856.

Report of the Secretary of War: Senate Executive Document 11 (35th Congress, 1st Session), 5 December 1857.

Rhodes, Charles D. *History of the Cavalry of the Army of the Potomac* ... Kansas City, Mo.: Hudson-Kimberly Publishing Co., 1900.

Robertson, James I., Jr. *General A. P. Hill: The Story of a Confederate Warrior.* New York: Random House, 1987.

Robertson, John, comp. *Michigan in the War.* Lansing: W. S. George & Co., 1882.

Rodenbough, Theophilus F. *From Everglade to Canon with the Second Dragoons* ... New York: D. Van Nostrand, 1875.

_____, and William L. Haskin, eds. *The Army of the United States: Historical Sketches of Staff and Line* ... New York: Merrill & Co., 1896.

Rogers, Ford H. *"Jeb" Stuart's Hat: War Papers Read Before the Commandery of the State of Michigan, Military Order of the Loyal Legion of the United States.* Detroit: privately issued, 1893.

Roland, Charles P. *Albert Sidney Johnston, Soldier of Three Republics.* Austin: University of Texas Press, 1964.

Ropes, John Codman. *The Army Under Pope.* New York: Charles Scribner's Sons, 1882.

Sanford, George B. *Fighting Rebels and Redskins: Experiences in Army Life of Colonel George B. Sanford, 1861-1892.* Edited by E. R. Hagemann. Norman; University of Oklahoma Press, 1969.

Schaff, Morris. *The Spirit of Old West Point, 1858-1862.* Boston: Houghton, Mifflin & Co., 1907.

Schutz, Wallace J., and Walter N. Trenerry. *Abandoned by Lincoln: A Military Biography of General John Pope.* Urbana: University of Illinois Press, 1990.

Sears, Stephen W. *Landscape Turned Red: The Battle of Antietam.* New York: Ticknor & Fields, 1983.

_____. *To the Gates of Richmond: The Peninsula Campaign.* New York: Ticknor & Fields, 1992.

Simpson, Harold B. *Cry Comanche: The 2nd U. S. Cavalry in Texas, 1855-1861.* Hillsboro, Tex.: Hill Junior College Press, 1979.

Skelly, Daniel A. *A Boy's Experiences During the Battles of Gettysburg.* Gettysburg, Pa.: privately issued, 1932.

Stackpole, Edward J., *Drama on the Rappahannock: The Fredericksburg Campaign.* Harrisburg, Pa.: Military Service Publishing Co., 1957.

_____. *From Cedar Mountain to Antietam, August-September* 1862 ... Harrisburg, Pa.: Stackpole Co., 1959.

Starr, Stephen Z. *The Union Cavalry in the Civil War.* 3 vols. Baton Rouge: Louisiana State University Press, 1979-85.

Stearns, Austin C. *Three Years with Company K ... 13th Massachusetts Infantry.* Edited by Arthur A. Kent. Rutherford, N. J.: Fairleigh Dickinson University Press, 1976.

Steffen, Randy. *The Horse Soldier, 1776-1943: The United States Cavalryman—His Uniforms, Arms, Accoutrements, and Equipments.* 4 vols. Norman: University of Oklahoma Press, 1977-80.

Taylor, Emerson Gifford. *Gouverneur Kemble Warren: The Life and Letters of an American Soldier, 1830-1882.* Boston: Houghton Mifflin Co., 1932.

Thomas, Emory M. *Bold Dragoon: The Life of J. E. B. Stuart.* New York: Harper & Row, 1986.

Thompson, Jerry. *Henry Hopkins Sibley: Confederate General of the West.* Natchitoches, La.: Northwestern State University Press, 1987.

Tobie, Edward P. *History of the First Maine Cavalry, 1861-1865.* Boston: Emery & Hughes, 1887.

Turnley, P. T. *Reminiscences of Parmenas Taylor Turnley* ... Chicago: Donohue & Henneberry, 1892.

Utah: A Guide to the State. New York: Hastings House, 1945.

Utley, Robert M. *Frontiersmen in Blue: The United States Army and the Indian, 1848-1865*. New York: Macmillan Co., 1967.

Wainwright, Charles Shiels. *A Diary of Battle: The Personal Journals of Colonel Charles S. Wainwright, 1861-1865*. Edited by Allan Nevins. New York: Harcourt, Brace & World, 1962.

Walker, Francis A. *History of the Second Army Corps in the Army of the Potomac*. New York: Charles Scribner's Sons, 1886.

Wallace, Edward S. *General William Jenkins Worth, Monterey's Forgotten Hero*. Dallas: Southern Methodist University Press, 1953.

Warner, Ezra J. *Generals in Blue: Lives of the Union Commanders*. Baton Rouge: Louisiana State University Press, 1964.

War of the Rebellion: A Compilation of the Official Records of the Union and Confederate Armies. 4 series, 70 vols. in 128. Washington, D. C.: Government Printing Office, 1880-1901.

Welch, G. Murlin. *Border Warfare in Southeastern Kansas, 1856-1859*. Pleasanton, Kan.: Linn County Historical Society, 1977.

Wharton, Mary E., and Ellen F. Williams, eds. *Peach Leather and Rebel Gray: Bluegrass Life and the War, 1860-1865*. Lexington, Ky.: privately issued, 1986.

Wickstrom, George W. *The Town Crier*. Rock Island, Ill.: J. W. Potter Co., 1948.

Williams, Kenneth P. *Lincoln Finds a General: A Military Study of the Civil War*. 5 vols. New York: Macmillan Co., 1949-59.

Wister, Sarah Butler. *Walter S. Newhall: A Memoir*. Philadelphia: The Sanitary Commission, 1864.

Index